- 8 JUL 2016

W

S

D1374934

Renewals

01159 293388

www.library.bromley.gov.uk

THE LONDON BOROUGH
www.bromley.gov.uk

Please return/renew this item
by the last date shown.
Books may also be renewed by
phone and Internet.

WITHDRAWN FROM
BROMLEY LIBRARIES

Bromley Libraries

30128 80141 239 9

Working in Science

A practical guide to science careers for graduates

Dr Tracy Johnson

Working in Science: A practical guide to science careers for graduates

This first edition published in 2013 by Trotman Education, a division of Crimson Publishing Ltd, The Tramshed, Walcot Street, Bath BA1 5BB

© Trotman Education 2013

Author: Dr Tracy Johnson

The right of Dr Tracy Johnson to be identified as the author of this work has been asserted by her in accordance with the Copyright, Designs and Patents Act 1988.

British Library Cataloguing in Publication Data
A catalogue record for this book is available from the British Library

ISBN 978 0 9568350 5 5

All rights reserved. This book is sold subject to the condition that it shall not, by way of trade or otherwise, be lent, resold, hired out or otherwise circulated without the publisher's prior written consent in any form of binding or cover other than that in which it is published and without a similar condition including this condition being imposed on the subsequent purchaser. No part of this publication may be reproduced, stored in a retrieval system or transmitted in any form or by any means, electronic and mechanical, photocopying, recording or otherwise without prior permission of Crimson Publishing Ltd.

Typeset by IDSUK (DataConnection) Ltd
Printed and bound in the UK by Bell & Bain Ltd, Glasgow

Contents

Acknowledgements

I would like to thank the staff at the University of Bristol Careers Service for all their help and support while I produced this guide, as well as all the students who teach me something new about careers guidance each day.

Thanks also to my family and friends who saw very little of me while I was busy on this project – writing a book makes you very antisocial!

Introduction

Welcome to *Working in Science*! This guide will provide you with an overview of the typical job roles available within the science sector, as well as comprehensive guidance to help you choose, find and maintain your ideal career. Whether you are currently a science student or have graduated and are still seeking inspiration, this guide will help you to identify roles that suit your skills and interests, as well as supporting the development of a professional approach to achieving your career goals. Below is a quick guide to what you will find in the two main parts of the book and how to use them, as well as a few essential pieces of advice to keep in mind as you progress.

Science graduates are very much in demand in the UK thanks to their valuable technical and transferable skills. The Royal Society of Engineering states that we need 100,000 science, technology, engineering and mathematics (STEM) graduates annually to keep the economy balanced. There is currently a shortage of about 10,000 graduates entering the science sector each year, so use this book to help you be best placed to seize available opportunities and secure the role you really want.

Part 1: The job roles

This section offers a broad overview of the typical roles available in different areas of the science sector. Each role offers a short description of the job, entry requirements, the skills required, salary information, typical activities and opportunities for training and development once established in your career. You will also find further resources linking you to relevant professional bodies and more detailed job information.

While the chapters in this section are organised by particular areas within the science sector, do bear in mind that **a degree in one subject won't necessarily rule you out of entering alternative jobs**. Most employers aren't as particular as you might expect when it comes to degree subject as long as you have the right skills, a positive attitude and some work experience on your CV. It is also possible to complete a master's degree to provide you with a more relevant skill set and career-specific knowledge. However, before you spend time and money on a higher degree, you should always check with potential employers whether this is necessary. While some employers will require the specialist knowledge developed through a master's, **others will be happy to train you on the job as long as you can demonstrate your aptitude and enthusiasm in your application.**

Take your time to browse through the job roles, even in areas you hadn't previously considered, as there may well be more career options available with your degree and experience than you think. Take the time to talk to a careers adviser at your university or college careers service if you are feeling completely undecided, and then work through Part 2, which will help you to plan your career and move towards your ideal role in the science sector.

Part 2: Starting your career and developing as a professional

Working in order through Part 2 will help you to get the most from the advice and guidance available here. This section will help you with your career choice and action planning, help you to develop your employability skills for science, make effective applications and survive the selection process. The final chapter also offers support on developing your professional skills during your first year in your chosen role, as well as advice on changing careers should your job turn out not to be what you expected. Even if you feel confident in your choice of job, working through the chapter on career planning will help you to identify your skills and better understand your motivations, which will ultimately help you write more successful applications, so please resist the temptation to skip over it! The chapter on developing professionally will help you to better understand the skills asked for on application forms and offers an insight into what an employer is looking for, so it's also well worth a read before you start filling out those competency questions.

While these chapters have been written to be as self-explanatory as possible, it is advisable to follow up on your career planning and discuss your applications with a careers adviser to receive valuable impartial and professional advice. You can also look at the 'Further reading and resources' section at the end for more specific information about topics you wish to look at in more depth, such as psychometric testing and finding work experience.

Essential advice

The following advice applies to the entire science sector and reflects important trends in the graduate market of which you should be aware as you work through this guide.

The value of work experience

The majority of graduate recruiters expect you to have some work experience on your CV when you apply to them, and you are likely to struggle in your search for employment if you have not held a holiday job, undertaken some part-time work or any volunteering activities. It would be ideal if you can find work experience in the same area as you eventually wish to have your graduate career, but most work experience can be valuable as long as you can identify the transferable skills you have gained and can apply them to the work you wish to do – you can read about how to do this in Chapter 15 on making effective applications.

If you wish to work in the health sciences, with the National Health Service (NHS) for example, then experience in a laboratory could be advantageous, as could any customer-facing roles if you want to work with the public, such as being a podiatrist or radiographer. Client-facing work is also recommended if you want to work in public engagement with science, as is volunteering at museums or science fairs.

Opportunities for casual work experience are not often advertised, although some larger organisations, such as pharmaceutical companies, may advertise more formal internship or placement opportunities. You will need to be confident and ask companies directly about undertaking work experience. Emails tend to disappear into a busy person's in-tray, so make some calls and show your enthusiasm. If a company can't pay you, then ask if you can have a day spent work shadowing, as this all adds up on your CV and shows commitment.

Apart from gaining valuable experience, spending time in a workplace that interests you can help enormously with your career choice. What if you spend time in a science museum and find that working with the public is something you don't enjoy after all? Better to find out now than invest in a master's in public engagement, start work and find out that you have wasted both your time and money.

Work experience can also provide you with valuable contacts for your future career development. Knowing people in your chosen field means that you can find out about upcoming vacancies, gain in-depth knowledge of the sector from experienced professionals, and gain some great potential referees for your job applications.

Developing your skills

You will find specific skills required for a particular career listed under each job role, but you can take for granted that most employers will also be looking for the following.

- Communication and interpersonal skills: it's incredibly important that you can communicate orally, electronically and in print in a clear and professional manner with people in your organisation, clients and external partners.

- Problem-solving ability: employers need to know that you see difficulties as problems that can be solved, and not as insurmountable obstacles. Problem solvers save organisations time and money, as well as getting noticed in the right way when promotions and projects arise.

- Teamwork skills: although you may work by yourself some of the time, you will always be working as part of a larger team and need to think about what contribution you can make. You may see this referred to in job descriptions as being able to work as part of a multidisciplinary team, and it is particularly important in the health sciences. What roles have you played in teams in the past? Can you adapt your work style to suit different projects and contexts?

- Self-management and motivation: every employer loves a self-starter who can motivate themselves and needs little guidance once they are up and running. Think about how you have achieved results in the past; can you set realistic goals and come up with a plan to meet them in a timely way?

Your degree, extra-curricular activities and any employment or volunteering experience should equip you with the above skills. It is advisable to think of several examples for each one that you could use in applications and interviews to provide evidence of your ability.

Using social media for job seeking

Finally, it is important to be aware that the graduate market has changed dramatically in recent years, and that traditional methods of finding work are being supplemented by increasing use of social media. This is covered in depth in Part 2, but it is crucial to start looking for opportunities beyond newspapers and websites. Many organisations advertise jobs using Twitter, as they expect enthusiastic candidates to be monitoring their feeds. Facebook also offers specific employer pages, and is a very immediate source of information about vacancies and training schemes. For example, the NHS Graduate Management Scheme has its own Facebook page where it provides regular updates about recruitment.

You can use professional networking sites such as LinkedIn not only to build your own profile and make valuable contacts but also to look at how people in the jobs you want to do entered their field. You can even ask questions about career development in the online forums. Ignoring social media as part of your job search strategy could leave you out in the cold, so it's crucial that you embrace it alongside all the other aspects of career planning that are covered here.

Those are all the essential pieces of information you need to work your way through this book. Take your time to find the best fit for you, seek professional advice when you need it and, above all, enjoy the journey towards the right science career for you!

Science, Technology, Engineering and Mathematics (STEM)

UNIVERSITY OF LEEDS

You could...

Take on a world of challenges with a STEM degree from the University of Leeds

...a wide range of degrees to suit all ambitions

Astronomy
Biology
Biomedicine
Chemistry
Computer Science
Ecology
Engineering
Environmental Science
Food Science
Geography
Geology
Geophysics
Genetics
Nanotechnology
Mathematics
Nutrition
Physics
Sports Science
Statistics
Sustainability
Transport
Zoology

Case study:
University of Leeds   UNIVERSITY OF LEEDS

The University of Leeds offers a wide choice of science, technology, engineering and maths (STEM) degrees.

These degrees provide the foundation for a diverse range of career opportunities. Our graduates have taken up exciting and challenging roles all over the world. You could too.

Rebecca Klein, BSc Zoology

Following her graduation in 1995 Rebecca worked in Thailand and Malaysia on a wide range of conservation projects. When she moved to Botswana in 2001 to work at Mokolodi Nature Reserve Rebecca became interested in starting up a conservation programme. Upon discovering that there were no conservation projects aimed at helping the endangered cheetah population she decided to establish the charity, 'Cheetah Conservation Botswana' in 2003 alongside Dr Kyle Good and Ann Marie Houser.

Botswana is home to one of the last free-ranging cheetah populations in the world. Rebecca said: 'The charity works with rural communities to try to reduce the conflict between people and cheetahs, through research, community outreach and education programmes. The zoology degree at Leeds was the foundation of my career and has enabled me to get skills and experience in my field to apply to wildlife conservation. I would encourage other university applicants to choose something that inspires you to work hard and take action. I aim to continue working towards the conservation of endangered species and habitats.'

The study of zoology is more important in the 21st century than ever. As a zoology student at Leeds you have the chance to explore evolution, animal behaviour, physiology and development, and have the opportunity to work out in the field in locations as diverse as Yorkshire, the Mediterranean and South Africa.

www.cheetahbotswana.com

Kath Leavy, BSc Mathematics

When Kath graduated with a degree in mathematics she was desperate to do something exciting and when she bagged herself what some people might call the 'coolest' job on earth, working for the UK Antarctic Heritage Trust, her dreams came true.

'I really wanted this job and put everything into it as I knew I just had to get it. The interview was an intense experience over two days; we were given all sorts of tests and challenges, woodwork, spreadsheets, electronics, sewing, team games and more. The most important thing was to pick a team that would get on together, so we were surrounded by people with clipboards, assessing our personalities. I was lucky enough to make the team, and headed south.'

Her job as base assistant with responsibility for finances and stock control means that she spends quite a lot of her time in Antarctica helping to maintain the first permanent British Antarctic base, which was built there in the 1940s.

'It wasn't at all what I expected, but then I had no idea what to expect. The surroundings are so incredible, it was awesome just to look around and see snow, ice, glaciers and mountains in every direction, as well as penguins, seals, whales and Antarctic sea birds.'

At the University of Leeds we create an environment which allows you to develop.

We give you the knowledge, skills and opportunities to be who you want to be. So whether you want to solve world hunger, create the next Google or cure cancer a STEM degree at the University of Leeds will prepare you to take on a world of challenges.

Mark de Jong, BSc Environmental Science

Mark chose to study environmental science at the University of Leeds due to its wide-range of options and flexible nature, enabling him to experience a variety of topics so that he could make an informed decision about his career. After graduating with a BSc in Environmental Science, Mark began work as a research technician at the Bermuda Institute of Ocean Science (BIOS). He spends most of his time visiting field stations around the island, maintaining scientific instruments and collecting samples of rainwater, aerosols and particulate matter for analysis in the lab. He also collects samples of atmospheric trace metals from the top of a 23-metre tower, 'where the views are amazing!' he says.

Mark took advantage of the industrial placement option on his degree and spent a year as an environmental engineer for a construction company. 'Taking an industrial placement was one of the best decisions I made about my degree', he says. His final-year dissertation involved research into developing a method for sampling dangerous airborne pollutants, using gas chromatography. 'It was both challenging and rewarding, and it helped me get this job with BIOS'.

Faith Bateman, MEng Electronic and Electrical Engineering

'The great thing about engineering is that it opens more doors than it closes. I wasn't certain about what career I wanted to pursue, so an engineering degree appealed to me because I could use the skills I would learn in a diverse range of industries. In essence I did not choose to be an electronic and electrical engineer; I chose a subject I found exciting which would enhance my knowledge and give me a valuable degree. It was the practical elements of the course at the University of Leeds that enticed me to apply, and the hands on experience helped me to cement the knowledge I gained in lectures and gave me a better idea of different ways I could use my degree.

'The university has strong links with industry, and thanks to this I obtained a summer placement with Ultra Electronics in London after my second year. This experience gave me a taste of what a career in engineering would be like. I am now undertaking a PhD and I am currently designing a microfluidic system to analyse immune interactions at the single cell level. This is an interdisciplinary endeavour which bridges engineering with cancer research. I was able to apply for my position thanks to my electronic and electrical engineering background and the "wet lab" experience I gained during my MEng research project on molecular scaffolding.'

Find out more about University of Leeds STEM degrees at www.stem.leeds.ac.uk

Part 1
The job roles

1

Scientists are not all the same

There are many different ways to have a career in science

The Science Council is the umbrella organisation of learned societies and professional bodies in the UK drawn from across science and its applications. It currently has 40 member bodies which in turn have more than 400,000 individual members who undertake a very wide range of roles within science and academia, schools, industry and the public sector. While it has been relatively easy to define science ('the pursuit and application of knowledge and understanding of the natural and social world using a methodology based on evidence' is a definition taken from www.sciencecouncil.org/definition) it is far from easy to define the role of 'scientist'. Since its foundation in 2004, the Science Council has been trying to understand more about the range of occupations undertaken by those with science qualifications and experience, and what roles they are likely to be required to undertake in the future.

Chartered Scientists

Our first step in developing our understanding the careers paths of those with science qualifications was to explore the roles currently being undertaken by the 15,000 registered Chartered Scientists. The competencies for a Chartered Scientist combine science knowledge and skills with a series of professional attributes governing how the individual practises science: knowledge plus competence and ethics. This combination of attributes is of course not confined to academia and Chartered Scientists can be found in all sectors of the economy.

Varied career paths

Starting with these three categories, further research by the Science Council showed that while many people tend to consider 'scientists' to be primarily an elite group of individuals with PhDs whose primary purpose is research, individuals who called themselves professional scientists were very much more varied in the roles they undertook. Each year some 175,000–195,000 graduates are leaving UK higher education with science, technology, engineering and mathematics (STEM) degrees and, while it was obvious that not all of these graduates entered research or even science-based careers, demand from employers remained consistently strong, especially as science is now involved in almost every part of the global economy. We needed to understand where the STEM graduates went, how many could be classified as in 'science' occupations and how many were undertaking other roles that may or may not draw on their scientific knowledge and skills.

This research showed that a science professional may have a career **as** a scientist, **in** science or **from** science.

Working as a scientist, the individual will probably be in a STEM environment where the role will be clearly recognised as a science role within what would also be classified as a 'science' sector of the economy, for example, research and development (R&D) in pharmaceuticals or materials, or as a biomedical scientist in the NHS or forensic lab, testing or developing new equipment or services. These jobs might even be called 'scientist'.

Working in science individuals would be in a science sector but they will have moved away from direct day to day science or laboratory activities and would be influencing, supporting, promoting, managing, leading and shaping the way science is delivered and used. Examples include managing a collaboration between industry and academia, leading a research or grant funding programme, shaping a new R&D investment or purchasing strategy, leading the roll out of a new application or project, developing sales and support literature, influencing the training, regulation or public policy related to a product or application of a research output, or perhaps being involved in science publishing or communication.

However, we also found that scientists moved into wider employment sectors where their science knowledge and skills were valued but neither the sector nor role would normally be classified as science based; for example psychologists working in marketing or customer relations, or mathematicians and IT specialists working in logistics in the retail sector or risk modelling in banking, sales and purchasing of high tech equipment in non-science sectors (including IT), in technology-dependent creative sectors such as film and TV, marketing, promotion and campaigning as well as advising non-governmental organisations (NGOs) and politicians.

We found that science teachers outside higher education are also not commonly classified as working in science, and that most of those working in the health sector are also overlooked in traditional labour market information (LMI) looking at science occupations. You can read the following publication, www.ukces.org.uk/assets/ukces/docs/publications/briefing-paper-the-supply-of-and-demand-for-high-level-stem-skills.pdf for more information.

In addition to all these different types of employment destinations for science graduates, we found large numbers who entered the economy in 'graduate' jobs where their science skills and knowledge were the key skills that employers sought, although the jobs may not be science or technically based: this is the group we would term **'from'** science occupations. The picture of this last group is changing rapidly as almost all sectors of the economy now depend on the application of science and technology and are recruiting graduates with a high level of science and mathematics literacy. We also know that while Chartered Scientists were those with considerable experience and postgraduate qualifications in science, there were many others in the UK economy and society who were also using science in their roles.

The UK science workforce

The Science Council has supported UK workforce research (see www.sciencecouncil.org/sites/default/files/UK_Science_Workforce_FinalReport_TBR_2011.pdf) that aims to provide greater depth of data on the size, age profile, distribution and qualifications of the UK science workforce and give us a better understanding of demand for science skills in the economy. The methodology takes account of the whole economy as well as roles as scientists and using science, dividing these into primary and secondary science, and employment sectors into core and related science, and non-science. The results show that there are currently 5.8 million people in the UK workforce using science skills in their current role in roughly equal proportions of postgraduate, graduate and non-graduates: that amounts to 20% of the UK workforce with science skills and training. However only 200,000 were employed in the areas traditionally considered the domain of 'scientists': 170,000 people work in R&D and a further 32,000 are in academia. It was immediately clear that science graduates were literally everywhere in the economy.

In this research the definitions used were as follows.

Primary science workers: workers in occupations that are purely science based and require the consistent application of scientific knowledge and skills in order to execute the role effectively, for example, biochemists, chemical engineers, science and engineering technicians and medical radiographers. There are in total 1.2 million primary science workers in the economy where the largest employment sectors are health (474,000) and education (72,000) and other key sectors include pharmaceuticals, chemicals and energy and environment.

Secondary science workers: workers in occupations that are science related and require a mixed application of scientific knowledge and skills alongside other skill sets, which are often of greater importance to executing the role effectively: for example, actuaries, animal husbandry managers, chiropodists, civil engineers, environmental protection officers, pharmaceutical dispensers, teaching professionals, regulation and monitoring, and software professionals. There are 4.6 million secondary science workers in the UK economy with a significant proportion in health (1.2 million) and education (1.3 million).

Activities using science within the wider economy include design, laboratory services, health, regulation, policy, business to business (B2B) services, risk, marketing, technical, law and creative sectors, all of which can draw down, and influence, the current demand for science research as well as for scientists. This is why demand for those with science degrees is so strong and why it is so important to for graduates to develop a better understanding of the overall landscape of jobs and opportunities beyond a future in R&D.

About a quarter of the UK science workforce have postgraduate qualifications and a further 30% are graduates: in total therefore there are approximately 3.3 million graduate or above science-related jobs currently in the economy. The workforce research predicts that this will rise to around 4.5 million jobs in 2020, reflecting both up-skilling of roles and increasing overall demand for science skills.

Is science a vocation?

There is an unhelpful tendency to use the language of vocations when talking about degrees in STEM, something that is not done when discussing humanities and arts degrees. Medicine, dentistry, veterinary science, nursing etc. can properly be considered 'vocational' where the qualification is also a licence to practise, or the first step towards this: typically 90% or more of these graduates would enter the linked occupations. Many degrees are certainly occupation facing, preparing graduates for a range of roles within an employment sector such as laboratory-based biomedical sciences, forensic science, engineering or in environmental sciences. Typically 50%–60% of graduates would find their way to roles directly linked to the degree but others will take the skills to related sectors. For example, a biomedical science degree will be aligned closely with some roles within the NHS but graduates with these degrees are also sought in other analytical laboratory and testing environments elsewhere in the public sector (for example in water and air quality testing), forensic science and analytical chemistry in industry.

Another group of degrees might be better described as 'academic' where the choice may be influenced by a love of the subject rather than with any particular career path in mind. Having a degree in physics, chemistry, biology, natural sciences or mathematics does not, of course, automatically create a physicist, chemist, biologist, natural scientist or mathematician in a career or professional sense and is no more 'vocational' than a history, anthropology, classics, language or philosophy degree. While those who wish to enter research careers in these areas are likely to require a specialist degree in the subject, for the most part the preparation will be good grounding for a very wide range of both science and non-science career options.

Defining scientist roles

The most obvious way to define science occupations is to draw on the central discipline underpinning the work: physics, chemistry, biology, soil science, psychology, etc. Professional bodies also work around sectors such as energy or water but this doesn't help to describe what people actually do in their work. In order to give some shape and understanding to this landscape the Science Council has identified 10 broad types of scientist that looks at the types of skills and aptitudes used in different types of occupation.

Even within these broad categories the roles differ but the following 10 types of scientist may help to illustrate the range and help individuals to visualise the types of roles for which they might be best suited. The 10 types are listed below.

1. Explorer

2. Investigator

3. Developer/translational

4. Service provider/operational

5. Monitor/regulator

6. Entrepreneur

7. Communicator

8. Teacher

9. Business/marketing

10. Policy maker.

The **explorer scientist** is someone who, like Columbus, is on a journey of discovery 'to boldly go where no man has gone before'. They will be undertaking research and most often this will be 'blue skies' research and they will describe themselves as a 'basic' scientist. They will rarely focus on a specific outcome or impact beyond the next piece of the complex jigsaw of scientific understanding and knowledge and their research is likely to be funded by a publicly funded research council (see www.rcuk.ac.uk for more information) or a charitable foundation. As a 'blue skies' researcher the freshness of their ideas and creativity of their hypotheses will mark them out but they can be of any age and there are several funding schemes aimed at fostering and developing these individuals who play a key role in global science. Such researchers often work alone and describe themselves as very focused and determined and their environment as very competitive, especially for funding and publication. Investment and funding can be unpredictable. Explorer scientists are likely to be employed in a university or research centre but may not be teaching or involved in science policy. A key output measure will be publications in learned journals.

The **investigator scientist** is the 'mapping' scientist and this group includes the majority of those involved in science research. Investigator scientists dig into the unknown observing, mapping, understanding and piecing together in-depth knowledge and data, setting out the landscape for others to translate and develop, such as the scientists working on the human genome project. They are often adaptable, moving between different fields of research and between funders and institutions. They will almost certainly be located in higher education or a research centre, but unlike the explorer scientist they will usually work in a team in what will increasingly be a multidisciplinary environment and getting published will be a key feature of their lives. While output measures include research publications they will often be multiple authors, international networks and more stable funding environments. The majority of the 170,000 individuals in UK R&D will be in this category so while there are relatively more opportunities than for explorer scientists, it remains a competitive pathway with opportunities limited by the level of funding available.

The **developer/translational scientist** is an 'applied' scientist whose depth of knowledge and skills in both the research environment and the potential user environment enables them to make use of the knowledge generated by others and transform it into something that society can use. They might be developing products, services, ideas that change behaviour, improvements in health care and medicines, new technology or the application of existing technology in new settings. They will be the interface between science and society, turning new knowledge and understanding of the world around us into benefits for society. For example, they may be working as a link between a university research team and a business user, or between a research team and the NHS as a new treatment for patients is rolled out. Developer/translator scientists are likely to have postgraduate qualifications but will have added to this a broader understanding of industry or the public sector helping them to draw down on research outputs and shape research and development inputs.

The **operational/service provider scientist** is one who provides scientific services in a wide range of ways. Rarely visible, these are scientists we have come to depend on within the health service, forensic science, food science, health and safety, materials analysis and regulation and testing but many also provide support in research and educational laboratories. This group of scientists will have strong laboratory skills, high levels of dexterity and attention to detail, and they probably do wear a white coat. They are more likely to work in teams and there are large numbers within pathology and biomedical services within the health sectors. But equally, they may also run their own business providing services to water and food industries, local government or agriculture. Many operational scientists are working within regulated sectors and examples include biomedical scientists, chemistry laboratories, public health scientists and school and higher education science technicians.

The **monitor/regulator scientist** is becoming increasingly important as we translate more science and technology into society, and as society needs the increasing reassurance that systems and technology are reliable and safe and seen to be reliable and safe. It is crucial for society that we build and maintain public trust and confidence in the applications of science so the monitor/regulator scientist must be able to communicate with the public as well as with the leading edge researcher, and establish credibility with both communities. They will have a mix of skills and may not be working in the lab very much although they will have a thorough understanding of the science and the processes involved in monitoring its use or application. Examples include the Food Standards Agency (FSA), government science services, the Human Fertilisation and Embryology Authority (HFEA) and a wide range of testing and measurement services.

The **entrepreneur scientist** plays a crucial role in making innovation happen. Their scientific knowledge and connections are deep enough to be able to see opportunities for innovation – not just in business but also in public sector and service delivery. They are able to blend their science knowledge and credibility with people management skills, entrepreneurial flair and a strong understanding of business and finance. They will need to know how business sectors work, how to secure investment and finance, and to oversee the innovation and development process bringing products and services through to market. Entrepreneurial scientists will need to explain or 'represent' the science thinking at Board level and to investors and are likely to have developed their knowledge across a range of disciplines and applications during a long career in science-based sectors. Technological developments are occurring everywhere in the economy where scientists have grown start-ups into large-scale companies in areas such as biotechnology, fuel and green energy solutions, satellite development and communication, transport innovation, fabrics and fashion and the development of app marketing.

Communicator scientists are a crucial group of scientists. A communicator scientist's career path may follow a variety of routes and for the majority there is likely to be some postgraduate science training. These are scientists who are able to combine their science and technological know-how with an ability to communicate and they need to be credible and trusted by both the science community and the public. Often undervalued by people who consider themselves to be 'pure' scientists, the science community has recognised the need to increase the pool of individuals with this combination of skills as all science sectors, not just research, need good science communicators. Robert Winston, Brian Cox and Alice Roberts are examples of scientists who manage to combine deep knowledge of and enthusiasm for the science with an ability to understand and respond to what audiences need to know but other roles would be in museums and science centres, journalism, working with NGOs and in fundraising, in government and in education.

The **teacher scientist** is an obvious category – people who are trained in science and who share this knowledge and enthusiasm to educate and train the next generation. Often forgotten, but certainly in my view fully part of the science community, these scientists will be working in schools, colleges and higher education and also in developing the tools for teaching and learning. Their knowledge of science is combined with pedagogy and hopefully, they play a key role in shaping education. The UK is short of science teachers, particularly in physics, and there are several schemes established to encourage good science graduates to consider teaching as a career option, such as Teach First.

The **business scientist** will be found in almost all parts of the economy where a high level of science and technology knowledge and skill is playing a part. The science and technology based sectors employ large numbers of different types of STEM graduates working in a variety of settings from R&D to marketing, especially in the B2B sectors such as IT and the chemical industries. STEM skills and knowledge are of course valuable in many types of non-STEM businesses – marketing, modelling, product development, finance, insurance, communications, risk management etc. – but in the STEM-related B2B environments a high level of technical and specialist knowledge is essential: examples would be pharmaceuticals, logistics, IT, chemicals and materials. These scientists must have sufficient scientific and technical knowledge to be credible with colleagues and competitors and over time they will have opportunities to progress through the company to higher levels at which their scientific knowledge is valuable but their management and business skills are essential. At senior management board or Executive Board level they may be in a minority of those with science knowledge and will have to lead discussions and decision making on new products, competition, health and safety etc.

The **policy scientist** combines science and technical knowledge and skills with knowledge and understanding of government and policy making, decision making and scrutiny processes to ensure that legislation and policy have a sound evidence base. They are employed and involved at many levels and in many environments including government and Parliament, NGOs and campaigning groups. Within this group of scientists, communication, people and negotiation skills are highly prized, as is their ability to live within an environment in which decisions have to be made on incomplete evidence or uncertainty. To be a government chief scientific adviser is perhaps at the top level and some have described this role as 75% scientist and 25% politician.

The 10 types of scientists described above serve to illustrate that not all 'scientists' work in a lab in a white coat and not all of them will have a PhD; but that a science degree can be a route to a very wide range of careers across all sectors of the economy. In exploring career options, graduates should consider whether they wish to combine science skills and knowledge with an interest in business, management, communication or policy and whether they want to work in a mixed environment with non-scientists. I am very grateful for the input from the Science Council's member organisations and to hundreds of individual chartered scientists who I have asked to describe their job and then to decide what type of scientist they are. Having started with three categories I ended up with 10, but was pleased to have avoided increasing this to a full football team of roles! I hope others find this outline of the 10 types of scientist helpful and can use it to broaden their careers information advice and guidance on STEM careers.

Chapter written by Diana Garnham on behalf of the Science Council, www.sciencecouncil.org.

2

Biology

The Society of Biology states that without a well-trained workforce of biological science graduates, we would not have clean water, carbon-neutral foods or carefully produced crops, and biology graduates are highly valued by employers. Biologists carry out an essential range of roles, including working with animals, plants, and marine life, as well as working in areas such as science writing, the media and medicine, and this chapter explores some of those options.

Getting into the field

Careers within the biological sciences are competitive, so it can be advantageous to obtain work experience in the areas that interest you before you graduate. Not only will this enhance your applications in terms of skills development, but it will also help you to establish which areas would suit you best. Employers include NHS trusts and private hospitals, pharmaceutical and biotechnology companies, universities and private research laboratories, and outreach organisations such as science centres and museums.

Postgraduate study

You may also wish to look into whether a postgraduate qualification in a specialist area could enhance your prospects, and this is where talking to relevant recruiters can provide you with valuable advice. For example, if you want to be become a university lecturer in your subject or a research scientist, you will need to have a PhD. If you wish to be a soil scientist, only the University of Aberdeen offers an undergraduate degree in this subject, so you may need a master's in soil science to progress in this field on top of a first degree.

More detailed descriptions of options in biology are below, and all salary information is derived from Prospects, the graduate careers website, which is regularly updated, unless otherwise stated.

The job roles

Agricultural scientist

An agricultural scientist tests out new methods of farming and tries these out on experimental farms, usually focusing their work on one specialist area. This work is varied, from working in a very practical way with farmers, to conducting scientific research. Work includes liaison with external parties such as manufacturers of animal feed and pharmaceuticals, as well as other scientists and horticulturalists. Due to the nature of this work, it may not be suitable for those who suffer with allergies.

Entry

Entry to this field is usually with a degree in agriculture or a related discipline, such as biology, animal science or horticulture. A postgraduate qualification, such as a master's in poultry science, seed or soil science could enhance your prospects. Practical experience of working on a farm or in horticulture is usually expected. Longer hours may be required for out of hours farm visits or when laboratory experiments require shift work. Entry to careers in this sector is competitive, but there is a wide range of potential employers, including: animal and plant feed manufacturers, agricultural consultancies, the Department for Environment, Food and Rural Affairs (DEFRA), and chemical companies.

 SOCIETY OF
Biology

The UK's largest
professional body
for the life sciences

Professional development

Professional recognition

Meet other bioscientists

**Continuing Professional
Development**

Chartered Biologist status

www.societyofbiology.org/join

Telephone: 0844 858 9316

Profile: The Society of Biology

The world is constantly changing and biologists play a vital role in keeping up with those changes – from developing medicines and producing enough food supplies for our growing populations, to tackling climate change and species loss.

The Society of Biology can help you in your career

Whatever stage you are at in your career, the Society of Biology is here to help. From practical tips for job applications and techniques for a great interview, to advice on your job search, we provide information and guidance on all aspects of careers in the life sciences. An excellent starting point is the *Next Steps* booklet – the ultimate careers guide for bioscientists, which can be downloaded at www.societyofbiology.org/nextsteps.

Visit our website to see the full range of careers resources we have to offer: www.societyofbiology.org/careers.

Our Life Sciences Careers Conferences are a great way to get information on the wide ranging careers available to bioscience graduates. Experts from across the biosciences will be there to share their knowledge and experience. You can meet with employers and get guidance on planning your career and improving your CV. For details of this year's events and to register, visit www.societyofbiology.org/lscc.

When searching for jobs visit jobs.societyofbiology.org the one stop shop for biology jobs. You can upload your CV, set up alerts and search online for the latest jobs.

Becoming a member of the Society of Biology helps you to get more out of biology

Becoming a member is a great way to demonstrate your commitment to your career and improve your CV. Members can apply for grants for overseas travel in connection with biological study, teaching or research, and the Society offers Undergraduate Research Bursaries to support students in gaining valuable research experience throughout their summer holidays. As a member you will have the opportunity to network with experienced biologists who could be your future colleagues and employers, both at events and online. Members can also stay up-to-date with the latest news with our award-winning magazine, *The Biologist*.

Join today

The Society of Biology is a single unified voice for biology: advising government and influencing policy; advancing education and professional development; supporting members, and engaging and encouraging public interest in the life sciences. The Society represents a diverse membership of individuals, learned societies and other organisations.

www.societyofbiology.org/membership

Skills

Candidates should be able to demonstrate skills in the following areas:

- personal organisation

- able to get on with different people

- able to adopt a flexible approach to work.

Salary information

New entrants to this field usually earn between £17,000 and £22,000 but this can rise considerably with experience. (Sources: inputyouth.co.uk and careersinagriculture.co.uk.)

Typical work activities

Typical work as an agricultural scientist can include:

- carrying out tests on feed content or pesticides

- researching subjects such as animal and plant diseases, or pest control

- developing new crops and more efficient methods for growing crops

- advising farmers on how to generate more from their farms

- writing reports and keeping up to date with developments in the industry.

Training and development

With a master's degree, four years' experience and some management responsibility, it may be possible to apply to become a Chartered Scientist (CSci).

Further resources

Careers in Agriculture: www.careersinagriculture.co.uk/careers/agricultural-scientist

Input Youth: www.inputyouth.co.uk/jobguides/job-agriculturalscientist.html

Science and Advice for Scottish Agriculture (SASA): www.sasa.gov.uk

Arboriculturist

An arboriculturist, also known as a tree surgeon, cultivates and manages trees in both urban and rural settings. They are required to work outdoors and at heights in all weather conditions, so applicants may find that an enjoyment of outdoor pursuits is advantageous. Employment is usually with local authority planning and environment departments, commercial tree care companies, conservation organisations such as the National Trust, and botanic gardens, schools and universities. Self-employment can also be an option.

Entry

Relevant degree subjects include the life sciences, agricultural sciences, and urban studies. Myerscough College in Lancashire offers a BSc specifically in arboriculture. Applicants can complete a National Diploma in Arboriculture, which is one of the key recognised qualifications in the field.

Skills

Candidates should also be able to demonstrate:

- a good level of physical fitness

- a clean driving licence

- a good head for heights

- previous climbing experience, if appropriate.

Salary information

Entry-level positions offer starting salaries of about £15,000, rising to about £21,000. Supervisory roles offer salaries of up to £30,000. Very experienced arboriculturists may be eligible to apply for teaching roles and this could attract a higher salary.

Typical work activities

An arboriculturist would typically:

- apply their knowledge of tree biology for effective tree maintenance

- follow and negotiate clients' requirements

- carry out tree inspections and surveys

- give pre-planning advice on topics such as the effect a proposed development may have on trees in the area.

Training and development

The International Society of Arboriculture offers a certification programme. Membership of relevant professional training bodies, such as the Institute of Chartered Foresters (ICF) and the Arboricultural Association, may also help career development to more senior levels.

Further resources

Arboriculturists Association: www.trees.org.uk

ICF: www.charteredforesters.org

National Careers Service: nationalcareersservice.direct.gov.uk/advice/planning/jobprofiles/Pages/Arboriculturist.aspx

Prospects: www.prospects.ac.uk/arboriculturist_job_description.htm

Case study

Dr Sanjay Mistry, Former Post-doctoral Researcher with Stem Cell Group, University of Bristol, and then Azellon Cell Therapeutics

Why did you choose a career in science?
Science was the only real subject at school that interested me and I think when given options, science was the only subject that I was interested in and wanted to pursue in the future.

What made you choose your particular area?
I started wanting to be a chemist at high school but I found A level chemistry too hard. However, biological sciences was something I started to do well in and when it came to applying to UCAS I applied for biological science courses. To be honest I didn't know what I wanted to do and admittedly a lot of the decisions were peer influenced at the time; I think I would have liked to have become a doctor or a pharmacist really but didn't know or seek advice on how or where to begin. I kind of went with the flow and did what sounded enjoyable. I ended up applying to study biomedical science at first then changed to physiology and pharmacology because I think on reflection I wasn't academically strong enough to get into medical school anyway!

What was your route in? Qualifications, experience, contacts?
With some difficulties I was having at the time I ended up with only one A level. However, I was lucky and managed to get onto a HND in Biological Sciences at the University of the West of England (UWE), which meant that once I had completed it I was able to get on to a degree programme and skip a year. I completed my undergraduate degree in Pharmacology and Physiology, with a year in industry working in ophthalmic research for the Bristol Eye Hospital in 2001, but without a plan! So for two years I was working in call centres and applying for jobs at the same time, getting the odd interview now and again but always unsuccessful. I realised something wasn't working in my applications and time was passing so I then decided to take a new approach and apply for lower paid laboratory assistant jobs to get into the industry before I ended up being a call centre manager. I managed very quickly to get a role for three years with the Academic Rheumatology group. I worked hard and obtained my PhD and five publications within five years while working with them. We were making the national and international news with some of the breakthroughs we'd made, and spreading the news at international conferences. From our successes my professor started up a spin-out company developing medical devices from stem cell technologies which I ended up getting involved in as a postdoctoral researcher translating bench side experiments to clinical trial technologies.

What is a typical day like for you?
You need to be self-motivated and driven. Work started around nine but academic research has no rules on time keeping. You are your own boss. I would start with emails and from that a list of duties for the day can begin. You need to fit in the odd experiment but these can be done over a long period of time depending on what the protocol is. You negotiate your time with the objectives you are trying to achieve with your mentor. Nothing is really set in stone.

What do you enjoy most about your work?

I enjoyed the successes we had before moving onto my next role; I achieved five publications and was in the press frequently. You get to travel and meet other scientists in your field at international conferences.

What are the challenges?

I found with time that academic life wasn't really for me, and the difficulties that came with going into the business and management side in the spin-out companies was something I also didn't want to do. Research is funded in short-term contracts and you are best to jump from city to city or even work abroad to really be successful. I have since taken my interest in biology to a different area and retrained as a physiotherapist where I can use my subject knowledge but work more directly with people.

What advice would you offer a current student/recent graduate aiming for a role in your field?

Find a subject that you are passionate about and really research whether academia is for you. A lot of postgraduates leave academia to do something bizarre like being an account manager in a scientific company, which to me makes no sense if you love science!

What would you do differently, if anything, if you were starting your career all over again?

Nothing, I've done what I've done and I wouldn't be where I am if I hadn't learned from what I know now.

Botanist

A botanist studies all forms of plant life, including plant anatomy and physiology, genetics, and the taxonomy (identification and classification) of plants. There are several specialisms within this field: botanists with an interest in ecology will look at the interactions of plants with the environment and other organisms, while a field botanist might search for new species or examine how well plants grow in different conditions. Others may look at how to incorporate plant extracts into household products and cosmetic manufacturing.

Botanical research benefits the way in which we make use of building materials, textiles, foods and medicines in society. Botanists can also advise on the management of parks and green spaces, as well as helping to alleviate pollution problems. Work is usually a combination of laboratory and field work, and hours can be long.

Entry

Much of the available information on working as a botanist pertains to the US, so it is recommended that you seek guidance on particular qualifications directly from the admissions tutors for botany courses that interest you. The Society of Biology can advise on choosing courses to advance your career in this sector. Generally, you will need a degree in botany, plant biology, plant science, environmental science or ecology in order to begin your career.

Skills

Applicants should be able to demonstrate:

- an interest in nature and the environment

- good scientific knowledge, especially in biology and chemistry

- research skills, and the ability to analyse and interpret data.

Salary information

According to the National Careers Service, starting salaries for botanists are around £22,000 per year, rising to £30,000 for botanists in research posts and £55,000 for senior lecturers working in universities.

Typical work activities

A botanist's work may include the following activities:

- conducting experiments to develop new or improved crops

- developing or improving products for controlling disease or pests

- studying the effects of pollution or building developments on plant life

- managing a botanical collection.

Training and development

It is possible to train in biological recording with the Botanical Society of the British Isles, or the Field Studies Council. The Society of Biology also offers training for continuing professional development.

Further resources

Botanical Society of the British Isles: www.bsbi.org.uk

Field Studies Council: www.field-studies-council.org

National Careers Service: nationalcareersservice.direct.gov.uk/advice/planning/jobprofiles/Pages/botanist.aspx

Science Buddies: www.sciencebuddies.org/science-fair-projects/science-engineering-careers/PlantBio_soilandplantscientist_c001.shtml#whatdotheydo

Society of Biology: www.societyofbiology.org

Microbiologist

A microbiologist studies the growth and development of microorganisms such as bacteria, viruses, and algae. They also analyse practical problems in agriculture, medicine and industry, look at how microorganisms can be used to identify the virus responsible for a pandemic, engineer new bacterial strains for food development and manufacturing, and look at how the clinical management of patients can be improved in relation to infections.

Entry

Candidates require a degree in a relevant subject such as: microbiology; biology (with substantial content in microbiology); microbial sciences and biomedical sciences. Microbiologists who are not medically qualified can work in a clinical setting either as a clinical scientist or as a biomedical scientist. A degree in biomedical sciences is recommended for entry as a biomedical scientist working in hospital medical microbiology laboratories, and career progression is via the NHS Scientist Training Programme (see Chapter 7 on working in the health sciences for more information). The Association of British Pharmaceutical

Industry (ABPI) provides details of employers offering summer work experience opportunities.

Skills

Applicants will need to show evidence of the following skills:

- a methodical and accurate approach to work

- very high standards of health and safety.

Salary information

A microbiologist working as a clinical scientist in the National Health Service (NHS) would earn between £25,000 and £34,000 while those working in public health laboratories or pharmaceutical firms can earn higher salaries of up to £37,000.

Typical work activities

There is a very wide variety of work in this area, and within it a microbiologist may typically:

- track microorganisms in a range of environments

- prepare reports and recommendations based on research findings

- use a variety of specialist equipment, such as electron microscopes

- develop and plan methods to prevent the spread of disease

- develop new medicines, vaccinations and pharmaceutical products.

Training and development

Within larger organisations, such as the NHS and other hospital services, there are more structured training opportunities, and microbiologists may be encouraged to undertake an MSc while working. Smaller organisations may not be equipped to offer structured training programmes, so it is important to identify what is available to you before choosing a post.

For later career advancement, qualification up to PhD level is essential for research positions. An experienced microbiologist may be able to move into other fields and put their specialist knowledge to use in patent work, teaching or pharmaceutical sales.

Further resources

ABPI: www.abpi.org.uk

NHS Careers: www.nhscareers.nhs.uk/explore-by-career/healthcare-science/careers-in-healthcare-science/careers-in-life-sciences/clinical-microbiologist/

Prospects: www.prospects.ac.uk/microbiologist_job_description.htm

Nature conservation officer

A nature conservation officer manages and improves areas of environmental importance. They can be involved in developing policy about the environment both locally and nationally. Nature conservation officers provide environmental consultancy to government departments, environmental charities and nature reserves. You may also find job titles within this sector such as: biodiversity officer, sustainable development officer or conservation technician. Typical employers include: charities, the National Trust, local authorities and conservation groups. Working hours can include bank holidays and weekends.

Entry

Applicants will need a relevant degree in a subject such as biology, zoology, environmental science, ecology, geography or sustainable development. Without a relevant undergraduate degree, a postgraduate qualification such as a master's may help your chances; some employers in this sector will expect a master's level qualification and entry may be difficult without one, so it is worth contacting potential recruiters to find out what is required.

Most candidates will have begun their career in this sector with volunteering activities, and any experience in conservation management, planning or education will be valuable to your application. This is a competitive area and full-time posts are rare, with more substantial roles going to those who have already demonstrated commitment through volunteering or short-term contracts.

Skills

Candidates will also need to demonstrate:

- communication skills, including working with the public through walks, talks and education programmes

- persistence and commitment

- knowledge of geographical information systems (GIS).

Salary information

Early career officers will start on £16,000–£18,000 rising to £30,000 after 10–15 years of experience. Experienced officers, taking on management roles, may earn more than £30,000 and salaries may be higher in the private sector.

Typical work activities

A nature conservation officer may typically:

- contribute to planning and policy development

- prepare conservation reports, plans and publicity materials

- carry out wildlife observation and species surveys

- provide advice to landowners, planners and developers.

Training and development

Nature conservation officers are generally expected to enter the profession fully. It may be possible to undertake short courses as part of on the job training, and the Countryside Jobs Service lists opportunities on its website. Promotion requires involvement in a range of projects, so it is advisable to get involved with local steering groups, or organisations such as Friends of the Earth. Career advancement usually entails taking on a management role and may involve relocation.

Further resources

All About Careers: www.allaboutcareers.com/careers/job-profile/nature-conservation-officer.htm

Countryside Jobs Service: www.countryside-jobs.com

Prospects: www.prospects.ac.uk/nature_conservation_officer_job_description.htm

TARGETjobs: targetjobs.co.uk/careers-advice/job-descriptions/276207-nature-conservation-officer-job-description

Soil scientist

A soil scientist evaluates soil conditions by analysing its chemical, biological and physical composition, in order to inform and influence issues such as environmental quality, agricultural production, climate change and biodiversity. They study the responses of crops to fertilizers and crop rotation, and consult on construction projects. Soil scientists can also work in areas such as overseas development, forensics, government policy, and archaeological excavations.

Entry

To enter a career in soil science, candidates need a good honours degree in a relevant subject such as: biology, botany, chemistry, ecology, engineering, geology, soil science and zoology. Soil science is usually studied as a component of another degree programme in the UK; the University of Aberdeen is the only institution offering a degree in purely plant and soil science. A master's degree in soil science may be helpful if the undergraduate degree is not so relevant to this career choice. Take advantage of opportunities to develop laboratory skills through degree coursework. Because of the field work involved, candidates are also required to be physically fit and possess a clean driving licence. Candidates with disabilities should not be deterred from entering this profession as barriers to practice are gradually being removed.

Skills

Candidates should also be able to demonstrate the following skills:

- willingness to work outside in all weathers

- the ability to plan and carry out research.

Salary information

Typical starting salaries for a new soil scientist are between £16,000 and £22,000 rising to £24,000–£52,000 after 10–15 years of experience in the role. Salaries will vary depending on location, and the private sector pays more than public sector work.

Typical work activities

Soil scientists would typically carry out the following duties:

- field work, including collecting and storing samples, and travelling to sites within the UK

- monitoring or supervising laboratory work

- investigating the responses of soils to specific farming practices

- integrating soil science research and knowledge into the management of land and ecosystems

- identifying degraded or contaminated soils and planning how to improve their composition and characteristics.

Training and development

Soil scientists train on the job, and will tend to meet the needs of the organisation for which they work. It can help to join a relevant professional body, such as the Institute of Professional Soil Scientists (IPSS) or the British Society of Soil Scientists (BSSS). Promotion can often happen within five to 10 years of working for non-academic research bodies and by moving into management roles. Academic posts in universities have a much more structured career progression but lectureships can be extremely competitive to secure, and researchers may initially take on a series of fixed-term contracts to establish themselves.

Further resources

BSSS: www.soils.org.uk

IPSS: www.soilscientist.org

Prospects: www.prospects.ac.uk/soil_scientist_job_description.htm

Science Buddies: www.sciencebuddies.org/science-fair-projects/science-engineering-careers/Geo_soilscientist_c001.shtml

Technical brewer

A technical brewer manages the production and packaging of beers and lagers, ensuring that the quality of these products is at a high standard. They are responsible for the raw materials, as well as for the operatives and technicians producing the beers, and for maintaining the safe running of the production plant. In a large brewery they may look after a specialist area, or they could be responsible for supervising the entirety of a smaller operation. The role requires good knowledge of biochemistry, as well as sound business sense.

Work may be spread over evenings and weekends in shift patterns to allow for continuous production, and brewers can be called in out of hours to deal with technical problems. The working environment is noisy and industrial, and protective clothing is usually worn. Good physical fitness is required for maintaining large machinery, and travel between breweries may be required when working for large organisations. However, even what have been termed 'micro-breweries' now run surprisingly large operations, and the number of breweries in the UK is currently the highest it has been for 70 years, according to a 2012 survey by the Campaign for Real Ale (CAMRA).

Entry

To enter this profession as a trainee brewer a relevant degree will be needed. Only Heriot-Watt University in Scotland offers a degree course specifically on brewing and distilling, but degrees in biology, biochemistry, microbiology, food science and applied chemistry, among others, offer a good basis for development. The University of Nottingham offers a master's in brewing science, which could be a useful option for those without a relevant first degree. It is important to be sure that the industrial brewing environment will suit you, especially female applicants, as women are under-represented in this sector. Graduate recruitment schemes are run by some of the larger breweries, such as Fullers, but places are limited.

Skills

Candidates will need to demonstrate the following skills and abilities:

- a good scientific knowledge of brewing and biochemistry

- an understanding of chemical, mechanical and electrical engineering

- business and commercial awareness

- creativity for devising new products

- physical fitness and stamina.

Salary information

Starting salaries for a technical brewer can be anywhere between £17,000 and £24,000. This can rise to over £40,000 for a head brewer in a large facility.

Typical work activities

A technical brewer may be required to:

- check the temperatures and samples of beers

- work with a laboratory team to improve product quality

- source suppliers and ensure that raw materials meet the required standards

- create new products and their packaging for specific markets or occasions.

Training and development

More structured training opportunities may be available at larger breweries, and there is a programme on offer from the Institute of Brewing and Distilling (IBD), through certificate and diploma level through to Master Brewer (MBrew), which is appropriate for those with at least five years of experience in a more technical management role. Promotion and progression in this sector usually relies on willingness to take on management and supervisory roles, with a shift of emphasis from production to strategy and staff management.

Further resources

All About Careers: www.allaboutcareers.com/careers/job-profile/technical-brewer.htm

IBD: www.ibd.org.uk

National Careers Service: nationalcareersservice.direct.gov.uk/advice/planning/jobprofiles/Pages/technicalbrewer.aspx

Prospects: www.prospects.ac.uk/technical_brewer_job_description.htm

Society of Independent Brewers: siba.co.uk

Zoologist

A zoologist studies animal behaviour, characteristics and habitats. They collect and analyse data, such as GPS tracking, and use modelling software to predict and monitor the migration patterns of particular animals. Zoologists collect test samples to determine animal health and can be involved in complex procedures such as in-vitro fertilisation. They work to improve general knowledge of particular species, as well as supporting governments with conservation plans and providing information to the public. A lot of work carried out by zoologists involves prolonged observation, so patience and concentration over long periods of time are essential to be successful in this role. Zoologists often work in multidisciplinary teams, depending on the research they are carrying out; for example, research into how water pollution affects marine life may require work alongside a hydrologist and marine biologist. Field work can be very demanding if you are away for long periods of time, working in challenging conditions. There is also some risk of injury when working with animals, and the work can sometimes require long periods of time spent alone.

The majority of zoologists will work in academic research positions, as well as for government agencies, pharmaceutical companies and organisations involved in biomedical research and development. Relatively few zoologists end up working in zoos or in conservation, as salaries are modest and posts are far outweighed by applicants. There are also options for working within animal rehabilitation.

Entry

To become a zoologist, a good first degree is required in a relevant subject such as biology, zoology, animal ecology, parasitology or animal behaviour. To pursue a research position, further study to doctoral level is necessary.

Skills

Candidates should also be able to demonstrate skills in:

- patience, perseverance and working alone

- carrying out detailed and methodical work

- working as part of a multidisciplinary team.

Salary information

According to the National Careers Service, zoologists working in research posts can earn about £30,000 per year, rising to £50,000 for senior staff. Salaries in the private sector vary widely.

Typical work activities

Depending on the balance between field work and research in the role, a zoologist may typically:

- present to schools and other education and research establishments

- estimate wildlife population and growth

- collect and catalogue specimens and prepare collections

- prepare grant proposals and apply for research funding

- care for ill or injured animals and release them into their natural habitats.

Training and development

Some zoologists continue to specialise in their research, or move into private sector or consultancy work. It is also possible to move into other jobs such as management, marketing or scientific journalism with the skills gained from working as a zoologist. There may also be opportunities to work or study overseas, at other universities, institutions or wildlife parks.

Further resources

Alec.co.uk: www.alec.co.uk/free-career-assessment/careers-in-zoology.htm

National Career Service: nationalcareersservice.direct.gov.uk/advice/planning/jobprofiles/Pages/zoologist.aspx

3

Chemistry

According to TARGETjobs, one in every five pounds in the UK economy is dependent on developments in chemistry research. With opportunities available in research, industry, the production of pharmaceuticals and medicines, textile development and the examination of patent applications, there is plenty of variety for the graduate who wishes to work with chemistry. Working in chemistry requires specific technical and laboratory skills, and the more client-facing positions will also need good communication ability. Chemistry graduates are valued by employers for their research skills, attention to detail and analytical ability, entering a wide range of careers every year, including roles within the public sector, finance and manufacturing.

Opportunities exist throughout the UK, although Prospects points out that some opportunities with chemical employers are focused in the north west of England, while the south east contains the triumvirate of Oxford, Cambridge and London, offering a concentration of research-based employers. Several of the key roles in chemistry are detailed below, and looking at the typical working activities and routes in should help you to identify areas within chemistry that interest you. It is a good idea to start talking to professionals in these roles to find out what their job is really like on a day-to-day basis, and to make potentially useful contacts for work experience. Salary information is derived from Prospects unless otherwise indicated.

Please also see Chapter 7 on working in the health sciences, as there are plenty of opportunities to use chemistry as part of medical research and in various roles within the NHS.

The job roles

Analytical chemist

Analytical chemists are employed by both public and private organisations to assess the chemical structure and nature of substances, so that they can determine how that substance might behave under different conditions. These results can be used in drug development, to ensure stability and quality of products, in toxicology and also in forensic analysis. Analytical chemists usually work in multidisciplinary teams, and are mainly laboratory-based, although more senior staff may carry out office-based work. Work is usually nine to five, five days a week, although longer hours may be necessary, depending on deadlines. Typical employers of analytical chemists include government agencies, hospitals, research councils, environmental agencies and private food and pharmaceutical companies.

Entry

You will need a very good honours degree to enter a career as an analytical chemist, as academic standards for this field are high. A 2.i will be required, and possessing a degree in any of the following subjects could enhance your prospects:

- analytical chemistry

- applied chemistry

RSC Membership
Scientific Excellence and Professional Recognition

Thinking about progressing your career in the chemical sciences?

Competition for the best jobs in the chemical sciences has never been more intense. Being a member of the Royal Society of Chemistry can help you demonstrate your commitment to practising the highest standards and serve your professional goals:

- Keep up-to-date with the latest research and developments through free-access to a wide range of publications

- Engage with our global community of 48,000 chemical scientists, connecting with potential collaborators, funders and employers worldwide

- Explore your options for a successful future in the chemical sciences with the support of our careers service

Visit the website for further details on the extensive package of member benefits and services.

RSC | Advancing the Chemical Sciences

www.rsc.org/members
Registered charity number 207890

Profile: The Royal Society of Chemistry

The Royal Society of Chemistry (RSC) is a vibrant worldwide community that is committed to advancing excellence in the chemical sciences through promoting knowledge and sharing ideas.

Who we are

The RSC supports the education, professional development and recognition of chemical scientists whilst promoting the chemical science's role in solving social and economic problems. With offices in North America, Brazil, China, India, Japan and the UK, its reach is truly international.

Over 48,000 individuals are members of the RSC community, which spans over 100 countries, and includes leaders in industry and academia, policy makers and school teachers, as well as students. RSC membership provides professional and personal support, including access to the latest scientific information, professional development resources and funding opportunities.

The Careers Service and professional development: reach your full potential

The RSC's Careers Service helps members explore their options whatever their career stage. It offers free, confidential consultations with specialist careers advisers and a variety of online career development tools such as CV guidance, interview advice and job searching strategies. Careers events are also run for members, such as the online careers fair ChemCareers and careers hubs, which are run at locations across the country.

The RSC also enables members to gain skills and qualifications that can actively enhance their career opportunities. As a professional body we can offer appropriately qualified members designatory letters and routes to highly regarded qualifications. So whatever your career stage you can demonstrate commitment and gain professional recognition, factors that can help you take the next step.

Resources, networking and support: member benefits that make a difference

The RSC is a leading international publisher and members can access a number of online resources for free including the Virtual Library, a collection of peer reviewed journals, full text e-books, and databases, the RSC Journals Archive and Publishing platform. This huge variety of resources ensures that members can stay up to date with the latest research.

Members also receive the award winning *Chemistry World* magazine on a monthly basis, and unlimited access to the *Chemistry World* archive. Chemistry World Jobs brings you the latest job vacancies, placements and postgraduate opportunities from key industry employers, universities and specialist industry recruiters. Our members find *Chemistry World* an indispensable way of keeping up with the latest chemical sciences news, research and job opportunities.

Other member benefits include access to the RSC Networks. Our associations with leading chemical societies around the world enable our members to connect to a worldwide community of 300,000 chemical scientists. The Networks provide an excellent way of interacting with others in your field, for example allowing you to raise your profile with influential contacts.

In addition to supporting members professionally the RSC also provides personal support. This includes access to the RSC Benevolent Fund, which provides charitable grants and guidance in times of need.

Join the Royal Society of Chemistry today

To find out more about membership or become a member of the RSC please go to www. rsc.org/members

Case study

Remya, Senior Development Technologist

Having completed a year out in industry when I started applying for jobs in my final year of university I already had some experience of the application process. It was all about visibility – getting my CV on job websites and sending a tailored CV and covering letter out to employers and specialist recruitment agencies. Phone interviews, interviews and assessment centres were all part of the process and eventually I was successful in gaining the role of development technologist for International Paint.

I work in research and development, trying to understand how components of coatings can affect properties, and my chemistry degree is essential in this. I need to understand the chemistry of the components and whether there might be a more efficient way of using them. Other key skills include communication, teamwork and results orientation. It is also important to be innovative, have a customer and quality focus and, most importantly, knowledge of health and safety requirements.

I was heavily involved with the Royal Society of Chemistry (RSC) during my time at university, and still am. Having been involved as a student, I was able to work on the Committee for Recruitment and Retention of Members (CRRM), which was great in helping me meet new people. I am now involved with the Membership and Qualifications Board and Younger Members Network and the North East steering group, which I chair. I also carry out visits to schools and meet other chemists to discuss how to spread the love of chemistry.

Being involved with the RSC has provided opportunities for networking and learning about career options and I have been able to build up experience and knowledge of chemistry nationally and globally. There are a lot of employers who value membership of a professional body and the associated benefits.

I work with marine coatings, trying to ensure that marine vessels have the best protection and functionality. There is no fixed routine to my day – I work on both team projects and projects by myself, working in the lab or spending time in the office. I also get the opportunity to experience the issues first hand by going out to shipyards, attending training courses and visiting different parts of the world to meet experts and understand what is needed.

What I enjoy most about my job is the diversity; I am not just the typical 'white coat' chemist that people normally associate with chemistry. I also like the responsibility, which gives me the opportunity to develop both myself and the technology. Working for a large company (parent company AkzoNobel is the largest coatings company in the world) also means that I have many opportunities for career development.

My advice to students is to get some work experience in the chemical industry. My placement year at Merck Sharp & Dohme Ltd gave me an insight into the industry, as well as valuable skills, and prepared me for the real world when applying for jobs.

- biochemistry

- chemistry

- forensic science

- geochemistry.

Jobs in research will most likely require a PhD, and a doctorate is usually necessary to advance into senior posts. Because competition in this sector is high, any previous laboratory or research work experience can be advantageous, so talking to your academic department about finding placements or making useful contacts is advisable. However, full training in use of specific techniques and use of instruments is usually provided on the job.

Skills

Candidates should also be able to demonstrate evidence of the following:

- a logical mind and problem-solving ability

- a systematic and methodical approach to work

- excellent IT and laboratory skills

- teamworking skills

- personal responsibility

- excellent communication skills

- ability to explain complex science to non-technical staff.

Salary information

Salaries will depend on the employer and location, but a typical starting salary would be in the range of £14,000–£20,000. With more experience, you could expect to earn £24,000–£35,000 rising to over £50,000 with significant experience and managerial responsibilities.

Typical work activities

An analytical chemist would typically:

- use a range of equipment, software and laboratory techniques to undertake research and analysis

- provide information on compounds based on analysis

- report results and interpret data in accordance with data storage and protection regulations

- develop techniques for analysing drugs and chemicals

- work in multidisciplinary teams and with suppliers and customers

- keep up to date with relevant scientific developments

- ensure that health and safety regulations are upheld

- prepare licence documentation for new products.

Training and development

Most training will be carried out on the job in the form of short courses and workshops. The Royal Society of Chemistry (RSC) provides training opportunities that can count towards continuing professional development needs, and the Analytical Science Network also offers networking opportunities, as well as training, via its Emerging Analytical Professionals (EAP) meetings. Larger organisations may be able to fund further study to master's and PhD level. Opportunities for self-employment are rare, due to the costs of maintaining and equipping a laboratory, but some consulting work may be available for experienced staff.

Further resources

Analytical Science Network: www.rsc.org/Membership/Networking/InterestGroups/Analytical/ASN.asp

Prospects: www.prospects.ac.uk/analytical_chemist_job_description.htm

RSC: www.rsc.org

TARGETjobs: www.targetjobs.co.uk/careers-advice/job-descriptions/277545-analytical-chemist-job-description

Chemical engineer

A chemical engineer, also known as a process engineer, is involved in the design and construction of industrial processes. These processes can help with the production of oil and gas, pharmaceuticals, food and drink, plastics and toiletries, as well as in the research and development of new products. This role is well suited to chemists wishing to work in a more industrial environment, who possess excellent analytical and problem-solving skills, as well as the ability to manage projects and work with diverse teams. Jobs are available in this sector across the UK, and work is mainly nine to five, five days a week, with some shift work depending on particular employers.

Entry

The usual routes into a career in chemical engineering are either a three-year Bachelor of Engineering (BEng) degree, or a four-year Master of Engineering (MEng).

Both courses should be accredited by the Institution of Chemical Engineers (IChemE), if you are aiming for chartered status, whereby you will be accredited by a professional engineering body and expected to develop innovative solutions to engineering problems. BEng students will need to take on additional study to apply for chartered status, and work experience will be required by all applicants. Chemical engineering, biochemical engineering and process engineering are the most common areas studied for the BEng and MEng routes, but degrees in chemistry and applied chemistry, polymer science, environmental engineering and nuclear engineering can also be suitable.

Work experience is rapidly becoming essential for entry into this field, and applicants are advised to apply for placement and internship opportunities in industry for the summers of their second and third years, as employers such as Unilever and Procter and Gamble are increasingly recruiting graduates from their placement programmes. Note that advertisements for summer placements and work experience can start appearing as early as September of the preceding year, so you will need to plan ahead and apply early.

Skills

Candidates should also be able to demonstrate the following:

- project management skills

- good grasp of engineering and mathematical principles

- an interest in chemistry

- problem-solving and creative thinking skills

- teamworking skills

- communication skills, both oral and written

- excellent attention to detail

- commercial and business awareness.

Salary information

Salaries vary depending on the individual organisation and location, but the average graduate starting salary for a chemical engineer is about £28,000. With more experience, salaries can rise to £50,000 and to over £60,000 for a chartered chemical engineer.

Typical work activities

A chemical engineer would typically:

- test and develop new products

- use computer modelling to devise safe and cost-effective production methods

- upscale laboratory tests to large-scale industrial processes

- oversee the running of processing plants

- work closely with health and safety staff

- design and install new production plants.

Training and development

Some employers offer on the job training, and the IChemE runs short courses, workshops and conferences that contribute to continuing professional development. Schemes that are accredited by IChemE are known as Accredited Company Training Schemes (ACTS) and can help to ensure that professionals develop their skills appropriately and satisfy training requirements for chartership. Career development in this field usually depends on becoming chartered and, once this status has been attained, opportunities in project management and in developing specialist roles can become available.

Further resources

IChemE: www.icheme.org

National Careers Service: nationalcareersservice.direct.gov.uk/advice/planning/jobprofiles/Pages/chemicalengineer.aspx

Prospects: www.prospects.ac.uk/chemical_engineer_job_description.htm

Colour technologist

A colour technologist works with the science and technology of colour application and performance across a wide range of sectors, including textiles, paper, furnishings, medical products, inks, toiletries, paints and cosmetics. They can help to develop dyes and pigments, as well as analysing people's perception of colour, and can work with both customers and suppliers if employed in the retail sector. Working hours depend on individual organisations and location, but colour technologists usually work nine to five, five days a week. Manufacturing work may require shift patterns, and the industrial environment is noisy as well as requiring the wearing of protective clothing. Employers include the textile industry, clothing and furnishing design companies and cosmetics manufacturers.

Entry

Relevant degree subjects for a career as a colour technologist include:

- chemistry

- colour science

- clothing and textile technology

- materials and polymer science

- chemical engineering

- physics

- biomedical sciences (for medical careers)

- production or manufacturing engineering.

An MSc in Colour Science or Technology may be advantageous if your first degree is in a different subject, and a PhD will be required for research positions. Any work experience in the area would also enhance your application, but is not essential.

Skills

Candidates should also be able to demonstrate the following:

- excellent colour vision, for shade and colour matching

- good teamworking skills

- business and commercial awareness

- relevant technical skills

- excellent attention to detail

- good communication and client-facing skills.

Salary information

Technician roles can start at £17,000–£20,000 depending on the employer, while a more experienced colour technologist can earn £30,000–£35,000. Larger chemical companies may pay more than smaller organisations, and pay in the academic and retail sectors is higher than in technical roles.

Typical work activities

A colour technologist would typically:

- develop or modify existing dyes and pigments

- oversee the measurement of colour and its communication to computer-aided design (CAD) systems

- use reference samples to identify colour requirements

- liaise with customers and suppliers

- monitor reliability, accuracy and colour-fastness of dyes during manufacture

- keep up to date with developments in colour science

- minimise the environmental impact of the processes involved in the manufacture of dyes and pigments.

Training and development

Much training is carried out on the job, although graduate positions may include a more structured training scheme, including short placements in different areas of the organisation. The Society of Dyers and Colourists (SDC) offers professional qualifications at varying levels that can lead to the status of Chartered Colourist. This entails professional recognition by the SDC and indicates outstanding experience and ability in the discipline. It is essential for colour technologists to engage in continuing professional development and to stay up to date with scientific developments in the field, by attending conferences, reading and publishing research.

Further resources

Prospects: www.prospects.ac.uk/colour_technologist_job_description.htm

SDC: www.sdc.org.uk

TARGETjobs: targetjobs.co.uk/careers-advice/job-descriptions/278995-colour-technologist-job-description

Patent attorney

A patent attorney, or patent agent, assesses whether an invention is sufficiently original and innovative to receive a patent, which is a limited-term (20 year) right to protect the exploitation of that invention. Anyone who invents something technical and practical, rather than a purely intellectual concept, can apply to the UK Intellectual Property Office (IPO) to protect that invention. The patent attorney uses science and law to assess the invention and will guide the inventor through the process to obtain the patent and enforce their rights if the patent is infringed.

Most patent attorneys work with private firms, with others employed by large manufacturing organisations or in government departments. They possess the same rights as solicitors to conduct litigation and act as an advocate for their client. Work is usually nine to five, five days a week, but longer hours can be required to meet important deadlines. Most traineeships are based in London, with the majority of jobs available in the south and south east of England. This role can be more solitary in nature than many science jobs, although teamwork is more common in industry settings.

Entry

To become a patent attorney, you need a good 2.i in a science, engineering or mathematical subject. Postgraduate qualifications are not essential for entry but could enhance your application. Languages such as French and German can also be advantageous, as they are the official languages of the European Patent Office (EPO). You will also need to demonstrate that you can learn the legal knowledge required to carry out patent work, through undertaking relevant work experience or through taking an optional unit in law as part of your degree, in addition to proving your scientific abilities. This is a very competitive profession to enter, and standards are very high, so application processes are rigorous and demanding. However, the work offers a unique blend of science, law and commercial applications and can offer a highly stimulating and rewarding career.

Skills

Candidates would also need to be able to demonstrate the following:

- an ability to express complex scientific and legal processes with clarity

- clear understanding of scientific principles and processes

- attention to detail and a methodical approach to work

- an ability to understand and apply complex legal arguments

- excellent oral and written communication skills

- willingness to accept responsibility and work under your own initiative

- an ability to work with a wide variety of clients.

Salary information

A typical starting salary for a trainee patent attorney would be £25,000–£32,500. Qualification takes four to five years, after which pay increases to £50,000–£60,000. Successful and very experienced partners in private practice may be able to earn as much as £400,000 a year, and employees in private practice may benefit from performance-related bonuses.

Typical work activities

A patent attorney would typically:

- discuss the possibility of an invention being granted a patent with its creator

- analyse scientific documents to ascertain if an invention is new and original enough to be awarded a patent

- write up descriptions of inventions using legal terminology

- respond to patent examiners

- apply for patents to the Intellectual Property Office (IPO) and European Patent Office (EPO)

- recommend any modifications to the invention to secure the patent

- work with legal staff to secure or enforce a patent

- keep up to date with legal developments and intellectual property knowledge

- train junior patent agents after developing more experience.

Training and development

Training is extensive and prolonged and usually comprises a combination of self-directed study, on the job training and external training opportunities. You will also study for the exams set by the Chartered Institute of Patent

Attorneys (CIPA), leading to acceptance onto the Register of Patent Agents. Most trainees take their first set of exams after their first year on the job, and the advanced papers after another three years. Most patent attorneys will achieve chartered status by becoming Fellows of CIPA.

Options for later career development include taking the European qualifying exam to become a European patent attorney. Attorneys who have completed their CIPA exams can take the route to become a partner in private practice, or specialise in a particular area of patents. It is also possible to become a patent examiner for the IPO and see the process from a different perspective.

Further resources

CIPA: www.cipa.org.uk/pages/about-careers

Inside Careers: www.insidecareers.co.uk/professions/patent-attorneys

IPO: www.ipo.gov.uk

Prospects: www.prospects.ac.uk/patent_attorney.htm

Product development scientist

A product development scientist researches and develops new production processes and modifies current manufacturing systems to improve overall efficiency and to maintain quality control. They usually work in the manufacturing industry on products as varied as food, paints and cosmetics, and can be responsible for supervising a number of projects at the same time as well as developing new products. They are also interested in increasing the profitability of manufacturing processes. Product development scientists usually work nine to five, five days a week, but longer hours may be necessary to meet important deadlines, and the work can occasionally be stressful when launching new products or managing several concurrent products. Travel between production sites is also common. Product development technologists are typically employed within the food, pharmaceutical and biotechnology industries.

Entry

Product development teams are multidisciplinary, so entry is possible with a chemistry degree among many others, including physics, biological sciences, food science, chemical engineering and electrical engineering. You will need at least a 2.ii or above for entry, and a relevant MSc or PhD can be advantageous, especially in terms of later career progression and development. Practical work experience in a laboratory or factory setting can also enhance your application, so do seek out placement and internship opportunities as part of your degree or during summer vacation periods.

Skills

Candidates will also need to be able to demonstrate the following:

- excellent teamworking skills

- a logical and analytical mind

- good communication skills for working with a diverse range of people

- very good organisation and project management ability

- well-developed IT and mathematical skills

- presentation skills for communicating ideas for modifying processes or creating new products

- problem-solving skills.

Salary information

Typical starting salaries in this role would be between £20,000 and £29,000. More experienced staff can earn between £32,000 and £39,000 with staff at a very senior level and with substantial experience earning £52,000–£60,000.

Typical work activities

A product development scientist would typically:

- plan and oversee production processes and trials

- make modifications and improvements to existing processes

- reduce the costs of certain processes and increase yields

- demonstrate that new processes are an improvement on older ones

- advise on modifying equipment

- present information and test results to senior staff and clients

- ensure that new processes strictly adhere to safety protocols and procedures

- liaise with a range of technical, engineering and production staffs

- supervise junior staff and their training

- keep up to date with technical and scientific developments in the field.

Training and development

Most training for this position will be carried out on the job, or in laboratories and workshops. This will cover areas such as product and process knowledge, quality control and plant operation. As well as the technical skills, it is also likely that you will learn more transferable skills such as project management, leadership and presentation skills, and it may be possible to study for a more specialised postgraduate degree, depending on your employer.

As your career progresses, you may well take on management and supervisory roles, as well as managing much higher-profile projects with more responsibility. Continuing professional development will be expected and several professional bodies, such as the Royal Society of Chemistry (RSC), offer training courses and workshops to facilitate this. It may also be possible to move into more commercial roles, such as looking into business development or supply chain management, finance and IT. Consulting work may be possible after many years of experience, but self-employment is a tricky option in this sector due to the prohibitively high costs of establishing and running a production plant.

Further resources

Prospects: www.prospects.ac.uk/product_process_development_scientist_job_description.htm

RSC: www.rsc.org

TARGETjobs: targetjobs.co.uk/careers-advice/job-descriptions/278209-product-development-scientist-job-description

Textile technologist

A textile technologist works on the development and production of fabrics, yarns and fibres, as well as in research and development roles, production management, engineering and quality control. They are usually employed by manufacturers in the textile industry, and work to improve the efficiency of production processes. The end products they create can include clothing as well as household and industrial textiles. They will also liaise with designers, develop new synthetic fibres and new colour recipes, and can devise ways in which to improve the look, feel and durability of fabrics.

Work is usually nine to five in this sector, although long hours are possible when deadlines need to be met. Most work is production-based, although office and laboratory work is also usually involved. Jobs are available across the UK but are more typically concentrated in manufacturing areas such as London, the North West, West Yorkshire, the Midlands, Scotland and Northern Ireland.

Entry

To work as a textile technologist, you will need a degree in any of the following subjects:

- chemistry

- textile technology or science

- polymer science or technology

- computing and mathematics

- fashion studies

- production engineering

- materials science.

A related postgraduate qualification is only really necessary if you do not possess an appropriate first degree. Work experience in the industry is advisable, and those who have completed a textile-related degree incorporating a placement will obviously have an advantage, but do seek out opportunities during vacation periods if you are on a less relevant degree programme. It is also advisable to join a professional body such as the Textile Institute, and to keep up with current sector information by reading trade publications such as *Drapers*.

Skills

Candidates should also be able to demonstrate the following:

- good teamworking skills

- knowledge of chemistry and physics

- an understanding of the manufacturing process

- strong negotiating skills for working with clients

- problem-solving and decision-making skills

- organisation and self-management skills.

Salary information

Starting salaries for junior textile technologists are around £16,000–18,000 rising to £25,000–£35,000 with more experience. Very experienced staff with substantial experience in a senior role can earn £40,000–£50,000 and salaries in this field have recently started to see an increase.

Typical work activities

A textile technologist would typically:

- develop new fibres and fabrics

- develop new chemical processes to improve fabric performance; for example, making fabrics water resistant

- design more efficient and cost-effective production methods

- oversee the production process

- conduct research into new ways of using yarns

- source fabrics

- respond to queries from clients and customers

- keep up to date with the latest garment trends and developments in production technology.

Training and development

Most training is carried out on the job by more experienced technologists, but graduate training schemes will offer a more structured programme of development and should cover essential non-technical skills such as management and leadership. Developing communication skills for working with suppliers, manufacturers and designers is also a crucial aspect of the role. The Textile Institute offers a range of professional qualifications, to support continuing professional development.

Later career progression can involve managing an entire department and moving up the ladder of management responsibility, or you could become a technical specialist in an area such as colour management or quality management systems. Freelance work is possible with greater experience and some technologists will become owner-manager of their own textile production company.

Further resources

Drapers: www.drapersonline.com

Prospects: www.prospects.ac.uk/clothing_textile_technologist_job_description.htm

Textile Institute: www.texi.org

4

Physics

Physics graduates are employed across a wide range of industries, including research, IT, business, teaching, defence and engineering, and are valued for their analytical and practical problem-solving skills in the workplace. Only a minority of physicists will pursue a job in which they will use their specific subject knowledge; many of these will also pursue postgraduate study in order to further specialise in their discipline. This chapter will describe some of the roles in which a physics degree will be relevant to the work, as well as how to get into the sector. Salary information is derived from Prospects, unless otherwise stated.

The roles of patent attorney and product development scientist are also open to graduates with a physics degree, and you will find these outlined in Chapter 3.

THE UNIVERSITY of York
The Department of Physics

Study Physics at The University of York

University of York ranked 1st in the United Kingdom and 8th in the World
(the Times Higher Education 100 under 50, 2012)

Why is York the right place for you to study physics?
We pride ourselves on the quality of the undergraduate experience we offer – as seen in our many satisfied graduates. The University of York has an enviable reputation for having high standards and offering a friendly and welcoming environment for students from all backgrounds, so anyone has the opportunity to excel and pursue their interests.

What can you study?
We have a flexible modular system, offering degrees in Physics, Physics with Astrophysics, Theoretical Physics, Maths and Physics and Physics with Philosophy. All are available as either a 3-year BSc or 4-year MPhys degree and there is an option for a 'year in Europe'. Transfers between degrees are allowed in the 1st year.

How do you study?
We teach via a mix of traditional lectures, small group tutorials, laboratories, workshops, practical sessions, and group and individual projects. Our teaching is flavoured by our research excellence. All our students carry out an in-depth research project in their final year – often thought to be the best part of the degree!

How can you find out more?
You are welcome to attend any of our Open Days, read our Undergraduate Booklet or visit our website: http://www.york.ac.uk/physics. You can also email any questions to physics-undergraduate-admissions@york.ac.uk.

Profile: University of York

The Department of Electronics at the University of York has been consistently ranked amongst the best electronics departments in the country for its teaching quality and world-leading research in electromagnetic compatibility, biologically inspired computing, music technology, wireless communications and nanotechnology. It currently has over 70 full-time staff and over 500 students on a variety of programmes, specialising in subjects from avionics to nanotechnology.

Study

Since 2008 the National Student Survey has put York in the top 3 for student satisfaction in Electronic Engineering in the UK, as published in *The Sunday Times*. To complement the highly rated teaching quality, the Department provides extensive laboratories along with specialist computing, nanotechnology, media and audio recording studio facilities. The degrees enable students to become the innovative engineers so keenly sought after by employers – or to pursue many other careers having gained a wealth of transferable skills.

All of the BEng/MEng degrees are fully accredited engineering courses, validated by the IET. This means they are suitable for graduates wanting to go on to become a Chartered Engineer. All degrees have a sandwich year option, which can be taken between the second and third years of all our courses. For those on a four-year MEng degree, the sandwich-year option can also be taken between the third and fourth years. MEng students can also choose to carry out their final year academic project within a company.

In the third year all MEng students participate in a major software project. This is organised in teams who operate as self-contained units. Teams can trade with each other and buy and sell software modules (with notional money!). The final product is a substantial working piece of software.

If students want to spend time further afield, they can study on a year abroad or perhaps just take the opportunity to learn a different language alongside their course.

Courses

The range of courses includes the following.

- **Electronic Engineering:** this course provides a very wide range of knowledge and techniques in modern electronics.

- **Electronic and Communication Engineering:** the Electronic and Communication Engineering course gives students a strong electronics background with an emphasis on its application to communication technologies.

- **Electronic and Computer Engineering:** this is a Computer Systems Engineering programme combining the use of electronics and computer hardware/software.

- **Music Technology Systems:** this course focuses on the internal design and function of contemporary music technology systems within an electronic engineering programme.

- **Music Technology:** the Music Technology course is a creative music technology programme for students who are not taking Mathematics at a higher level. The degree offered for Music Technology is BSc.

- **Electronic Engineering with Nanotechnology:** this course gives students a strong electronics background with an emphasis on its application to nanotechnologies.

- **Electronic Engineering with Business Management:** the Electronic Engineering with Business Management course comprises 35% business management, 65% electronics. It meets the needs of those with ambitions to progress to a management position.

- **Avionics:** this is an electronics degree with an emphasis on the design and application of equipment for the aerospace industries.

- **Foundation Year:** the Foundation Year is an entry route to all the courses for those who do not have relevant qualifications, particularly mature students.

Case study

Careers and industry

The placement and careers staff within the Department provide advice on a range of summer placements, sandwich years and graduate jobs. Companies visit the Department during the academic year to give talks on their careers opportunities and to talk to potential placement students. There are numerous close collaborations with industry ranging from basic research to product development, and a number of spin-out companies have been generated, often employing graduates from the Department.

The Department is an invited member of the UK Electronics Skills Foundation (UKESF). This is a collaboration between major electronics companies and the public sector, working with universities to promote the electronics industry. It offers a range of scholarships that include annual bursaries, paid summer work placements and industrial mentoring and may include 12-month sandwich placements.

The Electronics Buildings and the Heslington Campus

The University of York was founded in 1963, and has three main campus sites, one in the historic centre of York, and two larger sites in the outskirts of the city at Heslington. The Department is based at the Heslington West Campus. The central features of a landscaped garden have remained, and the university buildings line the winding banks of a lake, home to a large variety of wildfowl.

The Department of Electronics shares a building with the Department of Physics. The teaching tower is the tallest building on campus, with fine views over the lake. This houses the undergraduate teaching and project laboratories, as well as the audio studios and several of the Department's computing labs.

Facilities and services

The Department has a wide range of facilities used to support the teaching and research activities. Most of these facilities are also available in collaboration with industry, allowing direct input to project work.

- **BioWall:** an interactive development environment for bio-inspired computing.

- **Clean Room:** facilities for fabrication and measurement of nano-scale devices, used by students from the first year of the nanotechnology courses.

- **Computing Labs:** the Department's own PC labs with specialised hardware and software to support the teaching.

- **Applied EM Test Facilities:** anechoic and reverberation chambers and open-area test-site facilities for researching electromagnetic problems from 10 kHz to 100 GHz.

- **FPGA and ARM-based Development Systems:** a range of tools for programming FPGA and ARM-based processors and system development.

- **Audio Recording Studios:** facilities for recording and producing acoustic and electronic music along with immersive laboratories.

- **Teaching Laboratories:** for practical and project work and including iPad/iPhone workstations.

- **OPNET:** the Department is a University Partner for OPNET, the industry-standard network simulation software.

Additionally, the Department's Technical Support provides design and construction facilities for the Department and industry, including PCB design and manufacture, digital manufacturing technology, 3D printing and a surface-mount assembly line.

iST
The Institute of Science & Technology

Achieving recognition

Having the professional standing of our members recognised has been a goal of the IST for a long time.

We are delighted to now be able to award our members official accreditation as a Registered Scientist (RSci) or Registered Science Technician (RSciTech), under licence from the Science Council.

Technicians working in other fields can join the IST's Registered Practitioner Scheme to get MIScT(Reg) or FIScT(Reg) status. We've always known that technicians' knowledge and experience deserved professional status - now, by getting that accreditation, IST members can demonstrate that they are making a vital contribution in their fields.

www.istonline.org.uk

Profile: Institute of Science and Technology

The Institute of Science and Technology has been supporting specialists with the technical skills that the world's economy needs for more than 65 years. We represent all sorts of technicians, experts and managers wherever they work: from science labs and engineering facilities to recording studios and IT departments.

As technology continues to develop at a tremendous pace, the IST is there to help technicians be the best they can be. We encourage our members to further their careers by pursuing professional and personal development, and by attaining a professional status that recognises the value of their experience and expertise.

In that way, we are always thinking about the future for our members and the organisations they work for. It is our mission to ensure that industry, business, research, schools, colleges and universities have the staff they need to keep up with constant advances in science and technology.

Central to this is the IST's belief that technicians deserve formal recognition for the work that they do, the experience they've racked up and the expertise they have to share. We know that our members are skilled professionals, and now we can give them official accreditation as a Registered Scientist (RSci), Registered Science Technician (RSciTech) or Registered Practitioner (MIScT(Reg) or FIScT(Reg)) to prove it.

By registering, technicians are helping to promote the professional standing of themselves and their colleagues. They are showing that they are making a vital contribution in their fields and achieving a status that makes them a key asset for the long term.

We are working hard to bring technicians from all disciplines into our international community of specialists. Our members work across a wide range of fields, which gives each of them the chance to make contacts across business, industry, research and education, and address the challenges these areas face together.

There is advice and guidance available for members (particularly new or young ones) through the IST's Mentoring Support Network, while our work with organisations such as HEaTED and Unionlearn, promotes the professional development of technicians in all areas. Together, we are ensuring technicians get the support and opportunities they need to achieve their potential.

We know how important it is for technicians to be able to develop their skills and have their expertise recognised in 2013. We know too, as we look to the future, that many more highly skilled technicians are needed. That's why the IST has dedicated itself to continuing to raise the status of specialist, technical and managerial staff, and to continuing to support their progression.

The IST is an organisation run by technicians for technicians.

Case study

The number of skilled technicians joining the IST's registration scheme is growing fast. That's because more and more of our members are discovering the great benefits and opportunities that professional recognition can bring.

Earlier this year, the IST became one of the Science Council's Pilot Licensed Bodies. That means that we can now award Registered Scientist (RSci) or Registered Science Technician (RSciTech) status to experienced technicians.

To register, technicians must be able to show that they have the skills to qualify for professional status, while always continuing their professional development. A full explanation of what you need to do to get registered status can be found on the IST website: istonline.org.uk/professional-registration.

In addition, the IST has been running workshops in different organisations to explain the application process in more detail. If you are interested in one of these workshops, and there is enough interest where you work, email office@istonline.org.uk.

You can meet some of the people who have registered so far by visiting our website: istonline.org.uk/professional-registration/case-studies.

Clint Gouveia RSci, MRI & OEM Production and Test Manager at Varian Inc., saw the advantages of going for RSci

'I chose to become registered because I believe it provides professional recognition for someone like me, who has significant experience working in a scientific and higher technical position. Professional status helps to differentiate you from your peers and of course, within the broader job market.'

Ben Palmer RSci, Materials Characterisation Research Technician at University of Sheffield, said registering brought him many benefits

'I believe the key benefits of joining the register are accredited recognition of the wide range of skills and experience I have gained; it provides a means to develop myself professionally in the future given the constant need to show ongoing CPD; and improved job security in an increasingly uncertain market. There is also a benefit to the organisation in that the support provided by their technical staff will constantly improve as technicians on the register continue to develop themselves.'

Melanie Hannah RSci, Chemistry Senior Research Technician at the University of Sheffield got registered after doing all sorts of activities to continue her professional development

'I have found that a lot of my regular work comes under the remit of continuing professional development. I regularly research papers on the chemistry of the research group for writing protocols and designing experiments. I take advantage of free webinars from manufacturers to keep up to date with the latest technologies. I am always eager to learn new skills and when the opportunity presents itself in the department I am always willing to undergo in-house training. For more soft skills training I have made use of the panosphix courses through the HEaTED website [www.heated.ac.uk]. This type of online training suits me as I work part time and a lot of the more formal training offered by the University is at times that would be awkward for me to attend.'

The job roles

Acoustician

An acoustician, or acoustics consultant, regulates and controls the use of noise and vibration at home, in the workplace and the environment. Correct acoustic design reduces unnecessary and intrusive noise, and enhances our enjoyment of music in spaces such as concert halls and cinemas. An acoustician carries out noise assessments on buildings to check that sound insulation meets Building Regulations, tests how a building's design affects sound quality and levels, and advises on noise levels in disputes. Acousticians tend to specialise in one area of their craft, so working in architecture, in the aircraft industry, healthcare, telecommunications and music are all options with this job role. The job is usually nine to five, but can vary between working in a laboratory with computers and being out on location, and travel between sites for work is common. Late nights will be usual if working in the music industry.

Entry

To work as an acoustician, you will need a degree in any of the following subjects:

- physics

- acoustics

- mathematics

- environmental science

- mechanical engineering

- a construction-related subject.

The University of Southampton offers a degree in acoustical engineering, and the University of Salford offers a degree in acoustics, with both of these programmes offering an optional placement year. There are also master's courses available that would allow you to specialise in studying acoustics if your first degree was less relevant to the area.

Skills

Candidates would also need to be able to demonstrate the following:

- a good understanding of sound and acoustics

- an understanding of environmental legislation and standards.

Salary information

According to job guides website Input Youth, starting salaries for newly qualified acousticians are about £22,000 and can rise to £35,000 with experience. A very senior acoustician can earn up to £60,000 a year or more.

Typical work activities

An acoustician would typically:

- use computer modelling to design plans aimed at reducing machinery noise or vibration in the workplace

- advise in legal proceedings, such as noise nuisance disputes

- investigate the effects of sound vibrations on machinery and structures

- design and work with recording studio and broadcast equipment

- design medical instruments, such as ultrasound devices, to help doctor diagnose and treat patients

- carry out noise assessments on buildings and check these against regulations

- perform environmental noise surveys to check that levels are within acceptable limits.

Training and development

Training for new acousticians is usually on the job, and may be combined with an in-house training programme, depending on the size of the employer. There are also professionally recognised courses offered by the Institute of Acoustics (IOA). The IOA offers the chance to work towards a Diploma in Acoustics and Noise Control, as well as generally supporting the continuing professional development of acousticians.

Further resources

Input Youth: www.inputyouth.co.uk/jobguides/job-acoustician.html

IOA: www.ioa.org.uk

National Careers Service: nationalcareersservice.direct.gov.uk/advice/planning/ jobprofiles/Pages/acousticsconsultant.aspx

Astronomer/Space scientist

Astronomers, also sometimes referred to as astrophysicists, observe and collect astronomical data, and use the laws of physics and mathematics to study matter and energy across the universe. They can also apply their learning to solve problems related to space flight and satellite communications. They require excellent powers of observation and a great deal of patient, methodical work to do their job.

This role has become popularised in recent years. Astronomical research is credited with improving weather forecasting, as well as air and sea navigation, and has been fundamental to the development of space exploration. Hours in this job can be long and irregular, including weekends, evenings and nights, depending on the nature of the research being carried out. Travel between meetings and to conferences is also usually required.

Entry

You will need a minimum of a 2.i in a degree such as physics, astrophysics or geophysics to start training as an astronomer. It is also now the case that most employers prefer applicants to have an MSc or MPhys (Master of Physics) in this field and, for a research career, it would be expected that you would also begin working towards a PhD. Graduates with a degree in computer science, mathematics or engineering could also retrain to move into astronomy by taking a more specialised master's. The Royal Astronomical Society (RAS) offers information on appropriate courses and degree programmes, as well as information on work placement opportunities for A level students.

Skills

Candidates would also need to demonstrate evidence of:

- patience for carrying out observations

- knowledge of electronics and machining for constructing equipment

- ability to work with specialists from other disciplines, such as meteorology.

Salary information

According to the National Careers Service, a junior researcher in astronomy will earn about £20,000–£30,000 a year. A senior astronomer or researcher with many years of experience could earn up to £60,000 a year.

Typical work activities

Astronomers tend to specialise in particular areas, but would typically work either in observational astronomy, making measurements and recording data or theoretical astronomy, providing physical explanations for those measurements and using theoretical models to consider the implications of research findings.

An **observational astronomer** would:

- maintain existing equipment and develop new instruments

- use and develop software to interpret images captured by satellites

- use telescopes or satellite and spacecraft equipment to collect data

- test out theories and analyse received data.

A **theoretical astronomer** would:

- make observations and test out new theories

- develop predictions based on previous observations and data

- develop computer models to look at physical processes taking place in space

- analyse their results and relate back to what is already known about the universe, making predictions about future developments.

Training and development

Most astronomers would typically work towards completion of a PhD in order to develop a specialism in their particular field of interest. It is possible to work towards Chartered Scientist status as an astronomer, receiving professional recognition and accreditation for your work, and the RAS holds more information about this on its website.

Further resources

National Careers Service: nationalcareersservice.direct.gov.uk/advice/planning/ jobprofiles/Pages/astronomer.aspx

State University Careers: careers.stateuniversity.com/pages/386/Astronomer.html

RAS: www.ras.org.uk

Metallurgist

A metallurgist works with metals and alloys, analysing their chemical and physical behaviour, providing technical advice about the use of metals and creating designs for metal components. They can also be employed in research and development and quality assurance. Metallurgists can work with multidisciplinary teams of engineers, scientists and product developers, and are employed by metal manufacturing companies, and the Civil Service (especially the Ministry of Defence), among others.

Travel within the UK, between sites, can be required, as can international travel for large organisations. Depending on the role, some work may be conducted in noisy and hot conditions, whereas other types of metallurgy, such as plasma spraying, need to be carried out in a clean laboratory environment.

Entry

Applicants require a degree in a relevant subject such as:

- metallurgy

- materials science

- chemical engineering

- physics.

Research positions will require a master's or PhD, and metallurgists aiming for professional recognition as a Chartered Scientist (CSci), will also require a master's.

Skills

Candidates will also need to demonstrate evidence of the following:

- business awareness

- problem-solving and analytical skills

- creative thinking

- leadership potential.

Security clearance would also be required for a career in the defence industry.

Salary information

A metallurgist's starting salary would typically be between £20,000 and £25,000 rising to £30,000–£40,000 with experience. A very senior metallurgist could expect to earn up to £60,000, with 10–15 years' experience on their CV.

Typical work activities

A metallurgist would typically:

- undertake new product research

- liaise with clients over design requirements

- monitor and test for corrosion

- develop ways in which to make metals stronger

- investigate accidents that may be due to metallurgical failure, such as an air crash

- carry out research and produce reports

- write documents and manuals for customer use

- carry out structural analysis using computer software and modelling

- troubleshoot production problems.

Training and development

Most training is done on the job as part of a graduate training scheme, such as those offered by BAE Systems or Tata Steel, and all metallurgists are expected to maintain their continuing professional development by staying up to date with current research, joining professional bodies and attending relevant conferences. It is also possible to receive accreditation with two years' experience and an accredited degree from the Institute of Materials, Minerals and Mining (IoM3). Chartered Engineer (CEng) status may be gained via a membership scheme with the Institute of Corrosion (ICorr).

Career development can lie in production management roles, as well as in movement to non-technical roles such as working directly with clients, product and business development, or quality assurance.

Further resources

ICorr: www.icorr.org

IoM3: www.iom3.org

Prospects: www.prospects.ac.uk/metallurgist_job_description.htm

TARGETjobs: targetjobs.co.uk/careers-advice/job-descriptions/276123-metallurgist-job-description

Meteorologist

A meteorologist studies the atmosphere, climate and weather, making predictions based on their analysis of received information and data. A meteorologist may also conduct research into the weather's effects on the environment and also climate change.

As a result of the need for 24-hour information about the weather, meteorologists often have to work in shift patterns, including unsociable hours. Depending on the role, some hours may be spent in the field, and working outdoors in harsh conditions, collecting data and carrying out observations. Many meteorologists are employed by the Met Office, and their main headquarters are based in Exeter and Aberdeen.

Entry

To become a meteorologist, you will need a degree in a relevant subject, such as:

- meteorology

- mathematics

- computer science

- physics

- environmental science.

It is common for many meteorologists to hold a higher degree. The Met Office usually requires a 2.i or a First in mathematics or a physical science, while other employers prefer degrees in physics. A master's in a more specialised area could be an option if your first degree is not so relevant. Relevant work experience is a valuable addition to your application in this field, and the Royal Meteorological Society offers some work experience each year, as does the Met Office, although opportunities here can be limited.

Skills

Applicants for graduate work in this area would also need to demonstrate the following:

- excellent mathematical and computing skills

- solid written and oral communication skills

- ability to analyse complex data

- skills in working with a multidisciplinary team

- genuine interest in science and the environment.

Salary information

The Met Office would typically pay a starting salary of £21,000–£27,000 rising to £35,000 for an experienced meteorologist. Managerial positions may pay closer to £40,000 rising to over £60,000 with increasing experience.

Typical work activities

A meteorologist would typically:

- collect data from satellite images, radar and weather stations

- apply computer models to make weather forecasts

- supply weather information to customers

- investigate weather patterns and climate change

- apply research to practical problems, such as predicting extreme weather conditions.

Training and development

Employers such as the Met Office, the Royal Navy and private weather forecasting organisations usually expect graduates to work towards a QCF Level 5 Diploma in Meteorological Forecasting. Training is then expected to be undertaken as a regular aspect of continuing professional development. The Met Office offers further training, including a Professional Development Programme. Working with environmental consultancies or as a television or radio weather forecaster are also options. Joining a professional body such as the Royal Meteorological Society can support professional development.

Further resources

Met Office: www.metoffice.gov.uk

National Careers Service: nationalcareersservice.direct.gov.uk/advice/planning/jobprofiles/Pages/meteorologist.aspx

Prospects: www.prospects.ac.uk/meteorologist_job_description.htm

Royal Meteorological Society: www.rmets.org

Case study

Dr Stuart Newman, Senior Scientist, The Met Office
Why did you choose a career in science?

I've always had a keen interest in science and I wanted a career that would challenge me and maintain my interest for many years. There were other career options that would undoubtedly have been more lucrative but I was clear that a science-oriented job was a more appropriate direction for me.

What made you choose your particular area?

Although I had always identified the Met Office as a scientific institution I would be interested in applying to, I had doubts about whether my background was a good fit for a career in meteorological sciences. As it turns out the Met Office has an excellent graduate training scheme and they actively look to employ good science graduates from a range of backgrounds.

What was your route in? Qualifications, experience, contacts?

Having a PhD rather than just a BSc was a huge advantage, so I would say qualifications were the key asset for me.

What is a typical day like for you?

At the Met Office we work in an open plan environment, rather than individual offices, so there is the opportunity for many informative conversations between colleagues and exchange of ideas and so on. Although I attend regular formal meetings with my line manager, roughly fortnightly, I have the freedom to organise my time to fulfil agreed objectives. Mostly I work with measurement datasets and much of a typical day will be spent analysing data or writing software code for analysis, or else reading relevant scientific literature. If I need to consult with colleagues we might get together for a chat over coffee or in a meeting room. I am expected to write reports and papers on my research, including for peer review.

What do you enjoy most about your work?

My work objectives are to improve the science underpinning Met Office models, so I have a sense of contributing to an overall important goal. I work with a group of motivated and enthusiastic people which makes a huge difference as well.

What are the challenges?

There are significant time pressures for meeting deadlines for completion of certain projects, and I need to be disciplined to keep my research on track. The flip side of working on varied scientific topics is that I am sometimes required to become acquainted with new areas of science very quickly.

What advice would you offer a current student/recent graduate aiming for a role in your field?

As well as having a PhD, which is a key asset when competing with other applicants, a good knowledge of IT and scientific computing and programming is seen to be important. Having experience of independent research and publishing their work will stand an applicant in good stead.

What would you do differently, if anything, if you were starting your career all over again?

Purely from a career progression point of view it would have been better for me to seek to change jobs internally in the Met Office more often, and gain a wider experience in different departments. However, I remain motivated in what I am doing now, and have few regrets.

Nuclear scientist

There are several roles that fall under the heading of working in nuclear science. A nuclear engineer works in laboratories and with universities and government agencies on nuclear-related projects. These can include developing energy sources and looking into different ways of using radiological elements in healthcare and industry. Nuclear engineers can also be employed within the military, in power plants and in aerospace.

A **nuclear physicist** looks more closely at the particles within the nucleus of an atom, and can carry out their research in the fields of engineering, aerospace, healthcare and communications, spending much of their time in the laboratory.

In **nuclear medicine,** a scientist examines how to treat illnesses such as cancer and thyroid disease using radiography and medicine that contains radionuclides, as well as radiation therapies. They may also interpret images and data, working with other consultants as part of a patient's care programme. A nuclear medicine practitioner would also usually be a qualified doctor, as well as being trained in radiology.

Working environments and hours in these roles will depend on how much time is spent in the laboratory compared with time in industry or in a healthcare location. Long hours may be expected when important test results or data are required, and shift work may be necessary in hospitals. Many nuclear scientists do not deal directly with radioactive materials. Working conditions within locations such as nuclear power plants must adhere to strict protocols and are carefully monitored to ensure that radiation levels are safe.

Entry

Candidates will need a degree relevant to the area of nuclear science in which they intend to specialise. Nuclear medicine practitioners are usually required to qualify as a doctor, as well as in advanced radiation training, and most nuclear scientists will generally hold a master's in a more specialised area of mechanical or chemical engineering. Nuclear scientists embarking on a research career would also usually work towards a PhD in a specialist area. Typical first degrees would include:

- physics

- chemistry

- biology

- chemical or mechanical engineering

- mathematics

- computer science.

Skills

Candidates would also need to be able to demonstrate the following:

- excellent analytical thinking skills

- ability to work with a multidisciplinary team

- research skills

- excellent written and oral communication.

Salary information

According to Payscale.com, a graduate working in nuclear science could expect a typical starting salary of £23,151 rising to an average of £34,604 with several years' experience. The highest rate of the scale would be about £65,000.

Typical work activities

Specific duties would vary depending on the area of nuclear science, but typical work could include:

- monitoring nuclear facility operations

- staying on top of current developments in the field

- conducting experiments to learn more about safe use of nuclear materials

- examining accidents to obtain data

- writing operational instructions for those working with radioactive elements in industry and healthcare

- designing and directing nuclear research projects, and sharing the results with interested parties.

Training and development

All nuclear scientists would be expected to engage in continuing professional development to keep their knowledge and skills up to date, by reading academic work and attending conferences and workshops. Working towards a PhD may be a requirement for advancing in a research career.

Further resources

Some of the websites listed below are US-based. The skills information should be transferable to the UK, but it is advisable to check with British recruiters regarding qualifications and training schemes.

Education Portal: education-portal.com/articles/Careers_in_Nuclear_Science_Options_and_Requirements.html

eHow: www.ehow.com/about_4701549_nuclear-science-career-descriptions.html

Science Buddies: www.sciencebuddies.org/science-fair-projects/science-engineering-careers/Energy_nuclearengineer_c001.shtml

Department of Physics

B.Sc. and M.Phys/M.Sci. degrees in Physics, Physics & Astronomy, Theoretical Physics, Mathematics & Physics and Chemistry & Physics

Learning based on lectures, tutorials, labs and projects

Specialised courses include particle physics, cosmology and photonics

Excellent laboratory facilities include 4 modern telescopes

Supportive college system

Internationally renowned research department

http://www.dur.ac.uk/physics
Email: physics.admissions@durham.ac.uk
Tel: +44(0)191 334 3726

Ogden Centre for Fundamental Physics

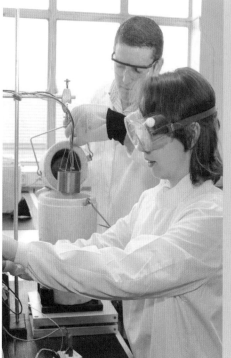

Be part of a thriving student community in the heart of the UK's fastest growing capital city and the Virgin guide's 'best-kept secret'.

At Cardiff School of Physics and Astronomy you have the opportunity to study mainstream Physics or Astrophysics in an internationally renowned, friendly research environment.

We offer:
- *A wide range of BSc and MPhys undergraduate degrees, with flexibility between schemes;*
- *Professional placement options;*
- *Final year independent research projects;*
- *An on-site astronomical observatory, laboratories, music studio and clean room facilities for state of the art research;*
- *A refurbished on-site library dedicated to Physics, Computer Science and Engineering with several study areas;*
- *Wi-fi access across the University campus;*
- *An active student society 'Chaos';*
- *Dedicated careers and employability support with our own in-house Careers and Industry Liaison Officer.*

For more information please visit our website www.astro.cardiff.ac.uk or email us to Admissions@astro.cardiff.ac.uk

Profile: Cardiff University

Overview

Cardiff has a large and successful School of Physics and Astronomy. There are 35 academic staff with a wide range of interests and specialist research areas. Most staff are internationally renowned in their particular area of research. Current research projects attract multi-million pound funding from numerous sources, the most important of which are from government and international space agencies.

Undergraduate programmes

Our degree programmes are designed to give you a thorough grounding in the fundamental aspects of Physics and Astronomy and to enable you to exercise as much choice as possible in your course content. Students can study for a BSc or MPhys degree, choosing from several single and joint honours programmes of three, four and five years' duration. Preliminary year studies are available as well as unique combinations, such as Physics with Music and Physics with Medical Physics. The core modules of the first and second years give way to a range of options in the later years. All of our courses are accredited by the Institute of Physics.

Careers

Physics graduates are highly sought after by employers in every sector from industry and education to commerce and healthcare. In 2011–12, 93% of our graduates were in employment or further study six months after graduation (DLHE data). Our dedicated Careers and Industry Liaison Officer is available to help support students with their career and work experience options. A series of Careers Management Skills sessions in the second year ensures that you are well equipped to apply for work experience and employment. We regularly invite recent Physics graduates to come back to talk to current students about their experience of working life, and these sessions, in addition to the Careers Fairs run by the Careers Service, mean that you will be well informed about, and inspired by, the many options open to you.

Teaching, learning and assessment

Traditional lectures, tutorials and laboratory work are complemented by computer, project and skills-based modules. Assessment is thorough and varied, taking into account different learning styles and needs. Assessment may be by exam or based on coursework, presentations, teamwork exercises, written reports or a combination of all of these.

Facilities

The School is part of the multi-million pound Queen's Buildings complex, which also houses the Schools of Engineering and Computer Science. It has modern well-equipped laboratories, lecture theatres, computing facilities, conference suites, and a project resource centre. Trevithick Library has been completely redesigned to offer a variety of functional yet innovative learning spaces. The School's on-site observatory encompasses CHaNT (Cardiff Half-metre Newise Telescope), a half-metre optical telescope for astronomical imaging in a city; a 12-inch Meade optical reflecting telescope; a solar telescope; a 3-m radio telescope. There are independent first, second and third year undergraduate Physics laboratories which allow students to gain experience with a variety of experimental methods and equipment. In their final years, students undertake major project work. The priority is to get students embedded into research groups within the school, giving a valuable insight into modern scientific research and also giving the opportunity to pursue a specialist field in depth.

Contact us

For further information on the range of programmes offered by Cardiff School of Physics and Astronomy, please visit www.astro.cardiff.ac.uk, call 029 2087 6457 or email admissions@astro.cf.ac.uk.

Case study

'When starting out as an undergraduate, you don't really grasp the significance of what you're about to undertake. As one of my fellow students aptly stated, a physics degree is "2,500 years of genius condensed into a four year course". That's a lot of genius, and a lot of physics to absorb in only a handful of years. This was a task not to be taken on by the faint-hearted.

'Along the way we met some of the founding scientists of modern physics, including Marie Curie, Paul Dirac, Albert Einstein and James Clerk Maxwell. Their powerful insights into the workings of the world around us led to some of the most fundamental developments in scientific history. They have provided us with the tools and techniques that have created almost all of the technology that we take for granted every day. These scientists not only shaped our degree, but also our daily lives, and we thank them for that.

Julie Gould, MPhys graduate with First Class Honours, 2012

'I asked some of my fellow students what they most enjoyed about their four years here at the School of Physics and Astronomy, and there was an unrivalled winner: project work. What we all really appreciated was being able to work on some real science and apply what we had learned in lectures. It was the sort of science that doesn't go according to plan, hardly provides any significant results, and is very unpredictable. Yet, at the same time it is also exciting, thoroughly enjoyable and very rewarding. Throughout the entire final year we were able to apply our own insights and ideas to physics that was being studied. We were able to build experiments tailored to our interests, test our theories, and gain a deeper understanding of the scientific method.

'What will we take away from our four years of hard slog through the 2,500 years of genius? We will not only take away an incredible amount of physics, but also a way of thinking. Science is not just a subject, it is a way of doing; think of science as a verb, rather than a noun. It teaches you to think methodically, to establish a rational and realistic view of how the world works. This scientific method can be applied to all walks of life, whether it be research, teaching or even politics.

'Many of our group are going on to quench their thirst for knowledge by studying for a PhD, some of us are going into more commercial routes of research, some of us are leaving science altogether, and the rest haven't decided yet. Maybe some of us will become Nobel Laureates, and some could be the next generation of influential politicians, but whatever routes we decide to take in life, we all know that we will succeed, no matter what. Studying physics has given us the confidence to tackle complex problems head-on, and find ways to overcome even the most challenging tasks that life throws our way.'

Julie is now studying for an MSc in Science Communication at Imperial College London.

5

Biosciences

Graduates with a degree from the biosciences, including subjects such as zoology, genetics, botany and toxicology, have a wide range of careers to choose from. As well as working in scientific research or in academia, bioscientists pursue options in the pharmaceutical industry and other laboratory-based work, the food industry, local government, sports sciences and the environment.

The roles of the biomedical scientist, forensic scientist and toxicologist are explored in more detail below, but bioscience students should also look at Chapter 7 on working in the health sciences, as many graduates will apply for roles within the NHS via the Scientist Training Programme (STP). All salary information is drawn from Prospects, unless otherwise stated.

The job roles

Biomedical scientist

Biomedical scientists work in a healthcare setting and test tissue samples and fluids to help clinicians in their diagnoses. Their work can be highly varied and most biomedical scientists tend to specialise in one of the following areas:

- medical microbiology

- clinical chemistry

- transfusion science

- haematology

- histopathology

- cytology

- virology

- immunology.

The work of biomedical scientists is essential to the effective treatment of patients with a wide range of conditions, including cancer, HIV and AIDS and diabetes, as well as supporting the work of blood transfusion teams, screening cervical smears and identifying viruses. Their work makes extensive use of technology and automated equipment and a keen eye for detail is required, along with an ability to work under pressure.

Entry

A biomedical science degree approved by the Institute of Biomedical Science (IBMS) is one route in. You must also be registered with the Health and Care Professions Council (HCPC), and it is possible to study for a biomedical science degree, which also allows compliance with registration with the HCPC at the same time. It is possible to enter with a degree in anatomy and physiology, biochemistry, molecular biology, immunology or medical microbiology, but further study of modules approved by the IBMS may be required.

Skills

Any relevant work experience can be beneficial to your application, and candidates should also be able to demonstrate evidence of:

- practical laboratory skills and manual dexterity

- an ability to take responsibility

- an ability to maintain confidentiality

- an ability to work under pressure.

Salary information

Starting salaries are around £21,000–£27,000 rising to £34,000 with more experience and up to £40,000 for a more advanced practitioner. Higher pay may be possible via allowances for night and weekend work.

Typical work activities

A typical day for the biomedical scientist may involve:

- testing human samples, such as blood and tissue

- working with computers and sophisticated laboratory equipment

- communicating test results to clinical staff

- ensuring that tests meet timed targets

- ensuring accuracy of testing through rigorous quality control.

Training and development

It is possible for biomedical scientists to move into management roles, education, research and more specialised laboratory work. Biomedical scientists can also work towards Chartered Scientist status later in their career, which is an internationally recognised standard of excellence.

Further resources

IBMS: www.ibms.org

NHS Careers: www.nhscareers.nhs.uk/explore-by-career/healthcare-science/careers-in-healthcare-science/careers-in-life-sciences/biomedical-scientists

Prospects: www.prospects.ac.uk/biomedical_scientist_job_description.htm

Forensic scientist

Forensic scientists apply science to the law, providing impartial evidence for use in court by the defence and prosecution. They examine and collect trace evidence such as blood and other body fluids, hair, textile fibres, and traces of flammable substances used to start fires. A forensic scientist may advise on the possible sequence of events at a scene and join in an initial search for evidence, and can also be involved in settling disputes for which damages are being claimed, such as road accidents. They usually present their findings in written form for the courts, but are occasionally required to appear in person.

Recent television crime dramas, such as *Silent Witness* or *CSI: Crime Scene Investigation*, have resulted in increased interest in this role, but they do not reflect the level of painstaking scientific detail that this work requires. Most of the work of a forensic scientist is also laboratory-based; only experienced forensic scientists may be asked to attend a crime scene. However, there has been an increase in available posts thanks to technological advances offering more research opportunities, and also due to increased storage of information due to the establishment of the National DNA Database.

Entry

An honours degree in life sciences such as chemistry, biochemistry, biology or pharmacology, as well as a postgraduate degree in forensics is the most common route in for forensic scientists who also want to be reporting officers who appear in court.

Skills

Candidates will need to demonstrate the following skills:

- **an enquiring mind and a persistent approach to work**

- strong written and oral communication when explaining scientific information to non-specialists and lay persons

- a high degree of accuracy and attention to detail

- objectivity and personal integrity.

Note that some labs also require good colour vision. A criminal record or a history of alcohol or drug abuse could result in exclusion from this profession.

Salary information

Salaries for trainee or assistant forensic scientists start at about £16,000. Salaries rise to £25,000–£30,000 after two to three years' experience, and senior forensic scientists can earn over £50,000.

Typical work activities

A forensic scientist may be required to:

- sift and sort through microscopic quantities of evidence

- apply techniques such as scanning electron microscopy or mass spectrometry

- attend and examine crime scenes

- input data into specialised computer programs

- present results in a written or oral form for court

- coordinate with external agencies, such as the police, and offer expert advice.

Training and development

Most graduate entrants to forensic science will undergo extensive on the job training and, if a forensic scientist's role becomes more research based, it may be possible to write this up for a PhD or master's qualification.

Further resources

The Forensic Science Society: www.forensic-science-society.org.uk

National Careers Service: nationalcareersservice.direct.gov.uk/advice/planning/jobprofiles/Pages/forensicscientist.aspx

Prospects: www.prospects.ac.uk/forensic_scientist_job_description.htm

Toxicologist

A toxicologist monitors and evaluates the impact of toxic materials and radiation on human and animal health. Their work is mainly laboratory based, planning and carrying out experiments and trials, devising and testing hypotheses, using appropriate techniques to identify toxins and analysing and interpreting data. They can work across a range of sectors including industry, in clinical settings, in the pharmaceutical sector, and forensics. Employers of toxicologists include: the Health and Safety Executive, the NHS, the Environment Agency, universities, hospitals and forensic laboratories.

Entry

Degrees specifically in toxicology are available, but any related degrees should include a significant toxicology component. These include: pharmacology, biomedical sciences, medical and veterinary sciences, medicinal chemistry and forensic sciences. A postgraduate qualification in toxicology or forensic science can be beneficial.

Skills

Candidates should be able to demonstrate the following skills:

- a logical and independent mind

- meticulous attention to detail

- an ability to collect and analyse large amounts of data.

Salary information

Starting salaries in the private sector range from £21,000–£26,000 while the NHS will pay a trainee clinical scientist on the Scientist Training Programme (STP) about £24,000. With experience, salaries can rise to over £34,000 with very experienced scientists earning about £70,000.

Typical work activities

A toxicologist would typically be required to:

- give evidence in court

- produce risk analyses and develop models to predict the long-term effect of chemicals and toxins within an ecosystem

- identify toxic substances and any harmful effect they may have on biological materials, animals, plants or ecosystems

- advise on the safe handling of toxic substances and radiation

- liaise with regulatory authorities to ensure compliance with national and local regulations.

Training and development

This is an expanding area of work with good opportunities for career development. Study towards a PhD may be helpful for long-term career progression, and it may be possible to gain sponsorship from an employer to fund this while working. To become a clinical scientist specialising in toxicology in the NHS, applicants need to obtain a role as a clinical scientist trainee and then engage in three years of formal training across laboratories and hospitals. Full details can be found on the NHS Careers website. Professional toxicologists can also achieve diploma recognition with three bodies: the Royal College of Pathologists, the Society of Biology and the American Board of Toxicology. This is achieved via training courses and examinations.

Further resources

NHS Careers: www.nhscareers.nhs.uk/explore-by-career/healthcare-science/
careers-in-healthcare-science/careers-in-life-sciences

TARGETjobs: targetjobs.co.uk/careers-advice/job-descriptions/
292569-toxicologist-job-description

UK Register of Toxicologists: www.toxreg.org.uk

6

Earth sciences and ecology

This sector offers a wide range of roles, with the opportunity to work towards doctoral status and consultancy. Graduates with degrees in earth sciences and ecology can choose from over 200,000 businesses operating in environmental and geological work, with graduate training schemes available with organisations such as CGG Veritas, DEFRA and the Forestry Commission.

Jobs in this sector require outdoor work and potentially long hours to get projects completed on time, sometimes against adverse weather conditions. Along with technical skills, business expertise is cited by Prospects as lacking in entrants to this field, so brushing up on your commercial awareness could enhance your chances. It is also worth reading journals such as *The International Journal of Earth Science* or *Environmental Earth Sciences*, as well as staying up to date with current affairs by reading a range of newspapers.

Some of the main roles available in earth sciences and ecology are outlined below to help you build an overall picture of the jobs available in this field. Salary information is derived from Prospects, unless otherwise stated.

Develop your career with the Energy Institute

Build your expertise among energy professionals of the highest calibre.

The Energy Institute (EI) is the leading professional membership body for the global energy sector, supporting individuals through learning, knowledge sharing and professional recognition at every stage of their career. We are licensed to register Chartered Scientists (CSci).

If you want to develop your scientific career within the energy industry and acquire professional qualifications, why not join the EI now?

Contact the EI Membership team:
e: membership@energyinst.org
t: +44 (0)20 7467 7100

www.energyinst.org

Case study: Energy Institute

Dr Shane Hattingh, CSci FEI, is Principal Reservoir Engineer at ERC Equipoise, an oil and gas consultancy working in the field of reservoir evaluation and analysis.

'I grew up in a South African gold mining town where my father's career in rock mechanics first sparked my interest in geology. I completed a BSc degree with geology, physics and applied mathematics, followed by a BSc Honours in geophysics.

'Having worked in mineral exploration for the early years of my career, where very little discoveries were being made, I found that the oil industry offered wider scope and more exciting prospects. In 1989 I joined the state oil company Soekor, moving into the discipline of reservoir engineering, which has been the focus of my career ever since.

'As the world's resources of oil and gas are consumed, the reservoirs that deliver their bounty are becoming scarcer. We therefore have to deal with geological structures that are more complex and difficult to understand. My day-to-day work mostly involves evaluating oil and gas resources and reserves and conducting technical geoscience-based studies. The evaluations involve analysing geoscience, engineering and commercial data, both raw and interpreted, to make estimates of the volumes of oil and gas that remain to be recovered from a field, to make projections of future oil and gas production rates, and to estimate ranges of uncertainty in all these parameters.

'As part of my role, I analyse laboratory experiments to understand the complex phase behaviour at high temperatures and pressure in the reservoir by applying the laws of chemistry. The industry is becoming more technically sophisticated and science provides the foundation for these advances. These studies are undertaken to increase our efforts to extract the maximum amount of oil from existing reservoirs in the most efficient, safe and commercially attractive way possible.

'I have always believed that scientific endeavour provides the avenue for solving many of the challenges that the world faces and it has been a priority for me throughout my career to maintain and continually develop my skills. This led to the application for Chartered Scientist (CSci) status with the Energy Institute. As a consultant this has been a great advantage. It provides recognition of my professional status, verifying knowledge and experience, and providing clients with a sense of confidence.'

For more information about achieving Chartered Scientist status with the Energy Institute, please visit www.energyinst.org/chartered-scientist

The job roles

Ecologist

An ecologist examines the relationship between animals, plants and the environment. Early-stage career ecologists carry out observation and recording work, eventually moving into management and policy work later on. It is important that all ecologists develop knowledge of environmental policies, as their work must adhere to relevant UK and European legislation. Working abroad is a possibility, especially for those with increasing specialisms and qualifications. Due to the need to travel between locations, a driving licence is usually required for this kind of work.

Entry

Applicants will need a degree in a biological or related science, such as:

- ecology

- zoology

- botany

- environmental science

- geography

- marine biology.

If you intend to work towards a research career, especially in academia, or a role as a consultant, then you will need a postgraduate qualification.

Skills

Candidates should also be able to demonstrate the following:

- ability to collect and interpret data

- knowledge of environmental legislation

- ability to identify different species

- knowledge of how to use statistical data and packages.

Salary information

Starting salaries are around £13,000–£20,000 initially, rising to £22,000–£28,000 with a few years' experience. £30,000–£40,000 would be the typical salary for those with 10–15 years' ecology experience.

Typical work activities

An ecologist may typically:

- carry out fieldwork, surveying and recording information on environmental conditions and wildlife

- use sampling and habitat survey techniques such as Global Positioning Systems (GPS), aerial photography and mapping

- use computer modelling to predict the effect of urban development on climate change

- test samples for evidence of pollution

- enforce legislation related to wildlife protection and endangered species

- monitor pollution incidents and their effects.

Training and development

Training is carried out on the job, and you can join a professional body to further support your development. The Institute of Ecology and Environmental Management (IEEM) offers professional development courses, as do the Field Studies Council (FSC) and Botanical Society of the British Isles (BSBI).

Further resources

National Careers Service: nationalcareersservice.direct.gov.uk/advice/planning/jobprofiles/Pages/ecologist.aspx

Prospects: www.prospects.ac.uk/ecologist_job_description.htm

Engineering geologist

An engineering geologist analyses earth matter before engineering works are carried out to ensure that any geological factors affecting this work are planned for. An engineering geologist can advise on the types of materials suitable for use during construction, as well as on any necessary safety procedures. They can also be involved in the development of environmentally sensitive sites. Work in this field can be physically demanding and carry a lot of responsibility, due to having to make professional judgements about developments. Travel is a frequent part of the work, and may require time spent away from home.

Entry

A range of honours degrees are appropriate to this career and include:

- geology

- earth sciences

- geography

- civil engineering

- mathematics

- geotechnology.

The Geological Society accredits certain degree courses, which can qualify holders for membership after a certain period of postgraduate experience: check their website for further information.

Skills

Candidates will also need to demonstrate the following:

- interpersonal skills

- good report writing ability

- a flexible approach to work

- good overall fitness levels.

Salary information

Starting salaries are around £25,000 rising to £40,000–£50,000 at more senior levels. Higher levels of pay are often found in the private sector, especially in oil and gas companies, and where work may be carried out in areas of high physical risk or in remote locations.

Typical work activities

An engineering geologist would typically:

- examine maps and photographs to determine site selection for development

- visit sites in various locations

- oversee specific projects and be involved in budgeting

- test and advise on construction materials

- advise on geological problems, such as subsidence, or environmentally sensitive issues.

Training and development

Training is carried out on the job, and attendance on training courses will be required. It is also possible to work towards Chartered Geologist status as you progress into your career, via the Geological Society. Joining professional bodies such as the Geological Society, Institution of Civil Engineers or British Geotechnical Association provides training and networking opportunities.

Further resources

Geological Society: www.geolsoc.org.uk

Prospects: www.prospects.ac.uk/engineering_geologist_job_description.htm

TARGETjobs: targetjobs.co.uk/careers-advice/job-descriptions/279445-engineering-geologist-job-description

Geochemist

A geochemist uses geology and chemistry in their analysis of the elements in rocks and minerals. Their research can be used in the following areas:

- oil exploration

- mining

- advising government and environmental agencies

- improving water quality

- designing plans to clean up toxic spillages.

Geochemists can help to minimise human damage to the environment, such as when extracting oil, and work may be available with companies interested in developing green technologies. Some of the work is laboratory-based, but geochemists also spend time visiting sites, including hiking and camping out, so physical fitness and being comfortable working outdoors are essential for this kind of work. Travel and irregular hours are a significant aspect of this role.

Entry

You will need a relevant first degree in a subject such as:

- geology

- geochemistry

- geophysics

- oceanography

- chemical engineering

- marine sciences

- mineral engineering.

Prospects points out that competition in this field is intense so early preparation for applications is essential, and a PhD is required for research careers in this field.

Skills

Candidates should also be able to demonstrate the following:

- project management and research skills

- attention to detail and a methodical approach to work

- physical fitness and stamina

- laboratory and analytical skills.

Salary information

Typical starting salaries are around £20,000–£30,000 rising to £32,000–£52,000 at senior levels. Higher salaries are usually paid by larger organisations, which may offer more pay for working in isolated or remote locations.

Typical work activities

A geochemist would typically:

- collect and analyse samples, including carrying out field visits

- use computer simulations to generate models

- work with specialist equipment, such as microscopes and mass spectrometers, to carry out research

- map exploration sites for analysis.

Training and development

Training is carried out on the job. Safety and outdoor survival skills will also be part of your training if there is a significant amount of fieldwork in your job. Developing business awareness, including knowledge of managing budgets, is essential if you are aiming for a role in consultancy later on. It is possible to work towards professional accreditation with the Geological Society and achieve chartered status after about five years in your career.

Further resources

Geological Society: www.geolsoc.org.uk

Prospects: www.prospects.ac.uk/geochemist_job_description.htm

wiseGEEK: www.wisegeek.com/what-does-a-geochemist-do.htm

Geophysicist

A geophysicist, or field seismologist, collects data on earthquakes and seismic waves, and then analyses and interprets those results. They use techniques such as gravimetry, analysing minute changes to the Earth's gravitational field, and geomagnetism, looking at magnetic differences between rocks to identify the intensity and direction of the Earth's magnetic field. Geophysicists have achieved a television profile in recent years, due to their role in analysing archaeological excavations in programmes such as Channel Four's *Time Team*.

Working conditions depend on whether you are laboratory-based or an exploratory geophysicist, which will involve periods of time out in the field and also out at sea. These trips can last for weeks at a time and involve long working hours. Physical stamina is therefore essential for field work and you need to be willing to travel regularly.

Entry

You will need a relevant degree in a subject such as:

- physics

- mathematics

- geology

- geophysics.

Postgraduate qualifications such as an MSc or PhD are desirable in this field, especially to advance in research positions, and may result in candidates being offered a higher starting salary. Joining a professional body such as the Society of Exploration Geophysicists (SEG) could also help with networking opportunities and career development.

Skills

Candidates would also need to demonstrate the following:

- foreign languages and cultural awareness could be an advantage when working overseas

- good overall physical fitness and stamina

- good colour vision for working with geological maps

- flexibility and ability to adapt to challenging working conditions.

Salary information

Typical starting salaries are around £22,000–£25,000 and £24,000–£30,000 for those with an MSc or PhD. With experience, salaries can rise at senior level to £40,000–£65,000. Salaries are higher in the private sector, particularly with oil companies.

Typical work activities

A geophysicist would typically:

- identify the appropriate measurement techniques

- use recording equipment in the field

- interpret and report back on collected and analysed data

- test and repair seismic equipment

- work on improving existing techniques for acquiring and analysing data.

Training and development

Larger graduate recruiters offer training schemes in all aspects of geophysics, including health and safety training. Smaller organisations will expect you to learn skills as you progress. There are no standardised qualifications for geophysicists but further training and networking opportunities are usually provided by professional bodies such as the SEG. Moving between organisations, especially due to fluctuations within the oil industry, and between countries may be required for career progression.

Further resources

Prospects: www.prospects.ac.uk/geophysicist_field_seismologist_job_description.htm

SEG: www.seg.org

Hydrogeologist

A hydrogeologist analyses the flow and distribution of underground water. This differs from a hydrologist, who applies scientific and mathematical knowledge to solving problems related to surface water, such as flooding, erosion and irrigation. A hydrogeologist constructs models of water flow based on data and information gained from maps and other documents, as well as designing projects to test out those models, and predicts the potential future impact on water flow and quality. Research carried out by a hydrogeologist can inform the management of natural resources and the protection of groundwater. UK hydrogeology employers include WYG Group, New Earth Solutions and the Royal Society for the Protection of Birds (RSPB).

Entry

You will need a first degree in a subject such as:

- geology

- environmental science

- engineering.

This will need to be supplemented by an MSc in a subject such as hydrogeology, geochemistry, engineering or another subject related to working with and managing groundwater. It may be possible to embark on a master's after obtaining a job and work through it with your employer's support.

Skills

Candidates will also need to demonstrate evidence of the following:

- mathematical modelling ability

- ability to conceptualise groundwater and geology across three dimensions

- business knowledge and commercial awareness.

Salary information

Typical starting salaries are around £20,000–£25,000 rising to £30,000–£45,000 for more senior and experienced staff. Salaries for those with many years of experience and management responsibilities can rise to £50,000–£60,000.

Typical work activities

A hydrogeologist would typically:

- manage projects and work with contractors

- undertake computer modelling to simulate groundwater flow

- produce reports for clients and stakeholders

- carry out field work and collect samples.

Training and development

Most companies, such as MWH or Carillion, will provide on the job training, and larger organisations will offer a comprehensive programme of graduate development. Joining a professional body such as the Chartered Institution of Water and Environmental Management (CIWEM) can offer training and networking opportunities. Joining CIWEM also offers the route to professional accreditation via chartered status.

Further resources

CIWEM: www.ciwem.org

Prospects: www.prospects.ac.uk/hydrogeologist_job_description.htm

USGS Water Science School: http://ga.water.usgs.gov/edu/

Mudlogger

A mudlogger plays an essential role in the extraction of oil, gathering and interpreting information relating to drilling operations. They monitor aspects of drilling such as the rate of penetration and speed of drill rotation, as well as using tools and laboratory techniques such as ultraviolet fluorescence to analyse collected samples. The work of mudloggers helps drilling to be more cost-effective and safe, with a reduced chance of well blowouts (the uncontrolled and highly wasteful release of oil or gas from a well).

Work is carried out at wellsites, so international travel is an essential aspect of the work, with mudloggers often working a two weeks on, two weeks off pattern on oil rigs and drilling platforms. During the two weeks on, working hours are usually 12 hours a day, seven days a week. Employers will cover the costs of travel, accommodation and food, and may pay extra for working in more remote posts. Working conditions can be intense, but employers usually try to make accommodation comfortable.

Entry

Most entrants into mudlogging hold a geology degree, but it is possible to start this career with a degree in chemistry, physics, geoscience or engineering. There are a number of online recruitment websites, including Oil Careers, that are worth looking at to find vacancies or names of companies to which you could make a speculative application.

Skills

Candidates should also be able to demonstrate the following:

- ability to work with technical skills from different disciplines, such as geology, chemistry and electronics

- ability to work under pressure in stressful conditions

- ability to work with sophisticated technology and learn new skills quickly.

Be aware that you will need to pass strict medical tests to an international standard to be deemed fit to work on wellsites.

Salary information

According to All About Careers, a fully trained mudlogger can earn £40,000–£60,000 a year. Given that your accommodation, travel and food costs are covered for a considerable portion of the year, there are also many opportunities to save money, and working with oil organisations can bring in higher salaries, especially if you are prepared to work in arduous conditions and remote locations.

Typical work activities

A mudlogger would typically:

- monitor computer recordings of drilling activity

- provide information based on received data to drilling teams

- carry out maintenance of electrical and mechanical systems

- uphold health and safety procedures.

Training and development

Training is carried out on the job, and includes survival training as well as the fundamentals of oil well drilling and use of computer systems. There is currently no system of professional accreditation for mudloggers but, with experience, it is possible to take on senior positions or to work in the oil industry, where it is possible to achieve accreditation.

Further resources

All About Careers: www.allaboutcareers.com/careers/job-profile/mudlogger.htm

Oil Careers: www.oilcareers.com

Prospects: www.prospects.ac.uk/mudlogger_job_description.htm

Seismic interpreter

A seismic interpreter assesses the amount of gas and oil present in rock. They interpret surveys that send pulses of sound energy through the layers of rock and record the energy that bounces back. The ease with which the oil can be extracted and any potential hazards which may be encountered can then be determined. They also work with 2D, 3D and 4D models to make estimates of mineral deposits, as well as computer modelling to replicate and anticipate seismic responses. Most UK jobs for seismic interpreters are based in London or Aberdeen, because of oil industry locations. International politics related to the oil industry can occasionally make this work rather pressured. Typical employers of seismic interpreters include oil exploration and extraction companies, British Geological Survey, research organisations and universities.

Entry

You will need a good honours degree in a subject such as:

- geophysics

- geology

- physics

- mathematics

- earth sciences.

Most companies will also expect applicants to hold an MSc in a more specialised area such as petroleum geology. The Geological Society holds a list of UK and international universities offering relevant courses, and you can also search recruitment websites such as Oil Careers for vacancies.

Skills

Candidates should also be able to demonstrate:

- ability to work in a variety of different environments

- attention to detail

- ability to work independently.

Salary information

Starting salaries are around £25,000–£30,000 rising to £50,000–£75,000 with more experience. Companies such as Exxon Mobil and Marathon Oil also often offer benefits such as private healthcare packages.

Typical work activities

A seismic interpreter would typically:

- use sound waves to produce geological maps

- produce maps and cross sections of the Earth's structure

- use seismic data to measure how much oil or gas may be present

- use computer modelling to simulate seismic responses.

Training and development

Technical developments move quickly in this field, so continuing professional development is essential to maintaining current knowledge of new equipment and techniques. Most initial training will be carried out on the job. There are no standard training courses for seismic interpreters; training will vary between organisations and will usually be tailored for individual needs.

Further resources

Geological Society: www.geolsoc.org.uk

Oil Careers: oilcareers.com

Prospects: www.prospects.ac.uk/seismic_interpreter_job_description.htm

7

Health sciences

This is one of the most diverse science sectors, covering life sciences, such as cellular science and genetics, the physiological sciences, careers working directly with patients, genetics and medical physics, and opportunities to develop new technology for supporting patient care. The health sciences are open to graduates from a wide range of science disciplines, including biology, chemistry, physics, immunology and pharmacology. This chapter presents an overview of some of the typical jobs within health science.

Graduate positions and essential work experience can be sought through relevant recruitment agencies, such as RIG Healthcare and CK Science. There are also options for careers within privately run organisations, such as pharmaceutical companies, research and development, and not for profit organisations.

The NHS Scientist Training Programme (STP)

The NHS is the main UK employer of scientists in the health sciences, and offers a three-year graduate-entry programme which can lead to more senior scientist roles. This is the NHS Scientist Training Programme (STP) (which replaced the Clinical Scientist Training Scheme in 2011), and it trains entrants to postgraduate level, leading to the award of a specifically commissioned master's, as well as developing your workplace skills. The STP is usually a balance of two-thirds work-based training to one-third academic study.

Entry to the NHS Scientist Training Programme (STP)

You will need a First or 2.i honours degree in a science subject related to the work for which you are applying. Applicants with a 2.ii will be considered if they have an MSc or PhD in the specialism in which they are interested (see below). The most commonly accepted degrees are:

- biology/biomedical sciences

- genetics

- biochemistry

- microbiology

- physics (pure or applied)

- mathematics

- engineering.

You will need to choose from the nine designated specialisms for your training (you may specify a maximum of two in your application), and these are:

- microbiology

- blood sciences

- cellular sciences

- genetic sciences

- neurosensory sciences (audiological, ophthalmic and vision sciences)

- cardiovascular, respiratory and sleep sciences

- gastrointestinal physiology

- clinical engineering (rehabilitations, clinical measuring and medical device management)

- medical physics (radiation safety and physics).

The NHS Careers website (www.nhscareers.nhs.uk) has full details. You will be required to register with the Health and Care Professions Council (HCPC) to be able to practise in most of the roles below.

All salary information below is derived from Prospects, unless otherwise stated.

Working with Science

The Department of Biomolecular and Sport Sciences at Coventry University encompasses biological, analytical and sport sciences,

Biological Sciences

The Biological Sciences are the study of all living things. Biology is a rapidly changing science and encompasses the disciplines of cell biology, molecular biology, microbiology and biochemistry. Our courses focus on the biological basis of human health and disease and we believe in hands on learning and our fully equipped biological sciences laboratories are the ideal environment for the study of life at every level.

Sport and Exercise Science

Our Sport and Exercise Science courses focus on the application of scientific principles to the promotion, maintenance and enhancement of sport and exercise related behaviours. Whether you are interested in how elite athletes perform, how to undertake exercise effectively for health and fitness or rehabilitation, or the prevention, treatment and management of injuries, we have several courses to prepare you for a wide variety of careers in this rapidly expanding area.

Environmental Health

Environmental Health includes the study of food safety, health and safety, housing, environmental protection, public health and health promotion and is essential for maintaining and improving the safety of the public. Our degree gives an excellent balance and prepares you for a range of careers within the field of environmental health.

Analytical Sciences

The analytical sciences focus on the analysis of the chemical composition of materials and include disciplines such as chemistry and forensic science. Our analytical sciences courses are heavily lab based with a focus on experimentation and methodical analysis of your findings, designed to give you an excellent platform for a future career in the analytical sciences, either in academic research or in the commercial sphere.

To find out more about our science courses please go to www.coventry.ac.uk and click course finder

Coventry University

Profile: Coventry University

Coventry University is an evolving and innovative university. Independent student surveys show that we provide a caring and supportive environment, enriched by a unique blend of academic expertise and practical experience. Three words set us apart – **employability, enterprise and entrepreneurship.** Our aim is to keep on improving. We're investing heavily in developing our state-of-

the-art facilities. By seeking to enhance the strong vocational emphasis of our courses and bolstering our links with the very best industry organisations, we're firmly focussed on preparing students for successful futures. Take a look at our courses and you'll see how we're preparing students for their future careers. The University occupies a purpose-built 33-acre campus in the heart of Coventry city centre. The campus buildings and environment are constantly being developed and improved.

As part of a comprehensive suite of science courses in the Department of Biomolecular and Sport Sciences our Environmental Health degree is managed and taught by qualified practitioners who are experienced within the local authority, and the Environment Agency, as well as in the private sector as consultants and contractors. This provides students with a more practical and applied course content, which will be of benefit in the workplace. In addition to this, other specialists in the field provide a varied and balanced view on current issues and practices by also delivering seminars.

As well as core materials in housing, health and safety, environmental protection, food and public health, the course uses a variety of problem-based and case study learning in both teaching and assessment. This approach means that students learn how to obtain and interpret information, and how to use this to solve a wide range of environmental health interventions. Our course also has a significant practical component including laboratory work and site visits to local industry to assess 'real life' environmental health. We also offer subjects that provide the student with the opportunity to develop additional professional tools such as communication skills, project management, report writing and marketing. This ensures the chance to become a graduate who will ultimately be employable based on their individual and broad skills in addition to the professional knowledge and application of their chosen discipline.

Coventry University has open days in June, September, October and November each year; see our website for full information and how to book a place.

For more information about the course the University and all our open days please go to www.coventry.ac.uk.

Case study

Simon Mortimer, Environmental Health

Being in environmental health comes from many routes and sources. In my experience you often get asked 'so what's that then?' or 'what do you do?' The answers to those questions are many. We often work in the background without people really seeing the important work that you do. Environmental health is only really in the public eye when something goes wrong.

The reasons for this are because environmental health practitioners are involved in your day-to-day life in nearly everything you do without you even knowing they are there. It could be your house, workplace, food and drinks, removing and controlling pests, removal of litter and waste, exposure to pollution or general public health issues such as obesity or smoking. A recent example of this is the horse meat scandal – you don't know work is being done to protect food safety on a daily basis until something goes wrong.

I started my career in 1999 whilst studying environmental sciences with an interest in working within the environmental management sector. I began working for a contracting firm involved in groundwork and foundation design and worked there through my undergraduate and postgraduate master's degree in environmental management for some three years. I was part of a team managing the company's environmental impacts from all their activities from storage of chemicals, transport and haulage, materials used, training and legal requirements with the aim of achieving the environmental management standard ISO14001.

Immediately following that I took a role as a consultant managing and supervising large-scale regeneration projects across the Midlands with regard to groundwork and the management of health and safety on site as well as the environmental impacts of the works being undertaken. I continued within this role for the next four years before being employed by a local authority environmental health department within the pollutions section looking at industry emissions, investigation of statutory nuisance cases, fly tipping investigation, contaminated land and also the management and implementation of the EMAS and ISO14001 environmental management schemes.

During this time I studied another master's degree, this time specifically in environmental health. On completion and professional accreditation to the Chartered Institute of Environmental Health (CIEH) I began working across the department undertaking health and safety inspections, food premises inspections (including restaurants and food manufacturers), environmental permitting inspections and management and extensive work in housing safety and standards. During this time I delivered periodic lecturers within environmental health at university on undergraduate courses. I worked within these roles for six years before moving on to full-time employment within a university setting.

My career to date has covered a multitude of working environments, subject areas and challenges. I have been able to work from the foundations to the very top of organisations to ensure that environmental management and performance are high on the agenda and that public health is a primary concern in all business activities to maintain the health of the populations that we serve.

Environmental health is a career, and way of life that you can take wherever you want to across many subjects, sectors and geographical locations the world over.

Profile:
British College of
Osteopathic Medicine (BCOM)

BRITISH COLLEGE OF
BCOM
OSTEOPATHIC MEDICINE

IN PARTNERSHIP WITH PLYMOUTH UNIVERSITY

A world leader in osteopathic education

The British College of Osteopathic Medicine (BCOM) is internationally regarded as one of the best specialist osteopathic education institutions. In its recent review for quality in osteopathic education, BCOM was awarded Recognised Qualification status 'approval without conditions' from the QAA RQ report for the second consecutive time – a sector-leading achievement.

Since its foundation in London in 1936, the College has become a world leader in osteopathic education and research. Based in Hampstead, north London, BCOM has been running its much-praised four-year undergraduate Masters in Osteopathy (M.Ost) since 2008. Its friendly campus has the most full-time academic staff in any UK osteopathic college.

Excellent Research Facilities
BCOM offers the most advanced osteopathic-research facilities in Europe, being the only specialist college to provide cutting-edge on-site human-performance and hydrotherapy laboratory facilities. Founder of the International Conference on Advances in Osteopathic Research (ICAOR), BCOM fosters a strong research environment that enables advances to be disseminated more generally, with the best student research being presented at leading international conferences.

BCOM works to instil a research ethos into all its graduates, increasing the clinical knowledge base and providing Continuing Professional Development.

BCOM's Holistic Osteopathic Approach
Particularly regarded for its uniquely holistic or naturopathic approach to osteopathic care, BCOM works hard at promoting the philosophy, science and clinical application of holistic osteopathy and naturopathy within the UK and throughout the international community.

BCOM's undergraduate and postgraduate students are an integral part of its teaching and research clinics.

Masters in Osteopathy

BCOM's four-year Masters in Osteopathy (M.Ost) aims to produce graduates suitable for registration with the General Osteopathic Council as safe, competent osteopaths in practice. The course integrates academic, scientific, anatomical, theoretical and research knowledge with applied clinical osteopathic and naturopathic skills, and is validated by Plymouth University.

Academic Degree and Rewarding Career

Osteopathy is an enormously rewarding career with 80% of BCOM graduates in work 6 months after graduation. The rewards of practising as an osteopath are many: a highly satisfying professional life; excellent financial rewards; a chance to be self-employed within a growing healthcare industry. Fully qualified osteopaths can also find employment in university-level teaching, corporate consultancy, work with animals and many other fields.

Contact

British College of Osteopathic Medicine
Lief House, 120-122 Finchley Road
London NW3 5HR
Tel: +44 (0)20 7435 6464
Email: admissions@bcom.ac.uk
www.bcom.ac.uk

Case study

Daniel Winfield, British College of Osteopathic Medicine (BCOM)

Daniel Winfield graduated from BCOM in 2012 and was the prize winner for Best Naturopathic Research project in his final year and also won the Presentation Prize at The 9th Chiropractic, Osteopathy & Physiotherapy Annual Conference.

Daniel began his career as a maintenance engineer and graduated with a degree in Building and Architectural Studies from the University of Brighton with a distinction. However, he wanted to achieve more and thought about a change of career direction.

After reading a naturopathy book by Sebastian Kneipp, Daniel was inspired to look further into naturopathy. Daniel said: 'Ever since my childhood I've had a passion for anything that involves working with my hands. I have a knack for problem-solving. I discovered that BCOM, with its long history of teaching naturopathy and osteopathy, offered the exciting prospect of graduating as an osteopath as well as a naturopath. I could work with people, work with my hands, be creative and use problem-solving skills, the things I had said I wanted. But this was Masters level. Was I capable of that? I took strength from my success at my previous studies.

'One of the best things about having studied at BCOM is the knowledge that I have had some of the most extensive training available to undergraduate osteopaths in Europe. I have heard of employers who wait for BCOM students to graduate before they advertise for associate osteopath positions. For a college of its size I found BCOM to be particularly well equipped for research.

'The staff were kind and supportive and of course there were wonderful patients who were so inspiring, and making a difference to their quality of life is, for me, one of the most rewarding aspects of osteopathy.

'The day I graduated and picked up my award was the proudest day in my parents' life. Even at 40, your mum and dad still feel pride when you do well. I was the first person to graduate in my family on both sides, ever – and I did it twice! It's never too late.'

BRITISH COLLEGE OF OSTEOPATHIC MEDICINE

Osteopathy
a degree and a career

Undergraduate Masters in Osteopathy

BCOM's M.Ost provides the best route into this fast-growing healthcare profession ... and beyond

"Approval without conditions" from QAA/GOsC quality review for osteopathic education - a sector leading achievement

For further information please contact

020 7435 6464
admissions@bcom.ac.uk
www.bcom.ac.uk

BRITISH COLLEGE OF
BCOM
OSTEOPATHIC MEDICINE
IN PARTNERSHIP WITH PLYMOUTH UNIVERSITY

The British College of Osteopathic Medicine Registered Charity No 312907
accredited by the General Osteopathic Council Degree validated by Plymouth University

The job roles

Clinical embryologist

A clinical embryologist specialises in investigating infertility and in assisting people to conceive and have children. As well as communicating with patients and other healthcare staff about courses of treatment, they perform clinical procedures such as in vitro fertilisation and monitor a successful implantation through pregnancy and delivery.

It is crucial to have an understanding of the law and ethics relating to this clinical specialism as well as knowledge of human reproductive biology, infertility and assisted reproduction. This area has been growing rapidly in the last 20 years and it is anticipated that more embryologists will continue to be needed in the future. Work may be available in overseas fertility clinics, and vacancies can be found with specialist recruitment agencies such as IVF.net.

Entry

The NHS Scientist Training Programme (STP) is the main route into embryology, and you will need a 2.i or First in a relevant science subject for entry. Relevant subjects include:

- biology

- reproductive biology

- genetics

- biotechnology.

Training lasts for three years, mainly in the workplace, followed by 18 months of specialisation. The training is salaried, as you will be employed by an NHS trust or local health authority.

Skills

Candidates must also be able to demonstrate:

- laboratory skills, including using lab technology

- research and record-keeping skills

- meticulous attention to detail.

Salary information

The starting salary is about £25,000 rising to £30,000–£40,000 with experience. Consultant practitioners can expect to earn over £77,000.

Typical work activities

This role includes activities such as:

- assessing the fertility level of individuals

- collecting eggs and sperm for processing

- embryo selection and transfer to recipient women

- complying with and maintaining knowledge of regulations, ethics and technology in this area.

Training and development

Pre-registration embryologists work towards a certificate and diploma over four years to become eligible for state registration with the Health and Care Professions Council (HCPC). Further training is required with the Royal College of Pathologists to become a consultant practitioner.

Further resources

All About Careers: www.allaboutcareers.com/careers/job-profile/clinical-embryologist.htm

IVF.net: www.embryologists.org.uk

Prospects: www.prospects.ac.uk/clinical_embryologist_job_description.htm

Clinical molecular geneticist

This role involves the use of biochemical and molecular biology techniques such as DNA sequencing to identify genetic abnormalities linked to diseases, including familial cancers, cystic fibrosis and Alzheimer's. The work usually falls under the areas of prenatal diagnosis, carrier testing and diagnosis confirmation, and is predominantly a laboratory-based role.

Entry

Entry is competitive and requires at least a 2.i degree in a life science or medical degree, including a significant genetics component. Relevant postgraduate study can also be advantageous. Employers include the National Health Service, private laboratories, government agencies, higher education institutions, and private pharmaceutical companies.

Skills

Candidates should also be able to demonstrate the following:

- laboratory work

- analytical thinking and problem solving

- project management.

Salary information

Starting salaries are around £25,000 rising to £30,000–£40,000 post-registration and up to £55,000–£98,000 for a consultant.

Typical work activities

This role includes duties such as:

- testing for genetic diseases

- conducting research and development

- recording and analysing quality control data

- attending conferences and maintaining subject knowledge.

Training and development

Initial training with the NHS lasts for three years, combining workplace experience with study for a master's degree. Specialisation usually takes place in the final 18 months of the training period. Clinical molecular geneticists are then eligible to apply for registration with the HCPC.

Training towards further qualifications is expected and supervisory roles may develop for post-registration practitioners. Senior post-holders may supervise teams and also contribute to policy formations with local authorities.

Further resources

Biotechnology and Biological Sciences Research Council: www.bbsrc.ac.uk

Clinical Molecular Genetics Society: www.cmgs.org

TARGETjobs: targetjobs.co.uk/careers-advice/job-descriptions/278985-clinical-molecular-geneticist-job-description

Prospects: www.prospects.ac.uk/clinical_molecular_geneticist_job_description.htm

Diagnostic and therapeutic radiographer

There are two types of radiographer: diagnostic and therapeutic. Diagnostic radiographers make use of imaging technologies, such as X-rays, ultrasound and magnetic resonance imaging (MRI) to diagnose and investigate a range of conditions, injuries and diseases. Therapeutic radiographers work with a team of oncology professionals to treat patients with cancer, delivering precise doses of radiation to tumours, as agreed with doctors and medical physicists. The NHS employs about 90% of the UK's radiographers, with the ratio of diagnostic to therapeutic being about 10 to one. There is some work available in private laboratories.

Entry

To practise as either a diagnostic or therapeutic radiographer, a degree approved by the HCPC must be completed; this can be done at undergraduate or at postgraduate/diploma level, and the HCPC has details of approved programmes on its website. Both routes require roughly 50% study and 50% work placement activity, with the courses lasting between three and four years. Applicants for diagnostic radiography may be asked for evidence of a workplace visit or work shadowing as part of the entry criteria.

Skills

Candidates will also need to be able to demonstrate the following:

- application of technical skills, alongside knowledge of anatomy, physiology and physics

- ability to work under pressure

- ability to reflect on your practice.

Salary information

Salaries for newly qualified radiographers range from £21,000–£27,000 rising to £25,000–£34,000 for senior radiographers and up to £67,000 for a managing or senior consultant.

Typical work activities

The therapeutic radiographer will be working daily with other healthcare and oncology professionals, as well as directly with patients, calculating and delivering radiation treatments. The diagnostic radiographer will assess patients in order to determine the appropriate radiographic techniques; perform a range of radiographic techniques; record imaging and patient documentation accurately and in compliance with data protection and confidentiality protocols, and regularly check and maintain equipment.

Training and development

Both types of radiographer can develop their career by taking on management, advisory and research roles.

It is also possible to develop specialisms. For the **diagnostic radiographer**, these could include:

- trauma/accident and emergency

- breast screening/mammography

- magnetic resonance imaging

- medical ultrasound.

For the **therapeutic radiographer**, specialisms include:

- treatment planning

- palliative care

- nuclear medicine.

There are currently only limited numbers of consultant and senior radiographer posts, so movement into higher levels may take time. However, because UK radiography qualifications are globally recognised, there are opportunities for career development in other countries.

Further resources

NHS Careers: www.nhscareers.nhs.uk/explore-by-career/allied-health-professions/careers-in-the-allied-health-professions/radiographer

Prospects (diagnostic radiographer): www.prospects.ac.uk/diagnostic_radiographer_job_description.htm

Prospects (therapeutic radiographer): www.prospects.ac.uk/therapeutic_radiographer_job_description.htm

Dietician

Dieticians make sense of and translate scientific information about food into practical advice to help people make informed decisions about their dietary habits and lifestyle. They also diagnose and treat diet-related health issues and increase awareness of the connection between food and health. They can assist patients with a range of conditions, including eating disorders, food allergies, diabetes, HIV/AIDS and various cancers. A dietician will have trained in both hospital and community settings to complete their course. Most UK dieticians are employed by the NHS, but there are opportunities in the food industry, in research, with charities, in the media and as a freelancer.

Note that a **nutritionist** studies the nutritional content of food, how this affects the body and how diet can be used to improve health. They are often employed in the food industry and by manufacturers, and have an increasing role to play in healthcare. However, they will not have trained in a clinical setting and may not possess the degree qualifications required to practise as a dietician.

Entry

To register with the HCPC, a dietician must have completed an approved course and details of approved programmes can be found on the HCPC website. Applicants can either complete a four-year degree in dietetics or nutrition and dietetics, or a two-year postgraduate diploma in dietetics, which also requires an undergraduate qualification with a significant component in biochemistry and human physiology.

Skills

Candidates will also need to demonstrate the following:

- willingness and ability to maintain knowledge on current nutrition information and research

- a supportive and motivating approach to working with people

- the ability to explain complex scientific information in a practical and intelligible manner.

Competition for work as a dietician is moderate, with a good match between candidates and available posts. The NHS advertises most of its dietician posts, so speculative applications will not be necessary, although they can be used in the private sector once qualified.

Salary information

The typical starting salary for a dietician is £21,000–£27,000 rising to £25,000–£34,000 with specialisms, and up to £40,000 at an advanced level.

Typical work activities

There is a broad range of work with this role and tasks can include:

- advising and educating patients with dietary disorders on how to alleviate their symptoms and improve their health

- assessing and calculating patients' nutritional requirements

- advising the food and pharmaceutical industry

- preparing information packs and materials.

Training and development

It is possible to progress in this career by moving into teaching and research, as well as by developing knowledge in specialist areas, such as oncology or gastroenterology, or by working with specific groups, such as children or the elderly.

Dieticians can register with the British Dietetic Association (BDA), which offers post-registration training and a five-year professional development award. The BDA also offers the Advanced Dietetic Practice Diploma, which can be taken at master's level, as well as a certificate or as individual modules. It is also possible to progress into management roles, or in an advisory capacity to the food industry.

Further resources

British Dietetic Association: www.bda.uk.com

NHS Careers: www.nhscareers.nhs.uk/explore-by-career/allied-health-professions/careers-in-the-allied-health-professions/dietitian

Prospects: www.prospects.ac.uk/dietitian_job_description.htm

Haematologist

Haematology is the study of blood and blood forming tissues, as well as blood-related disorders. This role can involve working with patients afflicted with blood and bone marrow diseases and conditions such as leukaemia, anaemia and sickle cell disease, as well as carrying out analysis of the structure and function of blood cells, and interpreting test results for abnormalities. Most haematologists are also involved in blood transfusion, blood type matching and in the provision of blood and its components.

Entry

With a 2.i in a relevant degree, entry is via the Scientist Training Programme (STP) with the NHS. It is also possible to enter via the biomedical scientist route, taking a degree in biomedical science approved by the Institute of Biomedical Science (IBMS) and the HCPC. Graduates with other life science degrees may be able to enter via this route, but could be required to top up their studies with prescribed biomedical modules.

Entry into NHS training schemes is competitive, and relevant postgraduate qualifications as well as work experience could be advantageous, as can involvement in research projects and publications.

Skills

Candidates also need to demonstrate skills in:

- the ability to organise and carry out research

- commitment to lifelong learning

- patience and emotional resilience when working with patients

- confidence with complex technology.

Salary information

Starting salaries are £25,000–£34,000 rising to £40,000 with experience and up to £97,000 for experienced, senior professionals in the field. There are some opportunities for private practice, such as undertaking outpatient consultations.

Typical work activities

Duties for a haematologist may include:

- analysing blood samples using manual and technology-assisted techniques

- receiving and preparing blood samples for analysis

- reviewing data for abnormalities

- cross-matching blood for transfusions.

Training and development

Following successful completion of the training period, progression in this role often requires moving between laboratories and hospitals. Further study is very likely, with many haematologists progressing to qualifications at MSc and PhD level. Research and publication in peer-reviewed journals can help professional advancement, as can networking and maintaining a professional profile through presenting research, applying for research grants and undertaking international work placement opportunities.

Further resources

NHS Careers: www.nhscareers.nhs.uk/explore-by-career/healthcare-science/careers-in-healthcare-science/careers-in-life-sciences/haematology

Prospects: www.prospects.ac.uk/haematologist_job_description.htm

Immunologist

An immunologist investigates the functions and disorders of the body's immune (defence) systems, and uses their knowledge to diagnose and treat a range of conditions, including HIV/AIDS, cancers and even hay fever. They measure and analyse cells, antibodies and other proteins. Immunologists often work within the NHS alongside other healthcare staff such as biomedical scientists, and opportunities also exist in industrial and academic settings. This is currently a growth area within the NHS, so there are opportunities to be working at the forefront of new research.

Entry

Candidates usually require a First or 2.i degree in a biomedical or healthcare science accredited by the IBMS in order to be eligible for the Scientist Training Programme (STP) with the NHS. You may be required to top up a different life science degree with core biomedical modules approved by the IBMS – see their website for more information. Most people entering this field will also have completed a relevant postgraduate qualification.

Skills

You will also need to demonstrate evidence of:

- confidence in working with technology, systems and processes

- an organised approach to work

- flexibility

- high levels of personal motivation.

Salary information

Salaries start at around £25,000 and can rise up to £100,000 for a senior consulting immunologist. Mid-level roles usually attract a salary of up to £37,000.

Typical work activities

More clinically based roles will require working with patients and running clinics; undertaking a range of laboratory activities, and liaising with other relevant healthcare professionals. Academic and research positions will also require applications for funding to support projects; writing papers for publication based on research, as well as making conference presentations; the preparation of tests and the analysis and interpretation of results, and the use of specialist software and equipment. Industrial roles involve client liaison, project planning, research into new products, and input into team activities.

Training and development

Management responsibilities usually increase with seniority, and continuing professional development is expected throughout an immunologist's career. Research-based immunologists may work towards a PhD over a three to four year period, and funding for doctoral study may be available from research councils, universities or trusts – the Biotechnology and Biological Sciences Research Council (BBSRC) is a key funder in this area. In industry, for example within pharmaceutical companies, technical training should be available to support knowledge and development within specific areas.

Further resources

BBSRC: www.bbsrc.ac.uk

British Society for Immunology: www.immunology.org

NHS Careers: www.nhscareers.nhs.uk/explore-by-career/healthcare-science/careers-in-healthcare-science/careers-in-life-sciences/clinical-immunology

Prospects: www.prospects.ac.uk/immunologist_job_description.htm

Medical physicist

A medical physicist uses their knowledge of physics in a healthcare setting, developing and testing new procedures and equipment to help prevent, diagnose and treat a wide range of conditions and diseases. They may also use computer simulations and modelling during their research, and train other healthcare professionals how to use techniques, including imaging, laser treatments, radio therapies and electronics. Medical physicists are also involved in planning and delivering patient treatment programmes within the NHS, and employment is also possible within medical equipment manufacturing companies and in academic research posts.

Entry

A physics degree is the preferred entry qualification, but degrees in electrical/ electronic engineering or computing engineering may be accepted. Work experience within a hospital medical physics department is recommended.

Salary information

Typical starting salaries within the NHS are around £25,000–£34,000 rising to £30,000–£40,000 following completion of Part 1 of the Institute of Physics and Engineering in Medicine (IPEM) training. More senior post-holders can earn up to £40,000, and consultants up to £100,000.

Typical work activities

A medical physicist's work can include:

- research and publication of findings

- development and maintenance of new technology and equipment to ensure safety

- drafting of policies for operating equipment

- commissioning of new equipment

- planning and explaining treatment programmes to patients

- processing complex image data.

Training and development

Continuing professional development and assessment is an essential aspect of career progression as a medical physicist. Following registration, reviews are conducted every two years to allow unsupervised practice; the Health and Care Professions Council oversees this. It is possible to work towards more specialist posts, such as radiotherapy physicist, as well as progressing towards a PhD.

Further resources

Medical Physicist: www.medicalphysicist.co.uk

National Careers Service: nationalcareersservice.direct.gov.uk/advice/planning/jobprofiles/Pages/medicalphysicist.aspx

Prospects: www.prospects.ac.uk/medical_physicist_job_description.htm

Case study

Dr James Matthews, Research Assistant, University of Bristol

Why did you choose a career in science?
I have always been interested in how things work, and wanted to find out about the natural world. I was always comfortable with maths, so maths and science subjects at school, and then at university, were natural choices.

What made you choose your particular area?
I am currently working in medical physics, but have worked in environmental physics. My choice of physics was due to an affinity to maths, and an interest in the basic forces that make the world work, in particular, electric and magnetic fields. A secondary interest to me, which has grown through my career, is how living things respond to electrical phenomena, and this is the current focus of much of my research. At one point I considered taking up medicine (due to an interest in how the human body worked) so it is satisfying to be able to contribute to a project that combines physics with medicine in a relatively unexplored way.

What was your route in? Qualifications, experience, contacts?
My first degree was in physics and music, and I found I had an interest in electronics while studying. I applied for a master's degree at the same university, which I paid for with a professional studies loan. My major project in this degree was the creation of a device that was used to irradiate a biological sample with electromagnetic radiation

Having graduated and found myself in a factory job, I was looking for research jobs and found a position at the University of Bristol. The position had already been filled by someone else, but I inquired whether there was any position for a PhD student within the group. The research was related to my final project in my master's degree so I took my dissertation with me to a meeting and left it with the head of the group to read. In time, he found some money to fund a three-year PhD researching atmospheric physics, and its relation to human health.

When I had finished my PhD, I was able to remain at the same research group to continue this research. After 18 months, a position in a medical physics project became available in the same research group, which I was able to take up. During this time, the academic in charge retired so the research was moved to a different department, but the project remained the same.

What is a typical day like for you?

It usually starts with a little admin, checking emails and highlighting those that need a response and checking through my week's 'to do' list. After that, it varies depending on what needs to be done. Some days I will need to spend time in the laboratory, either keeping experimental equipment in working order or running experiments. This can take anything from half an hour to a full day. I might spend some time behind the desk looking at data, both from my own experiments and archived from previous work by myself or colleagues, I would normally break this up with lab work or other admin.

I may also need to prepare work for dissemination, which could be through talks or posters at conferences, or written up for publication in a journal. Other written work can include reports for current grants, and applications for future grants. These jobs are often collaborative, so I may be asked for comments on other colleagues' work, and send my work to them, and senior academics, for their comments.

Some days will involve travel for measurements. My previous project involved field work taking measurements outside; my current project is a human volunteer experiment in collaboration with another university and a hospital. Work includes travel to the hospital to set up our equipment, and several days away from home while the experiment is in progress. Other days may involve meeting other academics, either informally or formally at conferences and academic meetings. At the end of the day, I will finish by checking my to-do list, backing up any work I may need to look at away from the office onto the memory stick that lives in my wallet, and I will check whether any of the important emails need to be answered.

What do you enjoy most about your work?

I enjoy the freedom I have in how I organise my time and which direction my research may take. At a fundamental level, I enjoy solving problems, so experimental work has its rewards, and finding out new things is rewarding.

I am very interested in cross-disciplinary work: I like to discuss problems with other researchers in different disciplines. Being a physicist currently working in a chemistry department on a medical physics project in collaboration with medics and clinical staff at a hospital means that I am working with different people. I am also finding time to explore new avenues of work, for example collaborating with some biologists looking at animal behaviour, or environmental scientists trying to estimate exposure to pollutants. Both sides benefit from these collaborations.

What are the challenges?

The largest personal challenge is the lack of long-term stability in my experience of university research. When a project expires, a researcher has to be prepared to move to find another position, if suitable grants can't be found where you are, and permanent positions in research are rare for people in the early part of their career.

A lot of my work has been self-led, so a level of self-discipline is needed to keep the work on track. I also have several strands on the go, so a level of organisation and multi-tasking is required.

What advice would you offer a current student/recent graduate aiming for a role in your field?

I think a PhD is the best route in to a university career in science, so if the student is approaching the end of their degree, it is worth enquiring at their university, or looking at other universities to see whether positions in a field that interests them are available. It is vital that the student has an interest in the subject they are hoping to study. Often, a science degree will include a major project in their final year, and this will enable the student to find out if they enjoy research. When approaching the end of the PhD, it is worth getting to know the other research groups and researchers in related fields, in order to build up contacts and networks, which may help in finding work when graduating from the PhD.

What would you do differently, if anything, if you were starting your career all over again?

I would attempt to get more publications in good quality journals earlier in my research career. The number of publications is often used as a crude metric for a researcher's progress, so a good publication record is a strong asset.

Occupational therapist

An occupational therapist assists in the assessment and treatment of a range of physical and mental disorders, using activity to promote independent functioning in everyday life. They can work with all age groups, as well as with people who have been disabled since birth, or with those whose disorders result from illness, accidents and lifestyle. They recommend personal treatment programmes and monitor a patient's progress, and can suggest changes to a person's environment as well as the use of any supportive equipment.

Places of work can include: GP practices, clients' homes, hospitals, prisons and schools. Occupational therapists may encounter some stressful situations and can also need physical strength and stamina to carry out their role.

Entry

Any BSc in Occupational Therapy should be approved by the HCPC. About one third of the programme will be spent on placement. Alternatively, a two-year postgraduate qualification – either a diploma or a master's in occupational therapy – can be taken. It is not essential to hold a relevant first degree, but subjects such as biological sciences, psychology, sociology or any health-related science would be useful.

Skills

Candidates should also be able to demonstrate the following:

- ability to build confidence and encourage their clients

- empathy and patience

- willingness to solve problems through assessment and treatment.

Salary information

Starting salaries are £21,000–£27,000 rising to the occupational therapist specialist grade of £25,000–£34,000 and then advanced at £30,000–£40,000.

Typical work activities

Activities may include:

- advising on home and environmental adjustments

- teaching anxiety management techniques

- coaching people with learning difficulties or helping with behavioural control

- managing a caseload and supervising the work of occupational therapy assistants.

Training and development

Occupational therapists can progress into managing other staff, research, and teaching in universities, colleges and hospitals. There are also specialisms recognised by the College of Occupational Therapists, including: accident and emergency, trauma, learning difficulties, neurology and mental health.

Further resources

College of Occupational Therapists: www.cot.co.uk

NHS Careers: www.nhscareers.nhs.uk/explore-by-career/allied-health-professions/careers-in-the-allied-health-professions/occupational-therapist

Prospects: www.prospects.ac.uk/occupational_therapist_job_description.htm

Physiotherapist

A physiotherapist treats people with physical difficulties resulting from illness, accident, disability, ageing and sports injuries. Physiotherapists maximise movement potential through health promotion, preventative healthcare, treatment and rehabilitation, and can work in many areas including intensive care, orthopaedics, learning difficulties, paediatrics and with the terminally ill. They work with the neuromuscular, musculoskeletal, cardiovascular and respiratory systems to develop and restore body function and overall wellbeing, devising and monitoring treatment programmes using manual therapy, therapeutic exercise and technological equipment.

Entry

A degree in physiotherapy accredited by the HCPC is required. It is also possible to take a fast-track postgraduate course with a First or 2.i in a degree such as biological sciences or sports science. Entry to courses is very competitive, so any pre-entry work experience will be advantageous, such as shadowing a physiotherapist or working as an assistant physiotherapist.

Candidates should also be able to demonstrate the following skills:

- listening skills

- patience and tact

- genuine interest in health and wellbeing

- keen interest in anatomy and physiology.

The work can also require physical strength and stamina.

Salary information

Starting pay with the NHS is £21,000–£27,000 rising to £34,000 for specialist physiotherapists and up to £40,000 for an advanced physiotherapist. Salaries are about the same in private practice.

Typical work activities

Typical daily activities include:

- assisting patients with joint or spinal issues

- writing up case notes and collecting patient statistics

- advising patients on how to look after or improve their conditions

- keeping updated on current developments in physiotherapy practice.

Training and development

Most newly qualified physiotherapists work within the NHS, experiencing different areas of practice through a series of rotations, each lasting three to four months. Continuing professional development is required after qualification, to stay registered with the HCPC, via short courses, on the job training and through supervision. The Chartered Society of Physiotherapy (CSP) offers a range of post-qualifying courses, and it is possible to study for postgraduate qualifications. Specialisms can be developed in areas such as: care of the elderly, occupational health, paediatrics and sports medicine. Self-employment is possible, but the CSP recommends two years of experience plus further training before going freelance.

Further resources

CSP: www.csp.org.uk

NHS Careers: www.nhscareers.nhs.uk/explore-by-career/allied-health-professions/careers-in-the-allied-health-professions/physiotherapist

Prospects: www.prospects.ac.uk/physiotherapist_job_description.htm

Podiatrist

A podiatrist, formerly referred to as a chiropodist, diagnoses and treats problems of the feet and lower legs, offering preventative care as well as carrying out minor surgery and treatments of infections and conditions. Podiatrists also work as part of multidisciplinary healthcare teams, alongside doctors, health visitors and orthopaedic specialists.

Employers include hospitals and clinics, health centres and GP surgeries, as well as private healthcare providers such as BUPA, Nuffield or Spire. Some podiatrists will work on a self-employed basis, and may move between locations as well as working from their own treatment room. They can also be involved in sporting events and in visits to schools. Because travel between locations during the working day is frequent, a driving licence is essential. Podiatrists in private practice can find that clients wish to see them outside of office hours for appointments and may have to work flexibly.

Entry

To become a podiatrist, you will need to complete a BSc in Podiatry approved by the HCPC. Competition is high for places on these degree courses because podiatry is also a second career of choice for many people. You will require occupational health clearance and an enhanced Disclosure and Barring Service (criminal records) check before being accepted onto a course. Most places on podiatry courses are funded by the National Health Service – see the NHS Business Services Authority website for more information.

Skills

Candidates will also need to show evidence of the following:

- enjoyment of working with all types of people

- manual dexterity for carrying out treatments and minor surgery

- good self-management skills and business knowledge, especially if self-employed.

Typical work activities

A podiatrist would typically:

- assess and treat footcare ailments, such as verrucas

- correct the anatomical relationship between different parts of the foot after analysing how a person walks or runs

- undertake nail surgery using local anaesthetic

- use equipment such as dressings, orthotics (inner sole) materials, surgical instruments and gait-analysis tools for assessing movement issues

- prescribe and fit orthotics and other appliances.

Salary information

Typical starting salaries for a podiatrist in the NHS are £21,176–£27,625. This increases to £30,460–£40,157 for a specialist podiatrist. Consulting podiatrists can earn considerably more, reaching about £90,000. Working in private practice pays more than working for the NHS, with sessions charged at about £40 each.

Training and development

The Society of Chiropodists and Podiatrists (SCP) is the main provider of continuing professional development (CPD) for podiatrists, offering regional and national training opportunities and programmes of study. It is also possible to study for a master's or PhD in aspects of podiatry, such as advanced podiatry or podiatry with diabetes. Training in business skills may be helpful to the self-employed, with providers such as Outset or GOV.UK. Experienced podiatrists may wish to pursue specialisms in areas such as biomechanics, high-risk patient management or dermatology, taking courses with the SCP.

Further resources

GOV.UK: www.gov.uk

HCPC: www.hpc-uk.org

National Careers Service: nationalcareersservice.direct.gov.uk

NHS Business Services Authority: www.nhsbsa.nhs.uk/816.aspx

NHS Careers: www.nhscareers.nhs.uk/explore-by-career/allied-health-professions/careers-in-the-allied-health-professions/chiropodistpodiatrist

Outset: www.outset.org

Prospects: www.prospects.ac.uk/physiotherapist_job_description.htm

SCP: www.scpod.org

P O d i B i A t R Y

where's the
science in that?

he world around us is dominated by science in one way or another, be it
ology in plants, the human body, **physics** in engineering or communications
d **chemistry** in food or DNA research.

Podiatry is no exception....
it's full of science!

or more information on podiatry please visit our website

contact:
e Society of Chiropodists and Podiatrists
ellmongers Path, Tower Bridge Road, London SE1 3LY
ephone: 0207 234 8620 ~ E-mail: enq@scpod.org

ww.feetforlife.org

The Society of
Chiropodists and
Podiatrists

Profile: College of Podiatry

The world around us is dominated by science in one way or another, be it biology in plants or the human body, physics in engineering or communications and chemistry in food or DNA research.

Podiatry is no exception . . . it's full of science!

To understand how the lower limb works and to help patients you need to know all sorts about biology, physics and chemistry.

Biology

Biology is probably the main science people associate with working in the medical profession. As a podiatrist it's really important to understand the structure of the body as well as how things interact. Podiatrists measure the blood flow in the legs and feet and to do this they have to know exactly how to find the arteries and veins. They can test blood flow in a number of ways by using their hands, ultrasound devices and blood pressure tests.

Treatment of painful or ingrowing toenails is achieved using simple surgical techniques. To do this podiatrists have to give patients injections of anaesthetic, which must be placed accurately near the nerves in the toe. To do the surgery effectively they have to understand the structure of the nail and surrounding tissues. So you can see how important it is to know your anatomy!

Physics

Physics is also important. Podiatrists treat a lot of different patients with biomechanical problems and understanding levers and forces really helps to diagnose the problem and work out how to treat the patient.

Participating in sports puts increased forces through the joints in the legs, which can cause pain and injury. Runners for example can develop foot or leg problems that may need treatment from a podiatrist. Using a treadmill, video equipment and their knowledge a podiatrist can assess the patient, diagnose the problem and potentially provide custom-made insoles that can alter the mechanics of the foot and reduce unwanted forces going through the foot.

Chemistry

Chemistry is also important in podiatry. Chemical reactions are essential for normal body function. Podiatrists need to know how illnesses and medicines may affect different chemical processes in the body to provide appropriate treatment.

Wounds in the skin contain all sorts of biochemicals. Podiatrists must understand what potential interactions there might be with anything they are using to treat a wound that would slow down the healing process. They need to know about different kinds of medication and how they react with the body.

For example understanding chemistry enables a podiatrist to calculate the maximum safe dose of anaesthetic for a patient.

If you would like further information about podiatry training please visit www. careersinpodiatry.com

BIRMINGHAM METROPOLITAN COLLEGE

BSC HONS PODIATRY

- 3 year full-time programme
- NHS Funded
- City Centre location
- Excellent transport links
- Superb facilities
- Fully equipped treatment clinic and operating theatre
- NHS placement supplied

BIRMINGHAM METROPOLITAN COLLEGE
shaping futures · changing lives

Matthew Boulton Campus
Jennens Road, Birmingham B4 7PS
For more information contact
Sandra Jevons
0121 446 4545 ext 8024
Email sandra.jevons@bmetc.ac.uk

f Birmingham Metropolitan College 🐦 @bmetc

Profile: Birmingham Metropolitan

What is podiatry?

Podiatry is a healthcare profession concerned with the assessment, diagnosis and management of pathologies within the foot and lower limb.

The BSc (Hons) Podiatry programme offered by Birmingham Metropolitan College and validated by Aston University provides an environment in which the student can gain knowledge, acquire skills and evolve into an independent and effective professional practitioner.

What subjects will I study?

Programme modules include clinical studies, regional and functional anatomy, research methods, pharmacology for podiatrists, health psychology and nail surgery under local anaesthetic.

What qualifications will I need to apply?

- Two A Levels at grade B and one A Level at grade C or above (280 UCAS tariff points). One of the B grades must be a science subject, preferably biology, human biology or chemistry.

- BTEC National Diploma/Higher National Diploma in a science-related subject

- Access to Higher Education course in an appropriate science subject (a minimum of 45 credits at Level 3 and 15 credits at Level 2 are expected from Access courses including all science-related modules).

Applicants must also possess a minimum of five GCSEs (or equivalent); two of which must be in English and mathematics.

International applicants or those applicants for whom English is not the first language must possess an International English Language Testing System score of 7.0, with an average of 6.5 in each subject area.

Employment and future career opportunities

Podiatry graduates can progress onto postgraduate and research positions. Career opportunities include employment within the National Health Service as part of podiatric and multidisciplinary teams involved in a variety of clinical specialisms including tissue viability and musculoskeletal care. Additionally graduates can work in private practice or undertake further training in forensic podiatry and foot surgery.

How to apply

Online applications can be made through UCAS (www.ucas.com)

UCAS Institution Code: M60 UCAS Course Code: B985

Start your journey at UEL

Our BSc (Hons) Podiatric Medicine degree will equip you with the skills and knowledge to practise as a podiatrist. On graduation you can apply for membership of the Society of Chiropodists and Podiatrists and Registration with the Health and Care Professions Council.

At our Stratford campus we offer an excellent teaching environment, including newly refurbished laboratories, computer suites, a new library and a purpose built Centre for Clinical Education.

To find out more:

Call: 0208 223 3333
Email: study@uel.ac.uk
Visit: uel.ac.uk/hsb

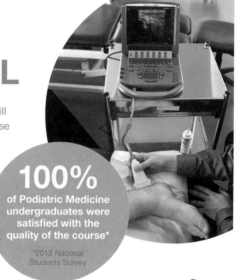

100%
of Podiatric Medicine undergraduates were satisfied with the quality of the course*

*2012 National Students Survey

UEL
University of East London

Be Driven Be More

Profile: University of East London

A Podiatric Medicine degree at UEL – preparing for a career in podiatry

UEL's BSc (Hons) Podiatric Medicine programme has been developed in collaboration with clinical staff, and has a strong practical element with students completing a minimum of 1,000 hours of clinical practice before they graduate.

This development of students' clinical skills is supplemented with clinical placements in each year of the programme. Students get a wide range of clinical placements that last between three and six weeks. Students gain experience of podiatric medicine in departments delivering the highest standards of care, covering the whole breadth of podiatric practice with hands-on experience ranging from basic foot care through to nail surgery and administering local anaesthetics, musculoskeletal practice, wound care and management of the high risk foot. Placements are offered within NHS Podiatry Departments across London and east England.

Our teaching is underpinned by our research. Podiatry research at UEL is housed within the Human Motor Performance Group (HMPG). This collective operates within a

143

multidisciplinary team and their emphasis is on research into motion analysis, neural control mechanisms, changes in skeletal muscle contractile properties and neural activation together with oxygen uptake as a measure of physical fitness.

What our students say

'Podiatry ticked all the boxes: as a practice it is wholly medical in its roots with surgical elements, and as podiatrist you are constantly working with people and there is a lot of scope for progression.'

Helen, BSc Podiatric Medicine Graduate

Find out more about studying Podiatric Medicine at UEL www.uel.ac.uk/ugpodiatric

Psychologist (clinical)

A clinical psychologist aims to reduce the psychological distress of their clients and improve their wellbeing. They make use of psychological research and treatments to make changes to their clients' lives, and can work with health problems such as anxiety and depression, neurological disorders, addiction, childhood behaviour disorders, adjustment to physical illnesses, and personal and family relationships. They operate mainly within health and social care settings such as hospitals, health centres, social services and with community mental health teams. Clinical psychologists are also occasionally on call for emergencies.

Entry

Candidates will need a psychology degree accredited by the British Psychological Society (BPS), with a classification of a 2.i, although it may be possible to apply for some postgraduate programmes with a 2.ii.

If a psychology degree is not held, or is not accredited, then the following options are available:

- sit the BPS's qualifying examination

- take an appropriate BPS-accredited postgraduate qualification

- take a BPS-accredited conversion course.

Another three years of postgraduate study leading to a Doctorate in Clinical Psychology are required for chartered status.

Candidates must also have a minimum of six to 12 months' relevant clinical work experience before applying for training; some course providers may be able to offer advice on what is appropriate for their programme. This work could involve being an assistant psychologist with the NHS, but can also include nursing, social work, and working with people with mental health issues or disabilities. Applications for the three-year doctoral training programmes are extremely competitive, with only one in six candidates being successful, and with many making several attempts at entry before succeeding.

It is crucial that before embarking on the process to become a clinical psychologist, applicants spend time with practising professionals to ensure that this is the right role for them and to learn about the realities of this demanding job. Experience of working with organisations such as Nightline or the Samaritans, or engaging in mentoring opportunities, can help to develop relevant skills and experience other people's problems first-hand.

Salary information

Trainee clinical psychologists start at about £25,000 on the NHS pay scale, rising to about £30,000 on qualification. With experience, pay can rise to over £45,000 and to more than £80,000 for very senior practitioners. Salaries within private hospitals and practice will vary.

Typical work activities

The activities of a clinical psychologist include:

- undertaking assessments using a variety of methods including psychometric tests, interviews and observation of behaviour

- producing and monitoring programmes of therapy and counselling, often in collaboration with colleagues

- counselling and supporting carers, and carrying out research, which can enhance practice.

Training and development

Continuing professional development is required by the BPS to maintain professional competence after qualification, and there are opportunities to move into specialist areas such as forensic psychology (looking in detail at criminal behaviour) and neuropsychology (specifically focused on the workings of the brain).

Further resources

BPS: www.bps.org.uk

Improving Access to Psychological Therapies: www.iapt.nhs.uk

NHS Careers: www.nhscareers.nhs.uk/explore-by-career/psychological-therapies/careers-in-psychological-therapies/psychologist/clinical-psychologist

Prospects: www.prospects.ac.uk/clinical_psychologist_job_description.htm

Sports therapist

Sports therapy does not deal with overall healthcare but focuses specifically on working with musculoskeletal conditions caused by sporting activities. A sports therapist will utilise sports and exercise principles to optimise performance, preparation and injury prevention programmes, as well as providing immediate care for injuries, including massage therapy. They will also design rehabilitation programmes and work with athletes to implement them. They may make use of some physiotherapy skills (see above), but are not qualified as such.

Most sports therapists work in sports injury clinics and can combine their practice with other roles within the sports sector, such as coaching, teaching or personal training. It is not unusual for a sports therapist to manage a 'portfolio' career in this way, and work for several clubs or gyms and therefore in different locations each week. If working with a sports team, then you will need to work weekend and evening hours due to competitions, while national and international travel may also be possible if affiliated to a team.

Profile: Bangor University

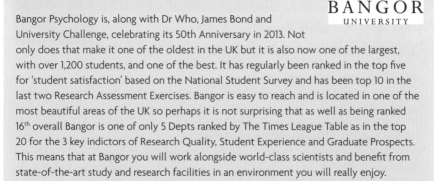

Bangor Psychology – world class at 50

Bangor Psychology is, along with Dr Who, James Bond and University Challenge, celebrating its 50th Anniversary in 2013. Not only does that make it one of the oldest in the UK but it is also now one of the largest, with over 1,200 students, and one of the best. It has regularly been ranked in the top five for 'student satisfaction' based on the National Student Survey and has been top 10 in the last two Research Assessment Exercises. Bangor is easy to reach and is located in one of the most beautiful areas of the UK so perhaps it is not surprising that as well as being ranked 16th overall Bangor is one of only 5 Depts ranked by The Times League Table as in the top 20 for the 3 key indictors of Research Quality, Student Experience and Graduate Prospects. This means that at Bangor you will work alongside world-class scientists and benefit from state-of-the-art study and research facilities in an environment you will really enjoy.

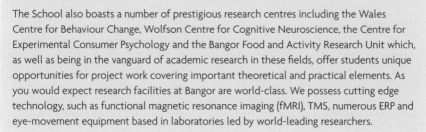

The School also boasts a number of prestigious research centres including the Wales Centre for Behaviour Change, Wolfson Centre for Cognitive Neuroscience, the Centre for Experimental Consumer Psychology and the Bangor Food and Activity Research Unit which, as well as being in the vanguard of academic research in these fields, offer students unique opportunities for project work covering important theoretical and practical elements. As you would expect research facilities at Bangor are world-class. We possess cutting edge technology, such as functional magnetic resonance imaging (fMRI), TMS, numerous ERP and eye-movement equipment based in laboratories led by world-leading researchers.

We are also a truly global community with staff and students from all over the EU and from countries as diverse as Australia, China, Israel, Iran, Japan and the US. The School forms a large part of the College of Health and Behavioural Sciences, a college that boasts a very strong research and teaching ethos, which translates into excellent course provision. Bangor is one of a select few UK psychology departments to appear in the CHE European Excellence Rankings, which is a good illustration of its international standing. The School is also renowned for being a friendly place to work and study, a fact that the department takes great pride in.

As well as undergraduate psychology degrees with a number of specialisms we also offer a range of postgraduate courses including Foundations of Clinical Psychology, Neuroimaging, Psychological Research, Consumer Psychology with Business and Applied Behavioural Analysis. The Department offers merit-based scholarships for outstanding candidates.

Many psychology students, undergraduate and postgraduate, do not realise the variety of career opportunities open to them. The study of psychology can lead to careers in education, marketing, human resources, government service, fundraising, creative arts and many other areas as well as the wide range of professional careers related to psychology. Very few disciplines offer the level of numeracy and literacy skills that are embedded in our psychology programmes.

Whether you are interested in psychology for research, as a stepping stone to a wide variety of careers or simply because you enjoy it, contact us to see what we have to offer.

Case study

Name: Declan McClelland
Age: 26
From: Anglesey, North Wales
Course: Consumer Psychology and Business MSc

Why did you choose Bangor?
I studied my undergraduate degree in psychology here. I also live locally, and many of my friends live in the area.

How did you feel when you started university?
Initially I was nervous when I began my undergraduate degree here, particularly because I wasn't going to be living in halls and I was slightly older than many of my peers when I started (23). However, when I began my MSc I was fine, I knew what to expect really.

The course . . .
The MSc is really interesting, the teachers and the modules are great and my course mates are fantastic.

Best thing about studying at Bangor?
Bangor really values the psychology department, so we have excellent facilities here. All the lecturers are down to earth and willing to talk to students, and there's a great sense of community here.

Life in Bangor . . .
Life in Bangor is great. Unlike a big city, when you meet people out in Bangor you are virtually guaranteed to see them again. This makes it really easy to make strong friendships and have a rewarding social life.

Plans for the future?
I hope to move into a more business-related field, such as marketing, which is one of the reasons I decided to study consumer psychology and business.

Any advice for prospective students?
I think Bangor is a great place to live and study, with a great sense of community. If you're interested in sports, we also have a great range of societies, and membership costs nothing. It's a great way to make friends, so get involved!

THINK PSYCHOLOGY
THINK BANGOR

Bangor Psychology is ranked 7th for research power and, as well as being ranked 16th overall Bangor is one of only 5 Depts ranked by The Times as in the top 20 for the 3 key indicators of Research Quality, Student Experience and Graduate Prospects. Why not join your future to ours?

Taught Programmes

MA Psychology

MA/Msc Consumer Psychology and Digital Media

MSc Psychological Research

MRes Psychology

MSc Neuroimaging

MSc/MA Consumer Psychology with Business

MSc Foundations of Clinical Psychology

MSc Foundations of Clinical Neuropsychology

MSc Applied Behaviour Analysis

MSc/MA Mindfulness-based Approaches

Doctorate in Clinical Psychology

Research Programmes

PhD - various specialisms

Please visit our website for more details.

www.bangor.ac.uk/psychology

Ysgol Seicoleg / School of Psychology

Prifysgol Bangor University, Gwynedd LL57 2AS

t. +44(0)1248 382629 **e.** psychology@bangor.ac.uk

Salary information

The typical starting salary for a sports therapist is about £16,000–£18,000. A therapist can earn closer to £35,000 by working with a professional team, but this would require considerable previous experience.

Entry

Sports therapy is not currently a registered state profession, and it is possible for someone to complete a weekend training course and call herself a sports therapist. It is preferable, in terms of professional credibility, to possess a relevant undergraduate degree or a postgraduate qualification in sports therapy, validated by the Society of Sports Therapists (SST). Many sports therapists come from a sports or athletic background, but this is not necessary to enter the profession. However, any previous experience in coaching or fitness training will be advantageous in understanding the therapeutic requirements of different sporting disciplines.

Candidates would need to show evidence of the following:

- physical fitness

- a flexible attitude to work

- empathy and sensitivity to the needs of an injured client

- good organisational skills.

Typical work activities

Progressing as a sports therapist may take time as individuals build up their client lists and work on a portfolio basis, supplementing their income with different types of work. It is essential to build and maintain a network of contacts in this profession in order to find opportunities, which may well not be advertised. Short-term or temporary work could lead to more secure employment. Moving into lecturing in further or higher education is also an option. A more structured training and development framework may emerge when the sports therapy profession becomes state registered and more carefully regulated.

Further resources

Prospects: www.prospects.ac.uk/sports_therapist_job_description.htm

SST: www.society-of-sports-therapists.org

8

Pharmacology and pharmacy

There are several options for the graduate exploring a career in this sector. If you are a pharmacology student or graduate, then you possess skills valued by employers including the NHS, the pharmaceuticals industry, the Department of Health and the Intellectual Property Office. To find employment in pharmacology and with pharmaceutical companies, as in most sectors any previous relevant work experience can be advantageous; volunteering or part-time work in a local chemist, with a practising pharmacist, can be useful to your application.

The two main career options in pharmacology and pharmacy are detailed below. Research careers are also a possibility, so see also Chapter 10 on working as a research scientist. Salary information is from Prospects, unless otherwise stated.

Please see also Chapter 7 on working in the health sciences, as well as Chapter 5 on biosciences, as there is considerable overlap between these areas.

The job roles

Pharmacologist

A pharmacologist carries out scientific investigations and analysis of chemicals, drugs and medicines to identify how they affect biological systems, and how they can be used safely. This investigation can be done *in vitro*, using tissue samples or cells, or *in vivo*, using whole animals for research purposes. Pharmacological research can also be used to develop new drugs.

Specialisms within pharmacology include:

- clinical pharmacology, looking at the effects of medicines on people using clinical trials

- neuropharmacology, analysing how the nervous system responds to chemicals

- regulatory pharmacology, which looks at whether drug treatments have other effects on the body than those that were intended.

Employers of pharmacologists include the NHS, pharmaceutical companies, the Medical Research Council, universities and government research facilities.

Hours are normally nine to five on weekdays, but longer hours may be required to complete experiments or clinical trials. Researchers in industry or universities usually work longer hours as routine. Some travelling, for conferences or for fieldwork purposes, may be involved.

Entry

Most entrants to this career hold a pharmacology degree, but it is also possible to enter with a degree in the following subjects:

- pharmacy

- biology

- chemistry

- microbiology

- biochemistry

- biomedical science.

A master's or PhD can also be advantageous and may lead to a higher salary; doctoral study will be necessary for a research career.

Skills

Candidates should also be able to demonstrate the following:

- meticulous work and attention to detail

- a logical mind

- ability to analyse and interpret data

- patience.

Salary information

According to the National Careers Service, typical starting salaries are £21,000–£28,000 rising to £35,000–£80,000 for a senior member of staff.

Typical work activities

A pharmacologist would typically:

- design and carry out controlled experiments

- analyse and interpret data, often using computers and sophisticated measuring equipment

- apply the results of research to the creation of new products and manufacturing processes

- oversee tests for new drugs and medicines, ensuring that quality control is maintained.

Training and development

Initial training usually takes place on the job in any required specialist areas or in the use of relevant technology. Maintaining knowledge and skills is an expected part of continuing professional development, and workshops and short courses are usually offered by science training centres and universities. The British Pharmacological Society and the Association of the British Pharmaceutical Industry (ABPI) also offer training opportunities, and it may be possible to progress into a research career by undertaking a master's and PhD.

Further resources

ABPI: www.abpi.org.uk

British Pharmacological Society: www.bps.ac.uk

National Careers Service: nationalcareersservice.direct.gov.uk/advice/planning/jobprofiles/Pages/Pharmacologist.aspx

Prospects: www.prospects.ac.uk/pharmacologist_job_description.htm

TARGETjobs: targetjobs.co.uk/careers-advice/job-descriptions/276303-pharmacologist-job-description

Pharmacist

A pharmacist is an expert in the use and supply of medicines and can advise other medical staff in hospitals, as well as work in community pharmacies in a retail environment. A pharmacist can check and dispense prescriptions, ensuring that legislation around the controlled use of medicines is upheld. Pharmacists may also offer advice and support directly to patients, and they can undertake further training to be able to prescribe medicines for specific conditions. Hospital pharmacists may also have responsibility for the use of medicines in health centres, nursing homes and GPs' surgeries.

Entry

To become a pharmacist, it is essential to complete a four-year pharmacy degree course (MPharm), which must be accredited by the General Pharmaceutical Council (GPhC). You then complete a one-year pre-registration training course, either in a hospital or a pharmacy, depending on where you intend to work, but it is also possible to transfer to a hospital pharmacy after completing the pre-registration year in community or retail pharmacy training. You must also pass a registration examination. Most MPharm courses need an A level in chemistry, plus two more A levels in physics, mathematics or biology for admission.

Skills

Candidates for a career in pharmacy should also be able to demonstrate:

- high levels of responsibility

- very accurate and methodical work when dispensing medicines

- good mathematics skills for calculating and using formulae

- an interest in people's health and wellness.

Salary information

According to the National Careers Service, a retail or community pharmacist would typically earn about £22,000–£34,200 a year. A junior hospital pharmacist would be paid according to the National Health Service pay scale, and would start on about £25,000 according to Prospects. With experience, this would rise to up to about £40,000 for a specialist pharmacist, to about £55,000 for an advanced pharmacist, and a pharmacist consultant could earn potentially over £80,000.

Typical work activities

A pharmacist would typically:

- check prescriptions for accuracy and dispense medicines

- provide healthcare advice to the public in a retail setting

- provide advice on medicine dosages and appropriate forms of medication

- discuss patients' treatments with doctors and medical staff, in a hospital, hospice or nursing home environment

- write guidelines for drug use within hospitals

- set up and supervise clinical trials, in a hospital environment

- training and development.

A qualified pharmacist would be expected to engage in continuing professional development, and the Royal Pharmaceutical Society (RPS) can provide information on courses and workshops. Hospital pharmacists usually take a certificate or diploma in clinical pharmacy, and can also work towards an MSc. All pharmacists need to stay up to date with developments in medicine and drug research, including new products and treatment methods.

Further resources

General Pharmaceutical Council: www.pharmacyregulation.org

National Careers Service: nationalcareersservice.direct.gov.uk/advice/planning/jobprofiles/Pages/pharmacist.aspx

NHS Careers: www.nhscareers.nhs.uk/explore-by-career/pharmacy/pharmacist

Prospects: www.prospects.ac.uk/hospital_pharmacist_job_description.htm

RPS: www.rpharms.com

Case study

Adam Hardy, Manager, Business Development (Proposals), inVentiv Health Clinical

Why did you choose a career in science?

I've wanted to work in pharmaceutical research and development since I was about 13. Of course, I didn't know much about how it worked and how many different jobs there were in it, but I've received a lot of advice and learned a lot since then and I'm still learning! I think the appeal to me was three-fold: the altruistic desire to 'do good', the fact that a career in science is generally well-respected, and I also thought it was a good way to put my brain to use!

What made you choose your particular area?

Alleviating suffering (both human and animal) directly. Although this could also be achieved by becoming a medical doctor, I felt that I wanted to be using my creativity and brain to devise new treatments and further the progression of the human race.

What was your route in? Qualifications, experience, contacts?

During work experience at 16 I was advised to go into the pharmaceutical industry as a scientist, so I studied pharmacology at university doing a course that also involved spending a year with a pharmaceutical company, which I knew would be invaluable and was a key determinant in my choosing my degree course. During this year, I was advised to do a PhD, so I did this too. During my PhD I was advised to gain postdoctoral research experience in an academic environment, preferably in a totally different field. I did this in Philadelphia. It was during this time that I realised that working as a bench scientist wasn't for me, and what I really wanted to do was to work in the business of making drugs, and advance drug discovery and development that way. Since then, I've worked for a small biotechnology company and I now work for a large contract research organisation that runs clinical trials for other pharmaceutical and biotech companies.

What is a typical day like for you?

My role involves managing the development process of proposals for clinical trials for which my company is competing with other companies. The proposal development process involves getting input from various senior management personnel in a timely manner, getting them to write text for the proposal and develop and review a budget for the trial. I am now a manager in the team and I help to oversee the development of proposals by other team members, as well as developing tools and processes that contribute to proposal development. The work involves managing a heavy workload to achieve deadlines, as well as drawing on a lot of interpersonal skills to achieve results from many more senior people. A typical day could involve elements of all of the above: holding teleconferences, developing budgets and proposals, and overseeing other staff members. I certainly don't see this as the end of the road though, but merely a stepping stone to gain skills and experience that will lead me into a more influential role in future years.

What do you enjoy most about your work?

I enjoy the satisfaction when I have produced a quality product, whether it's a tool for internal use or a client-ready proposal.

What are the challenges?

The biggest challenge is dealing with a heavy workload and achieving deadlines without getting stressed. It's also important to be able to manage other people's expectations of you.

What advice would you offer a current student/recent graduate aiming for a role in your field?

I think the biggest thing is to have realistic expectations. Expect that to start with your role will be routine, although very necessary. Then, as you gain experience and prove yourself, you'll be promoted to positions that involve less routine activity and that will draw more on your creative side (as well as paying more!). Also, don't be surprised if your career goals and ambitions change – when you're young, you can be more idealistic and altruistic, but as you get older you may become more realistic.

What would you do differently, if anything, if you were starting your career all over again?

I don't think there's anything I regret – I feel I've made the best choices at the time based on who I was at that time, and what information was available. With hindsight, it would have been good to know earlier what I was going to want (and need) later, as I perhaps wouldn't have spent time doing postdoctoral research had I known I would eventually end up away from the bench. However, there's certainly truth in the old maxim, 'you can't put an old head on young shoulders', so all-in-all, I don't have any regrets.

9

Mathematics and computer science

Mathematics, computing and information technology underpin the running of most businesses, and, according to Prospects, the IT and computing sector is forecast for continued expansion, with employment in this sector predicted to grow nearly five times faster than the UK average.

There is an enormous range of roles in this sector, including keeping the infrastructure operating behind the scenes of an investment bank, designing the next big-selling game for the Xbox, or working to protect the UK from terrorism, in roles such as forensic computing and cryptography. Computing and mathematical skills can also be put to creative use in sectors such as marketing and PR, art and design, and design engineering. Fundamentally, wherever business is being done, computing and mathematics graduates are needed to keep all systems working securely and efficiently.

Jobs are available with well-known corporations such as IBM, Microsoft and Cisco, and there are also opportunities within small to medium-sized enterprises (SMEs) and start-ups often established by computing and mathematics graduates looking to recruit new talent. There are also many opportunities for self-employment and freelance work, with some students beginning this kind of activity while still completing their degree and taking advantage of university support available for new entrepreneurs.

Graduates in this field also need to be committed to continuing professional development, as its rapidly changing nature involves regularly learning new programming languages and platforms; the ability to learn quickly cannot be overstated, and students aspiring to work in this sector should have clear evidence on their CV of being able to teach themselves new languages in their spare time, in addition to those acquired on their degree courses. Evidence of completing quality work, such as websites, open source coding or show reels, may also be necessary to demonstrate capability for the job. Contrary to popular stereotypes, the vast majority of jobs in computing and mathematics are not carried out alone, and the ability to communicate clearly with colleagues and clients is a must.

Selected profiles of some of the key roles in the sector are below. Salary information is derived from Prospects, unless otherwise stated.

The job roles

Actuary

An actuary uses their knowledge of mathematics, statistics and economics to advise on financial risks. They can help to solve business problems as well as forecasting long-term financial costs. Most actuarial work is carried out in insurance and pensions, and it is possible to move into working into investment banks later on. Actuarial work is also available in consultancy and in the Government Actuary's Department, which advises on costs for social security benefits, state pensions and healthcare. The UK professional qualification has mutual recognition agreements with international professional bodies, so overseas work is a possibility in this field. Hours can be long, especially for those in junior positions who will be studying alongside their work.

Entry

This profession is open to any graduate with proven numerical skills, but a degree in mathematics, statistics, economics, business, or in science and engineering could enhance your prospects. Most graduates entering this profession possess a First or 2.i honours degree. Postgraduate diplomas and MSc courses accredited by The Actuarial Profession are listed on their website.

Training requires a programme of study (about 15 hours a week) alongside working full-time as a trainee actuary, but exemptions may be made for those who have previously studied mathematics or economics, which can reduce training time. Reaching the minimum level of qualification (Associate member) takes between two and five years, while studying to advanced level (Fellowship) takes another three to seven years.

Skills

Candidates will also need to demonstrate evidence of the following skills:

- advanced skills in mathematics and statistics

- ability to explain complex information

- self-management and discipline for studying while working

- good business sense and an interest in the business world

- ability to take responsibility.

Salary information

Typical starting salaries are £25,000–£35,000 and are generally higher in London. This increases to £40,000–£55,000 for newly qualified actuaries, and can rise to £60,000 for people with 10–15 years' experience in senior roles. Salaries can reach over £100,000 for very senior actuaries.

Typical work activities

An actuary may typically:

- apply financial and statistical theories to assess the likelihood of an event taking place and its associated financial costs

- monitor risks within trading in investment banks

- advise on issues such as the administration of pensions and benefits

- present reports and advise on risk limitation

- value assets and liabilities

- analyse risks relating to catastrophe claims.

Training and development

Most entrants begin by working as a trainee actuary and then study for relevant exams in their own time. Their employer may offer study leave and help with meeting the costs of training, as well as mentoring and coaching opportunities. Following qualification, actuaries can take on management and supervisory positions, as well as mentoring trainees and leading projects. Some more experienced actuaries can move between areas of practice, such as from pensions work into asset management, or into related careers such as financial modelling, valuation work or investment systems.

Further resources

Institute and Faculty of Actuaries: www.actuaries.org.uk

National Careers Service: nationalcareersservice.direct.gov.uk/advice/planning/jobprofiles/Pages/actuary.aspx

Prospects: www.prospects.ac.uk/actuary_job_description.htm

Cryptographer

Cryptography (also known as cryptology) is the practice of concealing information and is a fast-growing area of work that attracts mathematics graduates. It involves the creating and breaking of codes, and these skills are required across a variety of employers who need to keep data safe, including government organisations such as GCHQ and the Serious Fraud Office, mobile technology companies, satellite television and internet service providers and banks. Cryptographers also help to design encryption software and must stay up to date with legal issues related to privacy issues. Related work in this area is also carried out in network and internet security.

Entry

Many security specialists begin work as network technicians and administrators, requiring an undergraduate degree in computing, or a related degree such as mathematics with proven practical computing skills. It is advisable to opt for degree units that cover security issues, if this is a career option you are seriously considering, or to look at a master's specialising in an aspect of computer security. Recruitment in this area can be carried out discreetly, due to the sensitive nature of the work, and contacting employers directly can be difficult, so it will be helpful to attend any campus visits that relevant employers make to your university, or attend any open days, so that you can ask about any particular qualifications you may need.

Once employed as technician or administrator, it is possible to study for a qualification in network security, such as Microsoft Certified Systems Engineer (MCSE), which can improve your prospects. Government agencies such as GCHQ also recruit graduates directly to their training programmes, especially postgraduate researchers on PhD programmes, as research skills are highly valued in this field. However, be aware that applying to government agencies requires discretion on the applicant's part and very thorough security checks as part of the recruitment process.

Skills

Candidates should be able to:

- demonstrate mastery of computer programming languages

- possess excellent mathematical ability

- demonstrate attention to detail

- concentrate for extended periods of time

- work alone, and be self-motivated.

In addition to technical skills, communication should not be underestimated as a critical skill in this field. Specialists need to be able to explain security needs to laypersons clearly, as the 'human factor' is often the weak link in security, with people using easily guessed passwords or maintaining lax data protection practices.

Salary information

According to IT Jobs Watch, network security offers a salary of £45,000–£50,000. Because of the level of importance attached to this kind of work, highly experienced security experts and cryptographers can be highly paid for their skills. Good security and cryptography consultants are also hard to replace, as they become very familiar with all the customised software put in place to meet a company's needs, so employers like to recruit staff who intend to stay in post long term.

Typical work activities

A cryptographer or security expert may:

- decipher codes or cryptograms

- create encrypted code

- monitor and maintain the security of data networks

- be responsible for data protection practices in the workplace, and communicating these to staff

- analyse and interpret large amounts of data from computer programs, weather patterns and computer viruses, for example, and predict future events or identify useful intelligence.

Training and development

Further career advancement, especially in research, may well require a PhD, and a minimum of five years' experience on the job. Maintaining current knowledge of developments in computing and mathematics is essential to this work.

Further resources

Careers That Don't Suck: careersthatdontsuck.com/2007/02/24/career-profile-cryptologist

e-how Internet Security Jobs: www.ehow.com/about_4796044_internet-security-jobs.html

International Association for Cryptologic Research: www.iacr.org

IT Jobswatch: www.itjobswatch.co.uk/jobs/uk/network%20security.do

University of Kent Careers: www.kent.ac.uk/careers/workin/forensiccomputing.htm

Computer games developer

A computer games developer is involved in creating and producing games that can be played on PCs, the internet, handheld devices, consoles and mobile phones. The work can involve creating new titles or updating existing ones, and roles within computer games development include:

- designer (coming up with the concept and look of the game)

- artist (creating visual characters, concept art and scenery)

- animator (bringing the characters and play to life using computer modelling and software)

- programmer (creating the code that makes the game work).

Games studios can be found nationwide across the UK, from Edinburgh to Brighton. There is the possibility of international work once a developer has acquired more experience, but most multinational games companies house their European headquarters in the UK.

Entry

The majority of people working in this industry are graduates with a degree in one of the following subjects:

- computer science

- computer games development

- multimedia design

- software engineering

- mathematics

- physics

- animation

- graphic design.

A relevant postgraduate qualification specialising in game design and development may help your prospects if you do not have a relevant first degree, but talk to games studios to find out what they require. Demonstrable practical skills and ability can be more relevant than qualifications in this field, so be prepared to show examples of your work in the form of a portfolio (for more artistic roles) or a working demo (for programming). You should ideally also possess a good working knowledge of key titles and be very familiar with playing them. Commitment can also be demonstrated by designing your own games, attending games festivals and networking with companies, and keeping knowledge updated with relevant websites and magazines.

Skills

Applicants should be able to demonstrate:

- ability to work alone and stay motivated

- creativity

- wide knowledge and understanding of computer games

- willingness to meet client demands and requirements

- ability to work under pressure.

For programmers: C++, C#, Java and ActionScript.

For artists: 3ds Max; Maya, Photoshop, DirectX, OpenGL.

Salary information

Typical starting salaries are around £18,000–£25,000 but could be lower if applicants start as a quality assurance tester and not as an artist or programmer. Salaries can rise with experience to over £70,000 for very senior managers, technical developers and production managers.

Typical work activities

Depending on their specialist area, a computer games developer may:

- generate game scripts and storyboards

- use 2D or 3D modelling software, such as Maya

- create the game's visual template at the concept stage

- work closely with clients to understand and meet their requirements

- solve problems and bugs within the game's code

- quality-test games in an organised and systematic way.

Training and development

Computer games developers are expected to engage in continuing professional development, staying up to date with new advances in the field, including learning new programming languages and packages, as well as staying in touch with market demands. Progression within this industry can be quick, with beginners moving up to senior level within 10 years. Higher-level specialists are currently in short supply, according to Prospects, so advancement can be rapid. The market for games on mobile and handheld devices is also expanding, and may continue to offer opportunities for development.

Further resources

Creative Skillset: www.creativeskillset.org

National Careers Service: nationalcareersservice.direct.gov.uk/advice/planning/jobprofiles/Pages/computergamesdeveloper.aspx

Prospects: www.prospects.ac.uk/games_developer_job_description.htm

IT consultant

IT consultants work with commercial and industrial partners seeking support with business and IT problems. An IT consultant can work to help improve the efficiency and structure of a business, as well as advising on the purchase of new equipment and hardware, the design and installation of IT systems, training users of those systems, and offering highly specialist technical expertise. IT consultants can also be involved in the sales and business development side of an organisation, as well as more technical roles. This work is usually contract-based, with IT consultants being hired for an agreed period of time to complete agreed tasks. Employers include software houses, management consultancy firms and financial organisations. Self-employment may be possible after experience in the industry has been accrued.

Entry

Working as an IT consultant is open to all graduates who can prove their computing skills, however a degree in computer science, software engineering, mathematics, operational research or information systems may enhance your prospects. Graduates with degrees in other disciplines, such as the arts and humanities or business, should be able to offer a 2.i, as well as proven technical skills. Postgraduate qualifications in IT are not usually necessary, but may be helpful if your first degree is not relevant. Any commercial experience is also valuable in understanding the needs of organisations and their customers.

Skills

Applicants should also be able to demonstrate the following skills and attributes:

- meticulous attention to detail

- excellent communication skills

- presentation skills

- ability to learn quickly

- ability to meet high client standards.

Salary information

According to Prospects, the average salary for an IT consultant is about £43,000, but this will vary depending on the individual consultant's experience as well as on the employer and location. Pay can also be performance based.

Typical work activities

An IT consultant would typically:

- meet clients and clarify project objectives

- plan the timescales of a project and decide on required resources

- make recommendations, both in written form and as a presentation

- design, install and test new IT equipment and systems

- organise and deliver training for system users.

Training and development

An IT consultant is required to undertake continuing professional development throughout their career, given continuing and rapid changes in technology, and most training is carried out on the job. Professional qualifications are available from the Chartered Institute for IT (BCS), and e-skills UK, a sector skills council, also offers support with training and apprenticeships. It is possible to either specialise in a particular area of IT, or to take on responsibilities such as management or staff training. Self-employment may also be an option with experience and the development of a solid professional reputation.

Further resources

Chartered Institute for IT: www.bcs.org

Prospects: www.prospects.ac.uk/it_consultant_job_description.htm

Startups: www.startups.co.uk/what-does-an-it-consultant-do.html

TARGETjobs: targetjobs.co.uk/careers-advice/job-descriptions/279915-it-consultant-job-description

Statistician

A statistician collects, interprets and presents quantitative information. They are employed across a range of sectors, including education, government, health and pharmaceuticals, finance, research councils and market research. A statistician usually designs surveys and data acquisition trials, collects the data, and then processes their findings depending on the context for which it was collected. They can then advise on these results and present any recommendations.

Entry

A first degree in a numerate discipline, or a degree with a quantitative component, is usual for entry into this sector. Relevant degrees include:

- mathematics

- economics

- statistics

- social and political science

- geography

- psychology.

If seeking a career in medical statistics, then an MSc in this subject would be advantageous. Competition for statistics posts in the Civil Service, with the Government Statistical Service, can be very high, so offering a First or 2.i degree in a subject with statistical content, such as mathematics or economics, is advisable.

Skills

Candidates also need to demonstrate the following:

- excellent numerical and IT skills

- sound understanding of statistical principles and concepts

- ability to work in a team as well as alone and using initiative.

Salary information

Typical starting salaries would be £22,000–£31,000 and closer to £22,000–£39,000 in London. At senior level, which would require more than 10–15 years' experience, salaries can increase to £30,000–£69,000 with some earning even more.

Typical work activities

A statistician would typically:

- design data acquisition trials

- use statistics to make forecasts

- advise policymakers on strategic decisions

- act in a consulting role.

Training and development

Most professional training for statisticians is conducted on the job. You would be expected to maintain current knowledge of trends within statistics work. The Royal Statistical Society (RSS) offers the opportunity to apply for the professional qualification of Chartered Statistician (CStat), requiring a portfolio of five years' professional experience; this is the highest professional grade achievable within the profession. Outside of the Government Statistical Service (GSS), promotion may require moving between organisations. It may also be possible to move into a research career, and this would require a PhD. In the GSS, promotion is made on merit, and statisticians are required to pass a formal promotion board. Most GSS statisticians would expect to apply for a senior grade (Grade 7 Statistician) within four to five years of appointment.

Further resources

Prospects: www.prospects.ac.uk/statistician_job_description.htm

RSS: www.rss.org.uk

TARGETjobs: targetjobs.co.uk/careers-advice/job-descriptions/279107-statistician-job-description

Software developer

A software developer, or software engineer, is instrumental in the design, building and maintenance of systems and computer programs that help organisations to run effectively. They can write and code individual programs as well as being responsible for providing a completely new software resource. Work can also include developing software for home entertainment consoles, designing databases for companies in the finance sector or for general administrative purposes, and designing computer controls for manufacturing machinery in industry. The case study below has been contributed by a graduate writing code within the financial services sector and provides more details of what is involved on a daily basis.

Entry

Applicants for software development positions usually have a relevant degree qualification, such as computer science, software development or software engineering. However, an employer may still recruit an applicant without a relevant degree onto a training scheme as long as they have demonstrable computing ability. It is also possible to study for an MSc in a related subject as a conversion course or to develop more specialist knowledge in a particular area of the field.

Skills

Candidates would also be expected to demonstrate the following:

- knowledge of the main programming languages and operating systems, such as Oracle, SQL, Java and C++

- ability to learn new programming languages and operating systems quickly

- ability to explain complex technical issues in a straightforward way to a client

- ability to work under pressure and to a deadline

- meticulous attention to detail

- business and commercial awareness.

Salary information

According to the National Careers Service, graduate software developers can expect a starting salary of around £20,000–£26,000 annually. This can rise to over £40,000 with more experience and to over £50,000 for developers who take on management responsibilities.

Typical work activities

A software developer would typically:

- review and update current systems

- write or amend the program codes and test the product before going live with it

- maintain a system

- produce training manuals for users

- fix technical problems.

Training and development

Because of the rapid pace of development in computing, it is essential that any software developer stays up to date with changes. It is also possible to take training programmes and qualifications to develop new skills with organisations such e-skills UK, the Chartered Institute of IT, or the Institution of Analysts and Programmers. Software companies such as Microsoft and Oracle also offer training courses and development products. Later in their careers, software developers can take on management and supervisory roles, as well as lead a team. It is also possible to work as a freelancer after gaining sufficient experience and developing a network of contacts.

Further resources

Chartered Institute for IT: www.bcs.org

CW Jobs: www.cwjobs.co.uk/careers-advice/profiles/software-developer

e-skills UK: www.e-skills.com

Institution of Analysts and Programmers: www.iap.org.uk

National Careers Service: nationalcareersservice.direct.gov.uk/advice/planning/jobprofiles/Pages/softwaredeveloper.aspx

Case study

Software engineer with a London-based software company in the finance sector

Why did you choose a career in science?

I chose a career in science and technology – specifically software – for a number of reasons. Firstly, I wanted to work in a technical capacity that allowed me to apply the practical skills I had worked hard to learn. Secondly, computing is an area I have always been particularly interested in along with finance; being able to couple computing with many subject areas also made it a very attractive opportunity when choosing a degree course. Finally, having a qualification in a tangible skill made job hunting much less hard work than it might have been in more creative or less capacities where skills can be much less quantifiable.

What made you choose your particular area?

I wanted to work in an area that really interested me so that I could enjoy both the technical challenges and the further softer challenges of building understandable and useful solutions. So, for example, the technical challenges of enterprise scalable software but also the real life challenges of suiting a user's needs and workflow, which is usually more challenging. The opportunities for career progression within the industry are good but you always have to continue evolving with the latest trends. Therefore, technology is an exciting industry to be in and keeps you on your toes.

What was your route in? Qualifications, experience, contacts?

I visited my current employer before starting university and was able to gain a good understanding and knowledge of the firm's business. I was fortunate enough to make a few contacts on my visit too – I retained these contacts throughout my career at university. They were able to help me with my application for this internship. I think therefore, it was the networking and maintaining contact along with some applicable work experience that allowed me to obtain the role I wanted.

What is a typical day like for you?

No two days are the same. However, they are usually composed of a mixture of some project work, a few meetings and odd jobs/bug fixes. That is, the developer is free to do as they please – pick up work as it comes in from clients/other programmers or just continue with ongoing projects. It is down to the individual to manage their time and ensure that their manager is informed of progress on all the projects.

Work is very fast paced with an emphasis on getting things done: clients are very demanding and want results instantly, which is very important for the way the business runs. Therefore, you can be on call 24 hours a day if your particular product breaks or is having client impacting issues.

The work is very enjoyable and dynamic. Being able to ship code the same day to paying customers keeps you on your toes and enables you to constantly improve things. The hours can be long (sometimes up to 12 hours a day), however no-one is clock watching and everyone wants you to succeed and be productive.

What do you enjoy most about your work?
Working with some of the best programmers in the world is what makes work most enjoyable. Everyone is striving to make the product as good as it can be and looking to help each other out. Being in the office is a genuinely enjoyable experience and something to look forward to every day.

What are the challenges?
The main challenge is getting things done correctly the first time – everything is constantly refined. Fortunately our lifecycle (working patterns) means that if you make errors then the issues will be picked up very quickly. Problems can very often creep in when you are building products very quickly and so it is important to maintain a clear head and run the right checks when deploying code.

What advice would you offer a current student/recent graduate aiming for a role in your field?
Showing a keen interest in a company and the people can get you a long way. At interview I was quizzed heavily on the role and position of the company I was applying for. Being able to talk intelligibly about the industry and current trends indicates your interest and desire to work there.

What would you do differently, if anything, if you were starting your career all over again?
Perhaps I could have explored the job market a bit more to see how many other roles there were out there. That doesn't mean to say that I didn't keep my eyes open at university but I always had the current role at the back of my mind as a great place to work and start my career.

10

Research scientist

Research scientists are responsible for designing controlled laboratory investigations, and analysing and reporting on their findings. These investigations can have a specific purpose or be carried out in the interest of widening scientific knowledge more generally. They work alone to carry out their laboratory and investigative work, but are generally also part of a larger research team that will share findings amongst themselves and with relevant external parties.

Typical employers of research scientists include:

- government laboratories

- universities

- pharmaceutical companies

- research councils

- hospitals

- food companies and producers

- utilities providers.

Research posts are extremely competitive, and postgraduate qualifications up to PhD level are usually required to be successful in this field. Most research scientists will also need to publish their findings in peer-reviewed academic journals to maintain their research credibility. They need to attend conferences and read academic journals to stay updated on current research, as well as maintain their knowledge of relevant areas of interest. Some international travel can be necessary for attending conferences or carrying out fieldwork.

Hours are mainly nine to five, but there may be a need for longer hours and weekend work to complete projects and meet deadlines, and some hospitals may require shift work patterns for researchers. Many researchers are also often hired on a fixed-term contract basis, although these contracts can last for several years at a time, and this makes the permanent research posts very competitive to acquire.

Entry

You need a minimum of a 2.i degree in a science relevant to the vacancy for which you are applying, while an MSc or PhD is required for permanent research positions. It may be possible to secure a post with an undergraduate degree and work towards a postgraduate qualification while working, but it is advisable to check with potential employers as to whether this is an option. Your undergraduate degree should generally be as relevant as possible to your chosen position, and first degrees can include:

- biochemistry

- biological sciences

- biomedical sciences

- chemistry

- natural sciences

- pharmacology

- environmental biology.

Experience of practical laboratory work can be helpful to your application, and academic posts will most likely also require postdoctoral research experience.

Skills

Candidates should also be able to demonstrate the following:

- a patient and methodical approach to work

- logical, analytical and critical thinking skills

- ability to work on own initiative and unsupervised

- presentation skills

- networking skills, for building professional contacts

- ability to work to a deadline and under pressure.

Salary information

Graduate research scientists typically earn around £18,000 according to Prospects, while holding a postgraduate qualification such as an MSc or PhD can increase your earnings to £22,000–£27,000. With more experience and evidence of responsibility, such as managing a laboratory or team, salaries can rise to £36,000–£60,000 over time. Private and public sector pay is roughly the same, although senior positions within the private sector can attract higher salaries.

Typical work activities

A research scientist would typically:

- design and carry out experiments

- record and analyse data

- write research papers, reports and bids for funding

- attend and present at academic conferences

- teach or demonstrate to students

- ensure that quality standards are met.

Training and development

Postgraduate researchers are expected to develop a broad range of transferable skills to enhance their work, such as project management, communication and presentation skills, as well as career management, and courses of this nature are offered by bodies such as Vitae. Research Councils UK also offer opportunities such as short courses. Promotion and progression within academia have defined pathways, and it is possible to aim for research fellow or professorial roles later in your career. Attracting funding is a key role for more senior post-holders, and managerial duties would also be common.

Researchers working in industry may find that they complete a range of placements as part of their professional training. Moving between industry and academia can be a way to make career changes later on, as well as to apply research skills to different contexts and purposes.

Further resources

National Careers Service: nationalcareersservice.direct.gov.uk/advice/planning/jobprofiles/Pages/researchscientist.aspx

Prospects: www.prospects.ac.uk/research_scientist_life_sciences_job_description.htm

Research Councils UK www.rcuk.ac.uk

TARGETjobs: targetjobs.co.uk/careers-advice/job-descriptions/278833-research-scientist-job-description

Vitae: www.vitae.ac.uk

Case study

Kate Benson, Senior Associate, Global Study Management, with Amgen Ltd

Why did you choose a career in science?

Originally, I chose my career because of my interest in learning more about 'myself' and how the human body works.

What made you choose your particular area?

Working in clinical research, I think that I am close to really making a difference for patients.

What was your route in? Qualifications, experience, contacts?

BSc (Biomedical Sciences & Chemistry)

PhD (Cell Biology)

Academic research (two years in the lab)

Industry laboratory research (three years in the lab)

Industry clinical research associate role (three years)

Industry role within clinical study management (two years – to present)

What is a typical day like for you?

I'm office based, managing Phase 3 clinical studies: coordinating the different departments involved in a large study e.g. data management, drug safety, labs, clinical site management, and drug supply chain.

We will be tracking the current status of the study and providing updates to senior management. We also manage 17 different countries within Europe and Australia for the study. I'm also involved in problem solving logistical issues with the sites to ensure that each patient receives their study drug on time and without issue.

What do you enjoy most about your work?

Solving problems, tracking progress, presenting at meetings, and seeing the results of the studies.

What are the challenges?

Solving the logistical problems in different countries to ensure that the data received in-house is as robust as possible.

What advice would you offer a current student/recent graduate aiming for a role in your field?

Clinical research is difficult to break into – persevere! Starting in an administrative role can help you to learn how clinical trials are run before progressing into the main role and then subsequently into project management.

What would you do differently, if anything, if you were starting your career all over again?

I would work abroad for a year.

11

Teaching science

Embarking on a teaching career requires a significant commitment to the education and development of others. While your teaching hours, either at school or university, will be clearly specified, teaching roles can require significant amounts of additional time spent on marking, preparing classes and carrying out other administrative tasks that require time well beyond the hours you will spend in the classroom or lecture theatre. All forms of teaching require stamina and the confidence to manage a class full of students, no matter what their age. For the right candidates, introducing school or college pupils to the study of science or sharing your knowledge with undergraduates and other adult learners, can be the most satisfying kind of work. It is a career option where it is possible to inspire others and make a genuine difference to their lives and aspirations.

Prospects for teachers

Teaching opportunities for science graduates are good in 2013, as there is a shortage of secondary school teachers in the UK who can offer mathematics, physics and chemistry as subjects, although this will vary by region and key stage being taught. There are also opportunities to teach in independent schools and some of the newly formed Free Schools, where there is more autonomy within the curriculum, as well as in local authority-run schools, so it is important to consider the kind of environment in which you would prefer to teach your subject.

For secondary school teaching, you will need either a four-year Bachelor of Education degree, or a first degree followed by a one-year teacher-training programme such as the Postgraduate Certificate in Education (PGCE). Academia usually brings research and publishing obligations alongside teaching and administration, and requires a PhD in the subject you wish to teach; you do not need a teaching qualification to teach in a university, although you would if you wish to teach in a further education college. In a further education college, the emphasis would also be more on teaching than on research.

However, opportunities to teach science are not limited to schools, colleges and higher education. You could also use your skills in prisons, in the armed forces, where you could teach the children of forces staff, with professional bodies, in nurseries with pre-schoolers, and in museums or science centres. Science outreach work and public engagement with science are growth areas, and more information about this can be found in Chapter 12. It is also possible to work in a more technical or supporting role in an education environment, as a teaching laboratory technician, for example. While a degree is not usually required for support roles, most applicants will have one and this can improve your chances of selection.

More detailed information about two of the main roles available to those wishing to teach science is below, as well as a case study by a secondary school teacher. All salary information is taken from Prospects unless otherwise stated.

The job roles

Higher education lecturer

Higher education (HE) lecturers carry out teaching and research duties within their subject. They deliver lectures, seminars and laboratory-based classes, as well as providing material that can be made available in multimedia formats that students can access on distance-learning courses or when they are away from the university on placements or a year abroad. They may also take students on field trips.

HE lecturers carry out research into their subject area with the aim of publishing their findings in peer-reviewed academic journals, in books and will also present their work at conferences. There are high levels of competition for publication in quality journals, as the funding allocated to university departments may depend on how successfully their academic staff are showcasing their research to their peers, and staff need to be seen to be 'research active' to maintain a successful career. Administrative duties also occupy a significant part of the job.

Staff may also be involved in the pastoral care of students, liaise with their university careers service to ensure employability is addressed in the curriculum, and engage with social activities and events as part of university life. Working hours can be flexible, although many lecturers will carry out research and administrative duties over evenings and weekends, and some classes may be held in the evenings, with university timetables becoming increasingly crowded.

Entry

Entry with a relevant undergraduate degree and PhD in your discipline is required for higher education teaching. However, some lecturers can come into higher education from industry if they possess the relevant knowledge to contribute to a programme or department. Candidates should start publishing their research during their doctoral studies, proving their ability to produce original work, when they should also have acquired some teaching experience.

Skills

Aspiring higher education lecturers should also be able to demonstrate the following:

- the ability to teach widely across the subject curriculum, at all levels

- project management skills

- ability to contribute to a department's research profile

- excellent interpersonal skills

- ability to supervise postgraduate students

- ability to manage a research budget.

Salary information

A typical starting salary for an HE lecturer would range from £30,000 to £40,000. Salaries for more senior academics can increase to £39,000–£48,000 or more. University salaries are paid according to an agreed national pay scale, and rates of pay will depend on the individual's experience and levels of responsibility.

Typical work activities

A university lecturer would typically:

- plan and deliver lectures and seminars

- attend academic conferences and present research papers

- carry out research, producing articles and books for publication

- set student assignments and assess them

- sit on examination boards

- carry out administrative tasks, such as admissions and committee work

- invigilate examinations

- supervise the research work of postgraduate students.

Training and development

All higher education lecturers are expected to undertake continuing professional development, attending courses where necessary to develop a range of skills, such as supervising postgraduate students. Many universities also now require new academic staff to complete a teacher-training course after being appointed, and this is completed alongside their usual work. This qualification is the Postgraduate Certificate in Higher Education (PGCHE) and is mainly delivered within the university by its education staff.

Academics will be expected to contribute their research to their department's output as soon as they begin work, so will usually concentrate on building their research profile in the early years of their career. They will also be expected to attend and participate in seminars and conferences, as well as contribute to department life by attending meetings and social events.

With experience, higher education lecturers can take on managerial roles such as becoming a programme leader, or they can progress to senior academic roles such as reader, professor or dean. However, vacancies for very senior positions can be quite rare, as people tend to stay in their posts for long periods of time once they are established. Additional roles such as examiner or reviewing for journals can also be adopted as part of the lecturer's work. Note that career breaks can have a potentially detrimental effect on an academic's prospects for promotion, as they can temporarily delay the output of publishable research.

Further resources

National Careers Service: nationalcareersservice.direct.gov.uk/advice/planning/jobprofiles/Pages/highereducationlecturer.aspx

Prospects: www.prospects.ac.uk/higher_education_lecturer_job_description.htm

TARGETjobs: targetjobs.co.uk/careers-advice/job-descriptions/280553-lecturer-higher-education-job-description

Times Higher Education: www.timeshighereducation.co.uk

Secondary school teacher

A secondary school teacher teaches one or more science subjects to school children aged 11–16. They may also teach A level students up to age 18–19. School teachers plan their classes to ensure that students learn what is required for their subject, assess their students and monitor their progress. In local authority schools, these classes must follow national curriculum guidelines, whereas in independent or Free Schools, there may be more scope for what is delivered and alternative qualifications to the GCSE, such as the International Baccalaureate, may be available. Teachers will also be expected to keep up to date with developments in their subject, to undertake regular training, network with other education professionals and meet with their students' parents.

Term-time hours can be lengthy, as teachers start work before school begins, run after-school clubs and need to work on class preparation and marking during evenings and weekends. Lunchtimes may also be used for extra-curricular activities or pastoral care. While teachers officially have 13 weeks' holiday, some of this time will still be used for marking and preparation.

Science subject shortages

There is currently a shortage of science graduates entering secondary teaching, and graduates who can teach mathematics or physics are in particularly high demand. Not only is there a great deal of scope for entering the profession, but the lack of teachers in these areas means that it may be easier to progress to more senior posts as your career develops. According to TARGETjobs, even if all the UK's current mathematics graduates trained to be teachers, there still would not be enough to fulfil current needs.

Other subjects in demand are chemistry, engineering, biology and modern languages. Teacher training bursaries of up to £15,000–£20,000 are available to physics, chemistry and mathematics graduates with 2.i and First class degrees, for those training in the 2013–2014 academic year. Full information about bursaries is available on the Department for Education website – see Further Resources.

Entry

There are several different ways in which to enter the profession. The main routes are to either complete a four-year undergraduate Bachelor of Education, which would give you Qualified Teacher Status (QTS), or to complete an undergraduate degree in the subject you wish to teach and then complete a one year PGCE for Initial Teacher Training (ITT), which would then award you QTS. The PGCE combines university study with time spent in the classroom.

Alternatively, there is an option to undertake school-centred initial teacher training (SCITT), where schools come up with their own training programme in collaboration with their local authority, but this route may not guarantee a PGCE and may be more suitable for applicants with previous relevant experience or who are making a career change.

The Teach First programme has also expanded significantly in recent years, and this charity places graduates with leadership potential directly into schools after six weeks of intensive training. The programme lasts for two years and, following completion, graduates are awarded a PGCE and can either stay in education, being well placed to advance in the profession, or can take their new skills into business and industry. Entry to this programme is very competitive and there is an emphasis on developing future leaders for business, policy development and education.

For all secondary teaching applications, candidates should show evidence of classroom experience, usually at least 15 days, acting as an assistant or an observer. Some universities also offer opportunities for classroom experience through programmes such as the Student Associates Scheme. Reading the education pages of national newspapers and publications such as the *Times Educational Supplement* can help you to make a well-informed application and demonstrate your interest in teaching.

Skills

Candidates should also be able to demonstrate the following:

- experience of working with children, such as through camps, youth clubs, tutoring, scouting and sports clubs

- knowledge of the national curriculum guidelines for your subject

- excellent communication skills

- stamina, confidence and motivation

- ability to manage a classroom and maintain discipline.

Salary information

A newly qualified teacher (NQT) will start at the bottom of a national pay scale, which for England, Wales and Northern Ireland, rises from £21,588 to £31,552. Pay is slightly lower in Scotland, but there are allowances for distance learning and remote schools, and slightly higher in London, due to the higher cost of living. Teachers who move into management roles, become key stage or year leaders or advanced skills teachers (in England and Wales) can earn considerably more, potentially over £55,000.

Typical work activities

A secondary school teacher would typically:

- design lesson plans and deliver classes

- mark pupils' work

- attend staff meetings and parents' evenings

- be involved in extra-curricular activities

- carry out pastoral care duties, such as being a form tutor

- manage pupil behaviour, and apply appropriate discipline

- network with other education professionals, such as careers advisers and education welfare officers

- participate in regular in-service (INSET) training as part of their continuing professional development.

Training and development

Newly qualified teachers (NQTs) have to complete a three-term probationary period after which their Qualified Teacher Status (QTS) will be confirmed. They will be monitored during this time and given a lighter teaching load. Some may also choose to study alongside their work for a Masters in Education (MEd) or Masters in Business Administration (MBA). With experience, teachers can progress into management roles and into headship, or pursue a curriculum specialism, such as teaching children with special needs.

It is also possible to transfer skills outside of school work and into other related jobs such as education policy development, school inspection, working as an examiner or as an education officer in a museum. Options in private tutoring are also available. Because teaching skills are so transferable, it is also possible to retrain and make a career change by moving to sectors such as law enforcement or social work.

Further resources

Department for Education: www.education.gov.uk/get-into-teaching/teacher-training-options.aspx

Prospects: www.prospects.ac.uk/secondary_school_teacher_job_description.htm

TARGETjobs: targetjobs.co.uk/career-sectors/teaching-and-education/287119-how-to-get-ahead-in-teaching-shortage-subjects

Teach First: www.teachfirst.org.uk/TFHome

Case study

Euan Cathro, Head of Science, Hawthorn High School, Wales

Why did you choose a career in science?

I was always the kid who asked 'why?' and science provided me with the answers and the ability to find out myself so I read a degree in it.

What made you choose your particular area?

I was asked by family friends to help their children with science study for examinations when I was sitting my Scottish Highers. I worked with them and got quite a thrill when they achieved higher than expected in their examinations. This led me to teaching in a very natural way.

What was your route in? Qualifications, experience, contacts?

Simple application after I finished my primary degree, followed by interview day and some shadowing at my local school.

What is a typical day like for you?

'Fire fighting' issues that have occurred due to student behaviour, delivering lessons, planning controlled assessments, analysing student progress and having meetings with other teachers about these things, as well as developing long-term targets for improvement in the department.

What do you enjoy most about your work?

The interactions with the students who are willing to share a bit of their lives with you and helping those that started off saying 'I don't get it!' to leave you saying 'Ah, thanks Sir!'

What are the challenges?

The growing decline in parents' abilities to parent and everyone expecting teachers to wave a magic wand and make the children behave better, as well as educate them in your subject, numeracy, literacy, curriculum cymru, citizenship, health etc. but in a very limited time frame.

What advice would you offer a current student/recent graduate aiming for a role in your field?

Make sure it is what you want to do and not what you just fancy trying. Teaching has such a huge amount of administration attached to it now that if you do not enjoy the teaching part enough to get you through the admin, you will be wasting your time.

What would you do differently, if anything, if you were starting your career all over again?

I may have chosen a more vocational degree such as pharmacy instead of choosing subjects I liked but as a first generation university-goer I never had the parental advice I could give my children now. They were just so pleased that I made it that far to do subjects I was good at.

12

Public engagement with science

If you enjoy working with the public, then there are plenty of opportunities to work in museums, science centres and university outreach programmes to educate the wider community about the role of science in culture. Working in public engagement with science can be a great option for those fascinated by their subject and who want to share their knowledge of scientific developments.

This chapter provides an overview of the sector, including two case studies from experienced professionals working in public engagement. If this is a career option that interests you, then start by volunteering or asking for work experience in local museums, science centres and at science fairs. You could also ask if your academic department has an outreach programme which you could get involved with.

bradford.ac.uk/wis

BE
OUTSTANDING

You'll earn more
than a degree at the
University of Bradford

Open Days 2014:
Friday 20 and Saturday 21 June
Friday 10 and Saturday 11 October

Profile: University of Bradford

The disciplines in the School of Life Sciences range from archaeological sciences through biomedical, chemical, forensic and clinical sciences to optometry and pharmacy.

Research-informed teaching

We believe that your learning should be informed by the latest world-class research and by clinical and professional practice. We will teach you in high quality facilities using a range of modern approaches, which recognise that different students learn differently. We place a strong emphasis on practical work, which is carried out in our own laboratories, on field trips and in work-related placements in the public and private sectors – some of which provide contact with patients from the first year of study.

Facilities

Our own state-of-the-art teaching facilities include modern biomedical science laboratories, the forensic enhancement suite, the University Eye Clinic (which is open to the public), a clinical skills suite with a simulated pharmacy and hospital ward as well as dedicated facilities for team-based learning and a wide range of well-equipped teaching laboratories in each discipline area. We have also developed an Integrated Learning Centre that features highly sophisticated human patient simulators and dedicated facilities for scholarship in pathology and anatomy – both in the context of modern healthcare and archaeological and forensic investigation.

Students will also work in the research laboratories of the Institute of Cancer Therapeutics, the Centre for Skin Sciences, the Centre for Pharmaceutical Engineering Science and Centre for Chemical and Structural Analysis. The quality of the research that you will experience in these areas is emphasised by the extent of the funding we receive from industrial partners, research councils and major charities including Yorkshire Cancer Research, the Leverhulme Trust and the Wellcome Trust.

Professional accreditation

The majority of our students are studying courses that are accredited by regulatory and professional bodies including the Institute of Biomedical Science, the General Optical Council and the General Pharmaceutical Council.

Postgraduate study

Our courses focus on applied science, clinical and laboratory practice, and the commercialisation of research. They share the following key features. They are all:

- designed to satisfy employers, the professions and ambitious students determined to develop their careers

- taught by a multidisciplinary team of internationally recognised researchers with extensive links to industry and the professions

- delivered in excellent learning facilities, modern and well equipped research laboratories and through industrial and fieldwork placements.

Courses are grouped into three themes:

- Medical and Clinical Laboratory Sciences

- Chemical and Pharmaceutical Sciences

- Archaeological Sciences.

For all of our students we believe that our approach, facilities and external contacts will help you develop not only your knowledge but your practical and employment-related skills and that after studying with us you will be able to look forward to a long and successful career. We look forward to welcoming you to Bradford.

Case study

Elliot Greenwood, BSc Biomedical Science

'While being at university I have managed to get involved in some amazing things. A great example of this is the extracurricular research project set up by students. The project looks at research from the field of tissue engineering. Not only did we receive funding for the project, we also travelled around the country and visited research labs that carry out experiments that shape the future of tissue engineering.

'Biomedical science is such a diverse degree that allows all kinds of doors to open for you. In my second year I spent a month volunteering in Morocco teaching children English. I travelled with two other biomedical science students and recommend doing something similar to everyone. I later started a six-month placement in a paediatric ward at Bradford Royal Infirmary as a volunteer play assistant. After I finish my degree I am hoping to continue my studies and do a PhD or apply for postgraduate medicine; but with biomedical science as my foundation I can't fail.'

Sokar Salam, Pharmacy (4-year)

'Deciding upon which university to attend to complete higher education is always a difficult decision. After carrying out thorough research and attending several open days, I chose to study Pharmacy at the University of Bradford.

'This is because of the excellence shown in the content of the course, the support provided by the staff and the ways in which student concerns are dealt with. The students and staff work extremely well together thus creating a friendly learning environment that works for everyone. A particular aspect that really stood out for me was that the University of Bradford has a 98% employment rate once a degree is achieved.

'The University of Bradford, unlike others, give their candidates the opportunity to choose between the sandwich and continuous course. As well as this, the staff guide and support the students in making an informed decision.'

Saanya Sequeira, MChem Chemistry with Industrial Experience

'I chose the MChem programme in Chemistry with Industrial Experience. It promised a strong foundation in chemistry and provided an opportunity to gain professional work experience in the final year. Staff are extremely approachable and support is always available when we need it. The university presents opportunities beyond academic studies; there are lots of sports clubs and societies to choose from.'

Undergraduate courses:

- archaeological sciences

- biomedical science

- chemistry and forensic science

- clinical sciences

- healthcare science

- integrated science

- optometry

- pharmacy

Postgraduate taught courses:

- analytical sciences

- archaeology

- archaeological prospection

- archaeological sciences

- biomedical science

- cancer drug discovery

- cancer pharmacology

- cellular pathology laboratory practice (new from 2014)

- clinical pharmacy (community)

- clinical pharmacy (hospital)

- drug toxicology and safety pharmacology

- forensic archaeology and crime scene investigation

- human osteology and palaeopathology

- pharmaceutical technology

- technology, science and entrepreneurship (new from 2014)

The importance of science in everyday life

Scientific research can seem abstract and beyond the grasp of the average citizen, yet it has the power to transform our daily lives. We only have to look at the staggering pace of change in mobile technologies to see how significantly our lives have changed thanks to the ability to access the internet on the move and stay in touch with our friends via social media platforms such as Facebook and Twitter. Advances in healthcare improve our chances of surviving previously fatal cancers or diseases such as HIV, whereas developments in textile technologies allow us to exercise in technical clothes that allow us to stay comfortable even during the toughest of workouts.

Science on screen

Science also has a much more visible profile due to a recent increase in television programming that allows us to hear about science from experts in a way that is intelligible and entertaining. While programmes such as *Tomorrow's World* gave us a taste of the future back in the 1980s, today's science programming introduces us to fascinating new developments such as neuroscience and the workings of the brain, as well as being able to reconstruct the era when dinosaurs walked the earth and bring us entire histories of scientific areas in an easily digestible format. While these programmes are entertaining, they also emphasise what science offers us in our daily lives, improve our understanding of the past and predict where developments might take place in the future. Increasing public interest in science via the media in this way can cement the understanding for continuing research, bringing in much-needed funding, and benefiting both UK society and the economy.

A number of charismatic television presenters have become associated with the public's increasing engagement with science, physicist Professor Kathy Sykes, anatomist Professor Alice Roberts, particle physicist Professor Brian Cox and quantum physicist Professor Jim Al-Khalili. Both Kathy Sykes and Alice Roberts work extensively in public engagement with the universities of Bristol and Birmingham respectively. Professor Sykes has contributed a case study about her work below, translating complex research into something we can better understand and of which we can more readily grasp the significance.

STEM subjects

Through working in science engagement, it is also possible to encourage more children into the study of science subjects. Getting more students into science, technology, engineering and maths (STEM) subjects at university level is crucial to filling the skills shortage that the UK is currently experiencing, with too few students opting for these types of degrees. Promoting science in an exciting way can help to change the perception of STEM subjects as 'too hard' or 'dry' compared to the humanities and social sciences, and as an opportunity to make a real difference to our immediate environment and lifestyles.

University of
Salford
MANCHESTER

College of
Science & Technology

❚ School of the Built Environment
❚ School of Computing, Science & Engineering
❚ School of Environment & Life Sciences

By applying a cross disciplinary approach, integrating real world situations into our teaching, research and enterprise, we're educating and inspiring the future generation of scientists, engineers, designers, technologists and so much more.

Contact us to find out more:
www.salford.ac.uk/cst
cst-enquires@salford.ac.uk 0161 295 4545

Profile: University of Salford

The College of Science & Technology at the University of Salford

The College of Science & Technology is a rich and diverse centre of quality teaching. Our aim is to produce graduates well equipped with the skills, knowledge and personal attributes to succeed in their chosen occupation. With a variety of undergraduate courses available across the spectrum of science and technology, award-winning lecturing staff and incredible facilities, your future starts here.

The College is comprised of three schools:

- School of the Built Environment

- School of Computing, Science and Engineering

- School of Environment and Life Sciences.

Employability is a key focus for the College – fieldwork and practical placements within our courses encourage the application of scientific techniques in the real world and are a core aspect of the learning experience at Salford. We place considerable emphasis on working with industry to ensure our graduates have the key skills employers require and a number of our courses are professionally accredited.

School of the Built Environment

The School of the Built Environment is a nationally and internationally recognised centre of excellence for built environment study.

It offers a range of modern, management-focused undergraduate courses developed in partnership with professional accrediting bodies and practitioner advisers, to meet the needs of a dynamic and innovative industry.

Courses include: BSc Architecture, BSc Architectural Design and Technology, BSc Building Surveying, BSc Construction Project Management, BSc Quantity Surveying, HNC Construction.

www.salford.ac.uk/built-environment

School of Computing, Science and Engineering

Our School of Computing, Science and Engineering has a wide range of undergraduate opportunities, covering traditional and innovative disciplines, underpinned by excellent facilities both at the University's main campus and at MediaCityUK.

Courses include the following:

Computing
BSc Computer Networks, BSc Computer Science, BSc Multimedia and Internet Technology, BSc Software Engineering.

Digital Media and Audio Acoustics
BEng Audio Acoustics, BSc Professional Sound and Video Technology.

Engineering
BEng/MEng Aeronautical Engineering, BEng/MEng Aircraft Engineering with Pilot Studies, BSc Aviation Technology with Pilot Studies, BEng/MEng/BSc Civil Engineering, BEng/MEng Civil and Architectural Engineering, BEng/MEng Mechanical Engineering, BEng Petroleum and Mechanical Engineering, Integrated Foundation Year courses for Aeronautical, Civil and Mechanical Engineering.

Maths and Physics
BSc Mathematics, BSc/MPhys Physics, BSc/MPhys Physics with Acoustics, MPhys Physics with Studies in North America, BSc Pure and Applied Physics.

www.salford.ac.uk/computing-science-engineering

School of Environment and Life Sciences
The School covers a range of academic disciplines across all areas of biology, environment, health, geography and wildlife conservation, providing an eclectic and stimulating interdisciplinary hub for undergraduate and postgraduate education and cutting-edge research.

Courses include the following:

Biology and Zoology
BSc Biology/Biology with Studies in the USA, Biology Foundation Year, BSc Human Biology and Infectious Diseases, BSc Zoology.

Biochemistry and Biomedical Sciences
BSc Biochemistry/Biochemistry with Studies in the USA, BSc Biomedical Science, BSc Medicinal Chemistry, BSc Pharmaceutical Science.

Geography and Environmental Management
BSc Environmental Management (with pathway in Environmental Health), Environmental Studies Foundation Year, BSc Geography (with pathway in Human Geography).

Wildlife
BSc Wildlife and Practical Conservation, BSc Wildlife Conservation and Zoo Biology.

www.salford.ac.uk/environment-life-sciences

Contact us
For further information, contact the College of Science and Technology at www.salford.ac.uk/cst or call the Enquiries Team on 0161 295 4545 or email cst-enquiries@salford.ac.uk

Women in science

Encouraging young women into studying and working in science is also very high up the careers agenda in the UK at present. The March 2013 issue of *Nature* magazine describes science as remaining 'institutionally sexist', pointing out that female scientists are still paid less, promoted less, and win fewer grants than their male counterparts, due both to discrimination as well as to the 'unavoidable coincidence of the productive and reproductive years' for women in scientific research careers. It is increasingly important that the gender imbalance in science is addressed, and that more women enter the sector and are promoted to more influential and senior roles in order for greater balance of opportunity and promotion to be restored.

Entering a career in public engagement with science

To enter this field, you will need a good degree in any area of science as well as a solid range of transferable skills for working with the public, such as good oral and written communication, and the ability to explain complex concepts with clarity to non-specialists. It is also possible to develop specialist knowledge in this area by taking a postgraduate qualification such as a BSc in Science Engagement and Communication, if you feel that you would like to offer something extra, as well as developing a deeper understanding of the history of public engagement with science.

Demonstrable research skills may be more relevant for roles within higher education or in government agencies, where policy-making and strategic decisions will be more integral to your work, and fewer client-facing duties are involved.

Salary information

Work requiring specialist knowledge and research skills will most likely pay more than public-facing positions. A museum exhibitions officer, for example, will start on about £20,000, according to Prospects and, with about 10 years' experience, can earn over £30,000; while someone on a structured graduate scheme engaged in research for the government, a think tank or a research council could potentially earn a higher salary and advance more quickly in their career to senior levels. Sign up for regular bulletins from online recruitment websites such as www.jobs.ac.uk, TARGETjobs or Guardian Jobs to see what kind of roles are being advertised, the qualifications and experience required, and the salaries available.

The two case studies below address different aspects of working with science engagement. The first, from Kathy Sykes, Professor of Sciences and Society at the University of Bristol, presents a more academic picture, while the second, from Dr Alison Rivett of Bristol ChemLabS, offers an insight into a more client-facing outreach role.

Case study

Professor Kathy Sykes, Professor of Sciences and Society, University of Bristol

Why did you choose a career in science?

I got switched on to physics by a brilliant physics teacher. I hadn't enjoyed science much up until then. But he got us doing open-ended practicals (experimental activities to encourage different approaches to learning) and showed us that science wasn't just learning lots of facts, but about finding out new things and exploring the unknown. In choosing a degree, I partly chose physics because I liked it best as a subject. I tried going on courses to find out about engineering and medicine, but always seemed to like the physics bits best. I also chose it because I thought it would leave me plenty of options about what to do afterwards.

What made you choose your particular area

It was physics I enjoyed most at school. I loved the way that with quantum mechanics you have to 'stand' having two different concepts about what is going on, and use the one that is appropriate. It suggests that there must be better ways of explaining things; we just haven't found them yet. I loved all the quirkiness of physics, the crazy ideas and thought experiments. I also loved the way physics could take this complex messy world and represent nature with really simple, elegant equations. So I did my degree and PhD in physics, both at the University of Bristol.

During my PhD I saw a woman, Sue Pringle, who was talking about chemistry with schoolchildren, what it was like to actually do chemistry and what it could reveal. She gave talks to many other groups too, like women's institutes, and tried to find ways to get others in the university to talk with the public and schools. I thought '*that* is the job I want'. It would bring together my love of science with communicating with a lot of different kinds of people. I asked her advice about how to get her job. She said there were lots of other jobs like it; I should go to conferences and meet people and try finding out what other roles I might play. She also said there was a lot of competition for this kind of work and I needed to get experience.

What was your route in? Qualifications, experience, contacts?

After my degree, I taught maths and physics A level with Voluntary Service Overseas in Zimbabwe. The experience I got teaching really prepared me for a role in science communication. I took Sue Pringle's advice, and started going to Science Communication conferences, to work out the current state of play, meet people and explore opportunities. I also started trying to get as much experience as I could in different forms of public engagement: I gave talks to schools and the public; I entered communication competitions; I wrote some web articles and I did work experience for BBC's *Tomorrow's World*.

I was hugely lucky to have a supportive and inspiring supervisor in the physics department, Pete Barham. He gave me material for talks to give to the public; he encouraged me, got me invited to conferences and critiqued public lectures I gave. I owe so much to him. He and Sue seemed to plot to try to help me find opportunities!

In finding my first job in public engagement in science, I'd seen that a new hands-on science centre was going to be built in Bristol, along with a wildlife centre and a centre for performing arts. I was desperate to work on it, thinking that I would happily devote myself to creating a science centre that would be a part of a new hub for science, nature and the arts, in what was then a derelict part of Bristol. I wrote to everyone involved in the project and asked them to let me work on it. Eventually, after a lot of letters and waiting, I was offered three months' work experience. In the meantime, I'd also been offered a job at the Science Museum in London, a fast-track training position that was meant to be permanent, but I couldn't resist the newer, but riskier project in Bristol.

What is a typical day like for you?

Each day working as Professor of Sciences and Society at the University of Bristol is different. I might be writing something, in which case I'll probably work from home to be able to focus on it fully. Or I might be preparing to chair a meeting, and need to read and understand a huge wodge of papers and plan with the secretariat how the meeting might go. Then, on the actual meeting date, I have to head off to London or Swindon and do the hard, but enjoyable work of keeping a group of very different kinds of people on topic and to time, as well as giving us all space to be creative. I might have an advisory group or meeting to attend, one in the university, or for a science festival or centre. Again then I need to read all the papers and have ideas and suggestions about strategies or visions for the future.

I spend a lot of time preparing and giving talks. Sometimes it might be at an international conference in some exotic country or city. Sometimes it might be for a group of schoolchildren, teachers, or people working in government. I may just spend a day catching up and handling all the emails and mail.

I do a bit of filming too. That means usually getting quite short notice about flying to some other country, reading about the subject and people I'll meet, and working out things to say. It usually means long, hard days which include waiting around for everything to come together then everyone is suddenly focusing on me to say the right thing at the right pace with an appropriate tone into the lens of a camera. It can be incredibly challenging, and you have to think on your feet, usually on very little sleep. However, you meet inspiring people and go to very privileged places that sometimes nobody else can go to, like way below ground inside a neutrino detector, or being driven by Google's driverless car in San Francisco.

I also spend some time training other people in science communication or how to chair meetings. I love doing this: it feels like a really tangible way of helping a new group of scientists communicate better.

I am one of the Directors of the Cheltenham Science Festival, which means helping to come up with ideas for the festival along with the team and the diverse and slightly crazily creative advisory group. It means keeping hold of the vision and thinking about how the festival can grow in the future. Then it means attending the whole festival, being welcoming to speakers, politicians and the public, chairing events and trying to help keep the whole atmosphere 'festive'.

What do you enjoy most about your work?
I love the variety in what I do. I enjoy working with different kinds of people to create different kinds of things. For instance, I love chairing meetings where scientists, social scientists, members of the public, policy-makers and business people come together to work something out or make something better. It's a huge challenge to make sure everyone gets heard and that people understand each other, but it can be humbling in what we all learn together.

Or, with filming, I love how the different skills of people come together to make something I could never do alone: there's a director who holds everything together and is a good storyteller, something which I am not; a camera man or woman, who has a great visual sense and knows what will look interesting or good to a viewer; the sound person, who hears things that none of the rest of us can, and an executive producer who steps in if things are going wrong and keeps the bigger picture. When it's working, it's a real joy.

What are the challenges?
Working out what to say yes to, and what to say no to. Keeping a healthy balance between work and 'life'. When you're doing something you believe in and that you enjoy, it's hard to get that balance right.

Academia can be a bit hierarchical at times, even though the UK is better than many countries, and even though science is a good leveller. Some scientists can at times look down on other subject areas, or people outside academia. I struggle with that. Some scientists can just be absolutely certain that they are right, when science should be more about being prepared to be wrong.

Not all scientists are brilliant at listening, and some think we don't need to listen to or talk with the public. I think listening is one of the most important things we do, and that listening to the public can give scientists new ideas. Being aware of societal concerns and hopes can help ground their work. That said, I work with some fabulous scientists and most are not like the above.

What advice would you offer a current student/recent graduate aiming for a role in your field?

Get experience and, ideally, a wide range of experience, so you can work out which things you enjoy most. Once you work out what you enjoy, throw yourself into finding a way to make it a focus of your work. Grab opportunities and keep an open mind about what you might do. Ask people for advice. Go to conferences and read to get a wide perspective on the area. There are master's courses in science communication. When I've been involved in employing people though, tangible experience has counted more than having done a master's course.

What would you do differently, if anything, if you were starting your career all over again?

I'd do the same things. I can't believe the things I have managed to do and the places I have got to. So much of it is serendipitous, but it's also based on seizing opportunities and being supported by some generous, inspiring people. Some academics advised me not to go to Zimbabwe between my degree and PhD, saying I would forget too much physics, but living in such a different culture and teaching people with such a different background taught me so much, and totally shaped what I did after my PhD.

What advice would you give female students/graduates trying to make a career in science?

Be persistent in trying to do what you want to do. Find other women in the same kind of position as you, and share what you struggle with and enjoy, and tactics if necessary. It may be that someone in a different subject area or different institution can give a valuable perspective, or allow you to discuss things which might be harder to share with a direct colleague. Find women who can act as inspirations to you, or as mentors. Ask them specifically to help you.

Don't let people get away with being sexist or being demeaning because you're female. Men and women should speak up. It's easy to let comments and actions slip by, but we are complicit if we let them be the norm. It can be really hard, especially if you're at the receiving end: you can think you're over-reacting, or it's somehow your fault or that you may risk your job, or you may wonder how you would prove anything. You may just be in disbelief and too shocked to respond appropriately. And so often the reply will be 'Oh, I'm just kidding, don't take it seriously'. But eventually, if enough of us make it clear what we find acceptable, people should get the idea. People have said to me before, 'Oh, he's just "old school", he doesn't mean anything by it'. But it's no example to be setting for the 'new school'.

I didn't go to any 'women scientist' groups, thinking that I didn't want to split the genders like that. But, in retrospect, I do think there are things women struggle with more than men and many things we can learn from each other and be inspired by.

Case study

Dr Alison Rivett, Science Outreach, Bristol ChemLabS & Science Learning Centre South West

Why did you choose a career in science?

I've always been curious and like finding out about things, and science allows you to always be discovering something new.

What made you choose your particular area?

Chemistry was one of the subjects I enjoyed most at school and college, so a degree in it seemed the most obvious option. I liked it so much I continued on to do a PhD in atmospheric chemistry research. During my PhD I realised I didn't want to stay in academia and continue with a research career. Then I had a chance to do some outreach activities and discovered (rather to my surprise) that I really liked it.

What was your route in? Qualifications, experience, contacts?

During my postgraduate studies I got involved with some outreach activities in the chemistry department, which gave me some experience. I continued to be involved voluntarily after I graduated while I was looking for a job in the public engagement field. Getting that job involved lots of applications, as I didn't have very much experience, but through that I made many contacts and got much valuable advice.

What is a typical day like for you?

Really varied – I might be out in a school delivering some chemistry outreach workshops or an assembly, I might be meeting teachers to find out what support they need for their science teaching, or I might be in the office organising an event.

What do you enjoy most about your work?

Being able to enthuse people about science – especially those who think they don't like it!

What are the challenges?

Balancing different roles and juggling lots of varied things.

What advice would you offer a current student/recent graduate aiming for a role in your field?

Get lots of experience! Get involved in as many science communication activities as you can, be that through your school, college or university, through a voluntary scheme such as the STEM ambassadors programme, or through working at a science centre or museum. Science communication master's programmes can be very valuable for making contacts and allowing you to explore different areas of the field.

To work in science outreach, you need a science background, but you also need to be able to show you have the ability to communicate, to share your enthusiasm and engage people and have an understanding of the audience you will be working with, whether that is children, schools or the public.

Science Degrees

Lancaster University is consistently ranked in the top 1% of universities globally

Students here develop their skills through studying in a collegiate environment, work experience, volunteering and social activities. Our degree schemes are taught by experts in their research areas. The latest degree schemes in Science and Technology include:

- MSci Biological Sciences
- MChem Chemistry
- MEng Chemical Engineering
- MSci Natural Sciences

www.lancaster.ac.uk

Profile: Lancaster University

An employment rate of 93%, teaching staff who are world leaders in their field, high research profiles, and seven departments covering an extensive range of leading science and technology subjects. That's why Lancaster University is 'the place to be' if you are passionate about working in science or technology.

Science and Technology | LANCASTER UNIVERSITY

The Lancaster Environment Centre is home to one of the largest groups of environmental researchers in Europe. We have more than 300 researchers, specialising in the disciplines of biological sciences, environmental science and geography.

InfoLab21 houses our centre for ICT research and the School of Computing and Communications, where our internationally renowned researchers collaborate with global companies including Microsoft, IBM, CISCO and Nokia.

Our new Chemistry Department teaches chemistry as an integrated and interdisciplinary subject.

Our teaching builds on current knowledge and extends into topics at the cutting-edge of modern science and technology.

We use various innovative methods to help develop skills and knowledge, including field trips, computer simulation, company and industry collaborations, traditional hands-on laboratory work and individually mentored final year projects.

A science or technology degree from Lancaster University is sure to lead to a really exciting career path.

Here's what some of our recent graduates do now:

- design engineer at Aston Martin

- structural design engineer at Airbus

- software developer at BSkyB

- systems analyst at IBM

- business analyst at Jaguar Land Rover

- research officer at Ministry of Defence

- physicist at CERN (European Organisation for Nuclear Research)

- assistant merchandiser at Arcadia

- land manager at Natural England.

This is what our students have to say.

Tom Walker, MPhys Physics

'The strong academic reputation of the University, combined with the quality of the accommodation, made Lancaster a good all-round option for me. I've now been offered and accepted a job starting in September, as a scientist for Mars. Hopefully I can apply many of the skills I've learnt here and pick up more along the way.'

Hannah Laurens, Space Science/Astrophysics

'The atmosphere at Lancaster is really friendly. The lecturers are all very approachable and we have similar interests. Lancaster was the right learning environment for me. I've just accepted a job for one year with the European Space Agency, for their Young Graduate Training Programme. I can't wait! Afterwards, I would like to complete a PhD in Space Science, possibly returning to Lancaster to do this.'

Emily Granger, Mathematics and Statistics

'I was quite shy before coming here but, by coming to Lancaster, I have been given opportunities such as being part of an executive for a society, completing an internship at the Uni and even living in Canada for a year! When I graduate I would like to become a medical or environmental statistician, or if not, work for a non-profit organisation such as Amnesty International or Oxfam.'

Part 2
Starting your career and developing as a professional

13

Planning your career: getting started and using essential tools and techniques

This chapter looks at the importance of laying solid foundations for career planning, and will cover:

- getting started – career planning, timing and your motivations

- external factors informing your career choices

- using available careers information, advice and guidance

- networking, making contacts and using social media

- making your decisions – goal setting and action planning.

> 'The most beautiful fate, the most wonderful good fortune that can happen to any human being, is to be paid for doing that which he passionately loves to do'.
>
> Abraham Maslow

Work is one of the most important aspects of our lives, and should be somewhere we can create meaningful activity for ourselves. Finding the right career in science is a question of equating what you are naturally good at and enjoy with something that pays what you feel is appropriate, in a working environment that suits you, along with colleagues by whom you feel supported. Whether you are educating children about science in a museum or working as a geologist in remote locations for weeks on end, your job should be something you look forward to and which provides feelings of achievement and satisfaction.

Getting started

One of the most frequent questions asked of careers advisers is, 'Can you tell me what I can do with my degree?' This is an unhelpfully limited outlook, as choosing your work is about more than the options you might have with your science subject, and studying for a degree in one area doesn't rule you out of working in another. If you're one of those people who has always had a clear career path in mind – you're studying chemistry and know you want to be a research scientist in a pharmaceutical laboratory – then that's great, but you still need to find out more about the reality of that job and build your network before you dive in.

If you're in the initial stages of not knowing what you want to do beyond 'working in science' then there is a range of tools available to help narrow down your options enough to start carrying out more detailed research. Taking the time to reflect and research will pay off long term – we really should be in work that makes us want to get out of the bed in the morning and that we find satisfying the majority of the time. As careers specialist John Lees puts it, 'Work is where you spend most of your waking life. It's where you put about 80% of your personal energy.'

Thinking about the career planning process

Too many students and graduates start the career planning process by looking at what's on offer and then filling in the application forms, rather than looking at what suits them first. The career planning process needs to start with some honest self-assessment, considering what you feel would be the best role for you as well as the best use of those waking hours at work!

A typical career planning process looks like this.

1. Carry out a thorough evaluation of your skills, preferences and values, by using online career planning tools and talking to career professionals.

2. Build contacts and develop a network (preferably gaining work experience).

3. Identify your options and available job roles.

4. Make your applications.

5. Go through the recruitment and selection process.

6. Start your new job!

When, at a future point in your career, you are seeking your next move, whether that means promotion, a sideways shift or even a complete change of sector away from the sciences, this process starts again. Simply applying for an advertised position without any knowledge of the organisation, role, or your suitability for it, is asking for a potential career mismatch and dissatisfaction, so take your time and make an informed choice.

Getting your timing right

If you are currently an undergraduate student in the sciences, then the ideal career development scenario may look like this.

- First year: spend the time becoming acquainted with your subject and enjoying extra-curricular activities such as volunteering or getting involved in societies.

- Penultimate year: apply for a summer vacation position during the autumn term or apply for your year-long sandwich placement in industry.

- Late summer/autumn term of your final year: apply for graduate positions and start going through the selection process.

Your second or penultimate year should be spent looking into your options and talking to people in the science sectors that interest you, starting to build your network of contacts and finding as much work experience as you can manage without compromising the quality of your studies. The majority of graduate employers will be looking for a minimum of a 2.i for you to be able to apply, but a 2.ii will not necessarily rule you out if you have excellent work experience and can provide solid examples of your skills.

The value of work experience

According to High Fliers, about three-fifths of graduate recruiters expect applicants to have obtained work experience, and the Association of Graduate Recruiters specifies that about a third of those employers expect that experience to be relevant to the job for which you are applying – see Chapter 14 on employability skills for science. Recruiters need to know that you understand the working environment and that you possess a professional mindset; and work experience is also an excellent way to decide whether or not a certain kind of role is really for you. Your enthusiasm for becoming an ecologist, for example, could wane if you find yourself spending more time outdoors in bad weather, rather than putting your laboratory skills to good use.

Alternative pathways to a graduate career

However, you may have a different timescale in mind to the one described above. You could decide to prioritise your studies to gain an excellent degree and wait until you have graduated before seeking work. Some career options, such as becoming an actuary, may require you to aim for a first-class degree, so giving your all to your subject may become your priority. In this case, you could be looking at finding work experience for six months to a year after graduation before you can re-join the graduate application cycle, but this could be time well spent if you learn from these experiences and fully explore your options.

Alternatively, you may have put in plenty of applications and simply been unlucky. These are increasingly competitive times for graduates with about 52 applicants per post, according to High Fliers, which is an increase of 11% since 2011. In this eventuality, employers will be looking for you to make the best use of your time while job seeking, gaining work experience and skills, doing research and cultivating that all important professional network. These are all activities that can provide structure and momentum to your day while you wait to reapply for available posts. If your applications are repeatedly bouncing back or you are not progressing past the interview stage, seek advice from a careers professional who can tell if there is a problem with the content of your forms or CV, and can coach you to perform at your best. Your university careers service should be able to help you as many of them continue to offer their services to graduates.

What's your motivation?

As well as starting your career planning early, it can also help to give plenty of thought to your own preferences, needs and working habits. Several large graduate recruiters have recently moved away from a competency-based interview, in which your skills relevant to the job are assessed, to a strengths-based one, where your preferences, innate abilities and motivations are discussed to see if these align with the company. This strengths-based approach can be a useful one to take at the beginning of the career planning process, as what you are naturally good at and gravitate towards is a good indicator of what you will find both motivating and rewarding in your work. A strengths-based interview could well include questions such as 'what makes you want to get out of bed in the morning?' or 'what would you do for a living if you didn't need the money?'

Psychologist Abraham Maslow's theory of the hierarchy of needs is often cited when we look at what makes people happy at work; once our basic needs for comfort are met, what appeals to us more personally in terms of our achievement, status and personal growth becomes increasingly important, and it's well worth taking the time to work out what aids your personal development before jumping into your job hunt.

What do you enjoy doing?

If you want to be happy at work, a good way of looking at the kind of career that will suit you is to look at what you enjoy doing in your spare time. The types of activities that really do make you want to get out of bed in the morning should be the ones you look at to see if you can map any of the skills used for these onto the scientific careers you have in mind. If you are a solitary person who likes working on detailed spare time projects, a career in science that requires constant contact with members of the public, such as that of a dietician or physiotherapist, may not suit you as much perhaps as a laboratory or research role where you can carry out work requiring meticulous attention with few interruptions. Job roles that are misaligned with your personal preferences and motivations, no matter how well paid, will leave you frustrated and dissatisfied.

Taking strengths-based thinking further

If you are interested in thinking about work from this more strengths-based and motivational point of view, then look in the 'Further reading and resources' section for books by John Lees, Carmel McConnell and Danielle LaPorte – all of these careers writers excel at helping you to match your work to what puts fire in your belly and could be a great place to start. *Skills for Success* by Stella Cottrell is also well worth consulting, as this provides a range of self-assessment tools designed to provide an overall picture of your motivations and how these can transfer into your employability, using personal development planning techniques that you may have already used as part of your course.

Finally, if your university or college offers any development awards, through which you receive credit for developing your employability skills, these can be well worth doing as a way of not only receiving training but also learning more about what you like and what you have to offer.

Your personal values and beliefs

As well as identifying your personal preferences and motivations, it's important to check in with yourself on your fundamental values and beliefs. This isn't something that many students factor into their career planning, but it's an essential component of your research into company cultures. We all have personal codes by which we live; they guide us and help us make decisions in everyday life, making up our own system of ethics. Ignore these when choosing your career and you could end up feeling very uncomfortable if the organisation you choose to work for has values that clash with your own.

It's extremely important that you look into what a company stands for and how it presents itself to the commercial world, as the work you carry out for the team you work within will be aligned exactly with these larger values; if you do not share these values, you will feel each day as if you are struggling with your job and employer.

When values conflict

A very basic example would be that you are looking for a career as a research scientist in a medical laboratory, but you have strong feelings about animal rights and welfare, ensuring that all your household and personal products are not tested on animals. It would make no sense at all to work for a laboratory that routinely experiments on animals in order to make breakthroughs in cancer treatments, if your values are being compromised each day, despite your dream to make a significant discovery in your field. Alternatively, you may feel very strongly about free healthcare being something that should be available to all, so becoming a radiographer in a private hospital would not suit you as well as working for an NHS-funded hospital.

These examples may seem obvious, but it's surprising how many people will look at a role simply in terms of skills and salary and discount how important an organisation's culture is; if you take the job, you will be expected to demonstrate company loyalty, so be sure to do your research and try to talk to people already there so that you make an informed choice. If this topic is particularly important to you, then use Carmel McConnell's book *Soultrader* to help you pin down your values before making your career decisions; see the 'Further reading and resources' section.

Using online career planning tools

Another excellent starting point are some of the online tools that your university or college careers service should be able to offer. For example, the planning tools available through both Prospects and TARGETjobs can help to confirm any existing career ideas you have in mind, as well as suggesting alternatives you may not have considered. Using these online tools may not help you fix on a particular role but they should help you to eliminate some options and leave others for you to explore in more detail.

However, you won't find more definitive answers to your career queries until you start speaking to people in your chosen roles and start researching the scientific community in more detail. It's also a good idea to book an appointment with a adviser to talk about the results obtained from using these tools so that you can start action planning and narrowing down your options.

Your 'fantasy career'

If you feel a little more imaginative, try an exercise called 'fantasy career'. This involves thinking less about identifying a particular job role and more about envisioning what your ideal working day would involve; this can then give you a measuring tool against which you can assess jobs that capture your interest.

Questions to ask can include the following.

- What's my working environment like? Am I at a desk, in a lab, working outside?

- How long do I have to commute for?

- Am I working at home?

- What am I wearing?

- Am I working in a large or small team? Am I working mainly alone?

- What's my salary?

- What does my typical day or week look like?

- What's my work/life balance?

If the idea of working away from home for periods of time, earning a relatively high salary and being very hands-on and outdoors appeals to you, this could mean that the life of a wellsite geologist could be for you. If you prefer a day spent working quietly in a clean, disciplined environment, then you may be more suited to a position as a research scientist. Again, answering these questions should help you to rule out obvious mismatches and then help guide you towards roles that better fulfil your personal preferences.

External factors informing your career choices

While you may now be clearer on what is important to you and how your values impact on the job you want, it's time to acknowledge other factors and deal with them accordingly.

The influence of the media

The recent economic recession has had an undeniably negative impact on the graduate labour market, with markedly fewer jobs being available and several industries contracting sharply, including sectors previously thought to be 'bulletproof' such as law. However, prospects are already looking up, with a slow but steady increase during the last couple of years in the graduate market, and with sectors such as IT and computing actually looking set to expand in the next few years, according to High Fliers.

However, there has been some unhelpful media reporting of labour market trends, and I have lost count of the number of students I have met who have decided not to bother making applications thanks to negative headlines, such as 'New graduates face tougher struggle in their search for jobs' (*Guardian*), or 'Graduate jobs rush has 83 chasing every vacancy at top firms' (*Daily Mail*). The market **is** crowded and highly competitive, but students and graduates **are** still being offered work. It's more important than ever that you not only make use of contacts to find opportunities in what is termed 'the hidden job market', or unadvertised positions, but also that you learn how to make high quality applications. It's fair to say that many employers complain about receiving very generic application forms, CVs and covering letters, where the name of their company could easily be replaced with another. It's essential that you learn how to tailor an application to a specific company and job role to give yourself the best chance of having your application progressed, and this is covered in Chapter 15.

'Graduates are perhaps spending less time on their applications. If I had one key message to get across it would be yes, there's competition, but just make sure that every single application they submit is the best they can possibly do.'

Graduate employer surveyed by the Association of Graduate Recruiters, 2012.

Don't listen to the media until you've done your own research: remain healthily sceptical, analyse the market yourself and submit the best applications that you can.

The influence of your friends

Sadly, even well-intentioned people can have a detrimental effect on your career plans. A friend may offer to have a look at your CV and give you some feedback. However, unless your friend is an experienced recruiter or career professional, the chances are that they don't know what a particular company is looking for at this level and could steer you down an unhelpful path. I base this on the large number of errors I have seen over the years on applications where a well-meaning friend has 'helped' with its production.

To be successful, your application must be explicitly mapped onto the requirements of the recruiting firm, with specific and crisp examples of your skills, written in clear, concise and accurate English. By all means get a friend with a sharp eye to check for errors of spelling and grammar, but make sure that an appropriately qualified professional provides you with feedback on the content. This is also where having a reliable network of contacts comes in, as you can ask someone in the particular field of science that interests you to have a look at your application, too, providing an informed industry viewpoint.

'A tailored application is key to convincing the employer you have the right experience, skills and attributes for the job.'

www.vitae.ac.uk

An alternative form of pressure that can come from your friends is when they all seem fixed on their career paths and are sending in applications left, right and centre, leaving you feeling left behind. This kind of pressure can be hard to resist, but it's crucial to take the time to work out what the right choice is for **you**. You may be a geology student sharing a house with four other geologists all applying for geophysicist positions but, if this isn't what you had in mind, you are unlikely to be successful in your applications anyway. Enthusiasm needs to shine through in your application form; no one wants to hire someone who isn't convinced that this job is right for them, so let your friends get on with their own applications and take the time to find your own path.

The influence of your family

Finally, and probably the most challenging influence on your career planning, is your family. Every careers service sees students upset about the fact that they are on a degree course they don't enjoy or with which they are struggling academically, but feel pressure from their family to continue because 'we are academics/physicists/chemists' or that certain degrees 'guarantee' certain professions. Sadly, there are no guarantees that even if you gain a First in your physics degree you will achieve a glorious career in any job, as there are so many other factors to take into consideration during the selection process. The graduate market is a constantly shifting entity and it will look very different now than it did to your parents, so it's crucial to seek impartial advice, no matter how well intended your family.

It can be very challenging to strike out on your own against family tradition, or to make a change of plan when your parents have funded your education. However, you are an adult who must make decisions based on your own preferences, or you could be looking at having to go through the same process of changing paths a few years into a career that you loathe, just deferred. Your university or college careers service should be able to help you talk through this issue and help you consider how to address it with your family, as well as helping you to identify the career path on which you really want to be.

Using available careers information, advice and guidance

There are many people whose knowledge and expertise could be crucial to the career decisions that you make. You may have your heart set on a specific job but, after talking to a science professional and finding out that work in their area is on the decline, it would not be prudent to pursue this line of enquiry and you would need to think where else you could best apply your skills and experience. There are many different people who can be of use to you – some will be impartial, and others will not, as we have seen above – so it's important that you can see the overall picture before making any major decisions.

Career coaches, consultants and advisers

You should have access to professional advice through your university or college careers service, but it's important to go in not only having done some preparation but also with the right expectations. It's essential that you must not expect them to tell you what job you should be doing. When you think about it, asking someone you just met to tell you what to do with your life doesn't make a lot of sense. It also raises ethical questions; what if they advised you to spend a large sum of money on a postgraduate course and you still didn't get the job you wanted? Or, what if you got the job and found you hated it? Whose responsibility is all of this?

> 'The adviser is there to guide and support you through those decisions but only you and no one else can take those decisions!'
>
> **UCLAN careers service**

A careers professional will ask a lot of questions and encourage you to reflect on all the issues covered above, before recommending that you research your chosen sectors and start making industry contacts. Thinking about some of these issues before your appointment can really help you to get the most from the session. Only **you** can decide which is the right path; it's about taking responsibility for your own decisions and by going through the complete career planning process from reflection to selection, you will have learned enough about it to be able to repeat it each time you wish to change roles.

Building your network and using contacts

'Networking' is a term that can make even the most experienced professional feel uncomfortable and, to be fair, the concept of developing relationships with strangers and asking them for help or advice can be challenging. However, the majority of people already employed in the sciences should be willing to offer you their views and encouragement if you approach them professionally and with genuine enthusiasm. Most people enjoy talking about their work, and are happy to hear from others eager to learn more about their field. However, while a career coach or adviser is obliged to offer you impartial advice, bear in mind that the information gleaned from your industry contacts may not be objective and will reflect the opinions and experience of a particular individual so, again, build up a clear overall picture of your chosen sector before you commit to any big decisions.

Building your network

There are many ways in which to start identifying potential contacts. Firstly, think about who you already know and who they might know. Your academic department may have industry contacts they can put you in touch with, especially if they offer placement or sandwich year programmes, or your university may have an alumni contact system. Also, don't rule out family and friend connections. You need to start asking around if people know anyone working in the field of science which interests you – let everyone know that you are actively seeking contacts and information. Once you start building a list of possible names, start a spreadsheet or chart that will help you keep track of contact details, when you contacted them, what their response was and what action you took. This will help you to avoid potentially embarrassing instances of emailing the same person twice for the same information, but it also enables you to let your contacts know what you've done with their advice and how you're getting on.

Networking works both ways; keep your contacts informed on your progress if they have tried to help you, and be sure to say 'thank you' if an opportunity comes your way as a result. Networks need maintenance, so avoid simply 'taking' from your contacts and make sure that you also give something back. At some point in the future, you will be the successful science professional being approached by a keen young undergraduate, and you will get your chance to pay back the favours.

Attend networking events

While the thought of this makes many people nervous, these evenings (or breakfasts!) are a great chance to get to know people and exchange information. Have a look online for relevant events and groups.

There is plenty of advice available online about how to manage a networking opportunity but some key points are:

- be interested in other people and ask questions

- be a good listener

- think about what you could do for them and not just what they can do for you.

It's a good idea to have a supply of professional-looking cards with you, as it makes exchanging contact details more straightforward, and there are plenty of companies that can produce these at a reasonable cost. If someone gives you their card, then follow up with a thank you email and say that you enjoyed meeting them. Again, it's all about cultivating good relationships if you want to be able to ask for help and advice.

'I started going to science communication conferences, to work out the current state of play, meet people and explore opportunities.'

Kathy Sykes, Professor of Sciences and Society, University of Bristol

Networking using social media

Social media tools such as Facebook and Twitter have rapidly become integral to the career planning and job searching process, as well as being an excellent way in which to contact industry insiders and find out more about what's going on in your chosen science sector. Here are a few basic guidelines on how to make the most of some of the most-used social networking tools.

Facebook

Keep your page professional

Despite being mainly associated with personal use, Facebook is a useful tool both for seeking contacts as well as providing information about yourself for those who look you up. If you are going to refer people to your Facebook page, then it helps to set one up specifically for this purpose so that you can keep control of the content. It's advisable to keep your personal page separate from your professional one, so that recruiters don't see party photos or comments you would prefer stayed between friends, so check your privacy settings. A professional-looking page can act as an effective online CV, so keep the content fresh and update when you can.

Check out relevant organisations

Many organisations and recruiters also have Facebook pages you can 'like', and receive information about their activities. The NHS, Soil Association and Institute of Physics all have Facebook pages, for example, and there are numerous entries on broader areas such as women working in science. It's not unusual for companies to advertise vacancies or work experience and recruit via Facebook, so it could well pay off to stay up to date.

Twitter

Many students and graduates avoid Twitter, as they feel they don't have much to say that people will want to read in 140 characters or fewer. However, you can be a 'silent' user of this useful tool and still glean plenty of relevant information. As with Facebook, you can learn a lot from following the feeds of others, and many organisations and individual industry players can become more accessible through the informality of this networking site.

Start by simply following people who interest you and reading their tweets. When you feel more confident, you can comment and reply, starting conversations about topics that catch your eye. Like Facebook, Twitter can provide valuable vacancy information that you could miss if you only stuck with newspaper advertisements, so choose your organisations and get following.

Make your Twitter presence 'employer-friendly'

- Put your job pitch in your Twitter bio

- Use a professional-looking avatar

- Tweet about your job search

- Include a link to an online CV in your bio

- Establish yourself as an expert in your field on Twitter.

Michael Gregory of marketing communications agency Freshfield, in a *Guardian* live Q&A

LinkedIn

LinkedIn is a professional networking site that allows you to maintain an online profile as well as read those of others. Reading the profiles of successful professionals can provide a wealth of information that you can learn from. As you build your network, you will be able to contact more people directly, or ask for introductions to people whom you may not know but would like to get in touch with. Make sure that your own profile is as complete as possible; LinkedIn runs its own online tutorials to help you make the best of the site, and these are worth a look if you are getting started.

As with Facebook and Twitter, you can also follow the feeds of other people and organisations to keep up with trends. LinkedIn offers other useful features such as 'Questions' where you can seek the advice of industry professionals or simply read advice already offered. You might also feel able to offer advice to someone else; this helps to build your profile and develop 'expertise' within the LinkedIn world, so explore the broader functionality and don't let your profile stagnate. LinkedIn also lets you connect to Facebook and Twitter, so you can update several profiles at the same time and not have to repeat yourself.

Blogging

If you enjoy writing, then setting up your own blog commenting on your studies or your chosen industry can be a great way to get noticed by potential recruiters. It shows that you are taking a deeper interest in your area and, because many blogs are by nature reflective and analytical, blogging demonstrates your willingness to express a point of view and think around a topic. If you intend to highlight your blog on your CV, then stay away from potentially controversial topics, such as the use of animals in research, or deal with them sensitively. If you experience a period of unemployment, then blogging about how you deal with this can be great evidence of your resilience. Accessible platforms are available through Wordpress, for example, so do give it a try if you like to write.

Keeping track of it all

Finally, with so much information available out there on the Internet, use online tools to help you stay organised. Applications that help you to bookmark useful sites, such as Delicious, can be very helpful in keeping things together and avoids that annoying feeling when you can't remember where you saw something useful. If you are a visual person who feels inspired by images or video, Pinterest is a site that allows you to virtually 'pin' things that you want to keep and remember on a board. New tools and variations on old themes appear continuously, so try them out and use what appeals to you most to organise your ideas and plans.

Putting it all together and moving forward

You should now be in a position to put together an action plan and start taking your career ideas forward. No matter where you are in the career planning process, it will help you to have some clear goals to work towards. This will provide you with some motivation as well as helping you to keep track of your progress.

How to action plan

- Identify the ultimate goal you are working towards. This could be a particular job, or it could be something more immediate, such as making your first contacts. Decide on the date by which you want this outcome to be completed and put it in your diary or calendar.

- Next, work backwards from that date to where you are now, identifying all the interim tasks that need to be achieved before the ultimate goal is attained, as well as the evidence you need to see to know that the task is complete.

- Now, add in the deadlines for all these smaller tasks. It's important for your morale to be able to tick these tasks off your list, as well as to break down what can seem an insurmountable obstacle into something much more achievable. You should now have a rough timeline of when everything needs to be done.

- Your next step is to identify the resources you need to achieve these tasks and reach your goal. These could include some of the online tools outlined above, books you want to read, industry publications or journals, or people you need to talk to. Don't try to pursue your plan without having the right resources in place, or you will waste time working without the right help, or miss crucial information and this could hold you back.

- Attach a reward for each interim goal that you tick off your list, especially if it's a challenging goal that you keep putting off, like attending your first networking event. This is a reinforcement theory known as Premack's Principle, where you can use a desired activity to make you carry out a less desired activity that you might be trying to avoid. Work in proportion: for small goals, attach small rewards like a night with your favourite TV show or a drink with friends, but, if you secure your dream job, by all means buy yourself a whole new working wardrobe, take a holiday, or whatever seems most appropriate!

- Finally, make sure that you regularly check in with yourself on your progress and make an honest assessment of how you are getting on; some people will try to do too much too quickly and will need to slow down, others will need to step up their activity and work harder. One way of ensuring that you stick to your plan is to share it with someone. Research demonstrates that telling someone you trust about your plans and asking them to help keep track of your progress increases your chances of achieving your goal, because you have shared and committed to it. Share your plan with a careers adviser if that helps, or with a trusted friend or family member who will give you the right kind of encouragement.

That's it!

You now have everything you need to make real progress with your career planning. The next chapter will help you to move on by identifying and developing the employability skills you need to succeed in working in science.

14

Employability skills for science: what employers want

This chapter explains the professional skills required by employers in the workplace and how to develop them. It will look at:

- your employability and the skills science employers value

- understanding graduate market trends and how they affect your job search

- the significance of 'soft' or 'transferable' skills to your science career

- taking responsibility for your development.

Being successful in your career requires you to take a broad look at your skills; you need to have more to offer a potential employer than skills that are only relevant to your subject. To get on in today's workplace, employers expect you to possess skills that enable you to work effectively in teams, deal with people both in your organisation as well as with external contacts, and manage your own workload, taking responsibility for your development and learning.

Recent reports discussing science graduates and their skills, such as the 2012 research carried out by the Lords Science and Technology Committee, highlight a growing demand from science employers for their recruits to not only be technically able but also to possess an understanding of how a business works. It is not enough to be able to do your job; to be successful in the graduate market you must also be able to demonstrate your understanding of how your job supports your organisation in its commercial endeavours, too. This chapter will help you to understand this broader skill set, how to start developing any weaker areas, and will prepare you for continuing professional development – an essential aspect of your career progression, no matter which job role you finally take up.

Your employability and the skills science employers value

In *Learning to Grow*, a recent report produced by the Confederation of British Industry (CBI), several priorities were identified by its employer members when recruiting graduates. 'Employability skills' – that broader skill set identified above – was highlighted as the highest priority, over 'degree subject' which was second on the list, reflecting the need for broadly skilled graduates who can be trained in more sector-specific skills while on the job. In many ways, it is easier to train someone in a 'hard' skill, such a laboratory technique, than it is to instil in them the value of working co-operatively and professionally with their colleagues. 'Relevant work experience' was third on the list, closely followed by 'degree result', 'university attended' and, finally, 'foreign languages'.

The need to employ professionally minded graduates is driving current recruitment practices, and this is something to keep in mind when making applications. While many application form questions will specify the skills an employer is looking for in particular, if you submit a CV and covering letter it is very important that you can address more than what you accomplished as part of your degree training, and that you highlight the transferable skills gained from a wide variety of your activities, including extra-curricular and social interests. This will help to demonstrate that you have an arsenal of potentially useful skills and are worth inviting to interview.

What is 'employability', anyway?

The Higher Education Academy's (HEA) definition of employability is:

'a set of achievements – skills, understandings and personal attributes – that make graduates more likely to gain employment and be successful in their chosen occupations, which benefits themselves, the workforce, the community and the economy'.

Possessing employability skills implies that you understand how to operate as a professional in the workplace, beyond deploying your technical skills, and that you make a valuable contribution, potentially even beyond your immediate work and into the wider community. Knowing what makes **you** employable is also an important aspect of maintaining your employability; if you don't know what you have to offer, then you can't sell it in the labour market, so it's worth spending time thinking about what you have learned from previous work and life experience, before you start completing any applications, as discussed in Chapter 13.

The difference between 'employment' and 'employability'

There is also an important distinction between simply 'being employed' and maintaining your employability.

> 'Individuals value employability, the opportunity to develop skills and experience, which make an individual a fit for a variety of roles. This makes employees feel more secure in their employment and opens up a range of possibilities both with their employers and in the wider labour market.'
>
> HR Magazine.co.uk

If you can keep your skills up to date and maintain your contacts, not only are you less likely to feel threatened by job insecurity, such as being made redundant, but you will also have a higher chance of finding new employment should you wish to or have to move on.

What skills should I be developing?

As well as looking at recruitment priorities, the CBI also identified a list of skills in demand from their member employers.

- Self-management: being able to get on with your work without constant supervision and manage your own deadlines often comes out on top of employer 'wish lists' for graduate skills.

- Teamworking: even in relatively solitary jobs, such as writing code as a software developer, you will still be part of a larger team and be expected to communicate with them on your progress.

- Business and customer awareness: understanding of the key drivers for business success and providing customer satisfaction. The selection process will often test your knowledge of a science recruiter's customers or clients, their nearest competitors and their unique selling points. Understanding how your job forms part of their business is crucial.

- Problem solving: analysing facts and situations and applying creative thinking to develop appropriate solutions. Problems come up very frequently at work, such as important research not proceeding as planned, and an employer needs to know that you can be trusted to try to solve them quickly, minimising the loss of time and money.

- Communication and literacy: writing professional reports is a key skill in many science careers, while any job involving research requires the production of academic papers. Being able to present with clarity to clients or your team is also a highly valued skill.

- Application of numeracy: most science graduates have good numerical skills, but can you use your mathematics in a more commercial context?

- Application of information technology: many science-specific roles will also require use of more sophisticated software packages, platforms, statistical information and use of specialist equipment, especially in the health sciences.

Source: CBI, *Learning to Grow* 2012

While these general employability skills will help you into your first graduate position, it is expected that you will continue to develop throughout your career, taking opportunities for what is known as continuing professional development (CPD). Most scientists will join a relevant professional body – ranging from the Geological Society to Royal Society of Chemistry – that offer courses to help you acquire the specialist skills you need. Some employers may encourage you to work towards an MSc, and this is very common in the health sciences, especially within the NHS. You may also wish to work towards attaining Chartered Scientist (CSci) status in your field as your career progresses. You usually need to have been accruing evidence of your professional abilities for at least five years before attempting to become chartered, but the qualification demonstrates that a professional body agrees that you have reached an advanced level of practice and can be a great career booster, enabling scientists to move into higher level roles.

Understanding market trends and how they affect your job search

As well as being aware of the skills employers are looking for in their new graduate recruits, it's useful to stay on top of labour market trends so that you can see what is influencing recruitment. Staying in touch with your contacts is one way to do this, as well as reading quality newspapers. Labour market research, such as that quoted above from the CBI, is regularly published. You should also be able to find information on science-specific websites (see the 'Further reading and resources' section for suggestions).

Trends worth noting

Some broader trends are worth noting here, as they have been developing for a few years and show no sign of disappearing in the short term, and could have an effect on the way in which graduates are recruited for the next few years.

Employers are increasingly recruiting their existing interns

First, there has been a significant increase in employers recruiting graduates who have already worked for them on internship or placement programmes. The 2013 High Fliers report (www.highfliers.co.uk/download/GMReport13.pdf) states that this trend is already observable in around one third of employers. Many employers now treat internships as an extended interview, so you get a chance to impress them on the job, and they are also a great way for you to see if a particular company culture is the right one for you. Don't be afraid to undertake several schemes and try out different organisations. Recruiting graduates from internship programmes is a much 'safer' way for employers in which to hire, so it could pay off to start your job search early; internship and placement schemes are usually open to second/penultimate year and final year undergraduates. If you graduate without a job, it's also worth asking around to see which employers offer graduate internships, as this can be a very useful way to get your foot in the door with a company.

Work experience is crucial to your CV

Second, if you have no work experience to offer at all, you could be putting yourself in a difficult position, with more than half of the recruiters in the High Fliers survey warning that graduates without work experience have 'little or no chance' of receiving a job offer from them.

However, it is important to bear in mind that you do not necessarily have to have work experience under your belt in the same industry that you wish to enter. For example, many of the pharmaceutical firms offer internship and placement schemes but your weekend or holiday job will have equipped you with some of the broader employability skills you need, such as teamwork and problem solving. As long as you can demonstrate in your application and interview that your existing skills are transferable to your chosen sector, you still have a good chance of making a positive impression.

You must be able to identify your skills and learning

Much of your success will turn on how clearly you can articulate your learning gained from one experience and apply it to a different context. Another candidate may have completed several pharmaceutical placements but be unable to provide examples of the skills they developed during their experience, and this could cost them dearly during the recruitment process.

So, while work experience within your desired field is the ultimate aim for your career development, any work experience can enhance your prospects as long as you can be clear on any learning and its potential application to your scientific field. Don't rule yourself out because 'I've only worked in a supermarket/waited on tables/worked behind a bar'. These roles provide many opportunities to develop valuable employability skills, so it's important not to undersell what you have to offer; dealing with a difficult customer could be useful to you in an application form when discussing how to cope with conflict. Employers are also offering more paid work experience opportunities than ever before, so take a chance and start applying (High Fliers 2013).

Graduate starting salaries have remained the same in recent years

Finally, here is one other trend to be aware of. How much you are likely to earn as a new graduate has remained quite static for the last four years due to the economic recession at around £25,000 per annum (at time of writing). This varies between sectors of course but, unless you plan to move from science to investment banking, where starting salaries are closer to £45,000, expecting somewhere around £25,000–£29,000 would be about right. You will generally earn more if based in London and the South East, but this will be balanced out by higher living costs. You may be asked in your application how much you are expecting to earn, which can often throw candidates who don't know the market rates for their desired role. Prospects is a very useful resource for salary information of this kind, and worth trying as a starting point to work out if what you are being offered is competitive (see 'Further reading and resources' for more information). Salary information, where available, has been included for all job roles described in Part 1.

The significance of 'soft' or 'transferable' skills to your science career

The CBI reported that science, technology, engineering and maths, or STEM, graduates 'seem to lack the employability skills' required to succeed in the workplace. Unfortunately, STEM graduates have developed a reputation over the years for being unable to communicate effectively, not adapting well to working in teams and being overly focused on their technical skills. Both my experience and that of other career professionals shows this to be a very broad and rather unfair assessment, but any noticeable lack of ability or confidence in STEM students could be attributed to the nature of their degree courses where, although group projects can be common, the kind of classroom debate required in the humanities and social sciences doesn't really happen. Final year science projects can be completed independently, which doesn't provide an opportunity to get used to making persuasive verbal arguments or working in a team to achieve results.

Seize any opportunities to develop your professional skills

Taking advantage of any skills development opportunities as part of your science degree is essential, as is signing up for workshops at your careers service, where you can meet employers who can demonstrate what is required for you not only to make it through their selection process but be successful in your job in your first few years. We've all groaned at the prospect of taking courses that don't seem particularly relevant to our degree subject but, in the long term, volunteering for that extra bit of presenting or taking the time to knock your CV into shape could make a difference to your employability, rather than spending more time in the lab.

Taking responsibility for your own development

You will probably still remember how university life differed from being at school in the first few months of your degree. Suddenly, no-one was reminding you to complete assignments or telling you what to do. Entering professional life requires the next step up, in that not only are you responsible for carrying out the work you have been contracted to do, but not completing it on time could cost your organisation significant sums of money, as well as the goodwill of its clients. Your role is not only to get your job done on time, but to preserve the commercial and business face of your company; this is why we spent so long looking at getting the right organisational 'fit' for you in the previous chapter, so that you feel loyal enough to the company you work for to want to get the work done to a high standard.

Any good employer will provide you with a thorough induction programme, but you are going to be asked to work independently early on so it's important to address any shortcomings that you feel are affecting your work right now. It's time for an honest look at where your strengths and weaknesses lie and how to work on any potential problem areas.

Self-assessment exercise

A good place to start would be with the list of skills from the CBI earlier in the chapter.

- Take each one and write them down or type them out, leaving plenty of space for comment.

- Take each skill and, on a scale of one to five, assess how confident you feel in this area, e.g. 'team working' gets a three, as it's not bad but there's room for improvement, and 'problem solving' gets a five, as you're the person people always seem to come to in a crisis and they value your advice.

If you rate your ability quite highly (either a four or five, roughly equal to being highly competent), then try to write down a couple of examples of when you put this skill to particularly good use, as you will find this to be a potentially helpful resource when dealing with applications and interviews.

An example could be: 'Communication skills – 4/5 Very good. Felt confident speaking to a member of our project group who didn't seem to be doing any work. Got to the bottom of the problem (they didn't really understand the task) and sorted out new deadlines for everyone, with their agreement.'

Creating a repository of examples now can save valuable time when you are juggling the completion of lengthy applications with your coursework deadlines in your busy final year.

Improving weaker skills

However, if you rate yourself between one and three for a skill, then this requires development. If you have already started looking into potential job roles, then you may have an idea of the particular skills required for the science career you have in mind, and this can help you to decide how urgently and in what depth you need to develop them. If you're not sure, then look at Prospects (www.prospects.co.uk), LinkedIn and Google to see what you can find out, as this will help you to avoid wasting time on areas that you won't need to be competent in for certain jobs. Asking your contacts about the skills they use each day in their work and what new recruits are expected to be able to do can also help you to prioritise. You may be a very nervous public speaker, for instance but, if it's not something you'll be asked to do in your proposed line of work (maybe you'll provide an online presentation instead, using digital media), then don't waste your time on that skill.

Having worked your way through the list, you should have a clearer picture of where your strengths lie, with reassuring examples of when you have put them into practice, as well as some areas for improvement. Act on those trouble spots immediately or you could find that your next application for work experience requires a skill in your problem area and you could stumble at the first hurdle.

Help with skills development

Think about where you can get some support in dealing with any tricky skills areas. Does your course provide any optional or open units that are more professionally oriented? Does your careers service or Students' Union offer any workshops or training courses? Some further education colleges offer a range of vocational programmes, while smaller providers are worth investigating, but check their qualifications and credentials. There are also many online courses available, and YouTube can be a valuable source of accessible information from experienced specialists wanting to showcase what they have to offer. Don't forget books, either, as there are some excellent skills development guides out there – have a look at the 'Further reading and resources' section for suggestions to get you started.

Effective action planning for development

The final step in taking your skills development forward is to devise and carry out an action plan; please revisit the guidance offered at the end of Chapter 13. Remember to:

- make your goals specific

- give them all individual deadlines

- work backwards when planning your timeframe

- identify the resources you need

- schedule in time to check on and evaluate your progress

- plan some rewards for a job well done!

Chapter 15 will now guide you through making effective job applications, drawing on the self-assessment of your skills above, as well as looking at how to present what you have to offer an employer in the way they expect to see it.

15

Making effective applications

This chapter explains how to put together effective and carefully targeted applications that will enhance your chances of gaining an interview. We will cover:

- what you need to know before beginning your applications

- dealing with application forms and competency-based questions

- how to produce an effective CV and covering letter package

- how to write a personal statement

- no vacancy being advertised? Make a speculative application.

> 'The biggest mistake that people make is to believe that their CV is the beginning and end of the process. That isn't the case. The [CV] is simply a door opener, much like an enlarged business card.'
>
> **Dave Jensen, 'CVs that open industry doors', www.sciencecareers. sciencemag.org**

The first point to bear in mind when you start filling out your applications is that what you submit won't get you the job – it's about getting you the interview. Your job application is all about making a potential employer interested enough to want to meet you and put you on their interview shortlist; after that, it's down to how you perform on the day compared with the other candidates. You need to answer their questions relevantly, as well as demonstrating that you understand their organisation, and provide examples of your ability to do the job required. It's a challenging task requiring careful preparation.

What you need to know before you begin your applications

Preparing to complete a good quality application requires careful and thorough foundations. The correct approach to take is similar to that when you were completing university assignments – make sure that you have all the information you need before you start writing and that your research is complete before you begin.

It will take much longer than you think

Writing applications is an extremely time-consuming exercise – each one will take several hours longer than you think, so plan ahead to allow enough space in your diary. Your first application can take anything up to eight to ten hours, allowing for review, editing and rewrites, so be prepared. Answering questions within a word limit requires skill and patience, as does drafting a tailored CV and covering letter from scratch. Make sure you have all the information you need to hand as you write.

A useful rule for time management is to estimate how much time you think you need for a task, and then add another 50% of that time, which should get you closer to the time you will actually take.

Last minute applications are not to be recommended

It is not recommended that you attempt to complete an application from scratch the night before the closing date. This really is a futile exercise, as it's highly unlikely that something thrown together at the last minute will make it through any initial screening. It's also advisable to allow a couple of extra days to get the application looked at by a careers adviser or some of your professional contacts, and allow time to make any changes or corrections resulting from their feedback. If you are emailing your CV or form to a contact, be sure to give them plenty of warning as you will be eating into their busy schedule. Do also be clear with them by when you need their comments back.

The three key topics you need to prepare

Preparing applications requires a certain amount of revision, just like preparing for an exam, and there are three key topics you need to be clear on before you start writing: yourself, the organisation to which you are applying, and the broader industry or sector within which that organisation operates.

Know yourself

How well do you know yourself? Your ability to 'sell' what you have to offer is crucial to any application, and this means thinking back to extra-curricular activities and work experience to identify the skills you developed and what you learned about yourself. Too many candidates will simply state what the duties of a job role involved, but this isn't what is required. Several people can perform the same job, but each one will learn something different from their experience and apply it to their new role – that is what the employer wants to know about, as those are the skills and learning that they will be gaining from recruiting you. So it's really worth taking the time to ask yourself, 'What are the three key things I learned from this job/activity?' For example, working at a museum in your holidays may well have equipped you with the communication skills, organisational ability and patience you may well need to work in a science outreach role as a graduate.

Use the job description as well as the skills and values that should be posted on your intended employer's website to help you to highlight the skills required for your desired job, to ensure that you are adequately 'mapping' what you have to offer onto what the employer wants; there will be more on how to do this, with examples, in the section below on completing application forms.

Know the company or organisation

The second topic you need to know about is the organisation you are applying to. Using the content of their website is not enough to make you stand out; this is what most people will rely on, and you need to show that you have gone the extra mile. Make sure that you perform a thorough search on the internet and in quality newspapers for current news items about the organisation, looking for positive comments by people in the science sector, any initiatives it has started, awards it has won, or projects it is involved in.

If you are applying for a graduate training scheme, then be sure you are as familiar as possible with what this involves, so that you can be prepared for questions that test your understanding of the role. Industry journals are a good place to look for current information, as well as more general business magazines (see the 'Further reading and resources' section for suggestions). Use social media tools such as LinkedIn and Twitter to help you to spot trends and identify key people.

Know the industry

Finally, you also need to be able to demonstrate your understanding of the broader industry and where your chosen organisation fits within it, providing evidence of your commercial awareness. For example, if you are applying for a role with a pharmaceuticals company, you need to be able to discuss their nearest competitors, and what makes that company distinct from its rivals; what is the unique research it carries out, and what are its key products? Who are their clients and main market? Have you met one of the company's representatives? Did you visit their stand at a careers fair or attend a company presentation?

You also need to be able to answer one of the questions that applicants frequently find challenging: 'Why do you want to work for Company X?' You will not be able to answer this question with conviction unless you have done your homework. In practice interviews, it is often the question that reveals a lack of candidate preparation and can bring home how hard it is to answer without a solid grounding of the key trends and news in your chosen area of the science community.

Be able to speak with authority in your applications and interviews, carry out your own research and then conduct a SWOT analysis: look at that pharmaceuticals company from all angles and identify its strengths and weaknesses, as well as potential opportunities and threats. Any employer will be more impressed by your own appraisal than by a rehash of something available online.

Dealing with application forms and competency-based questions

It has become very common for employers, especially those offering graduate training schemes, to provide an online application form for candidates to complete, rather than asking for a CV and covering letter, although the latter have not yet disappeared.

> By using a form, the recruiter will be able to focus on the skills, experience and attributes they wish you to provide evidence for, rather than relying on you to produce a CV and covering letter that may not target what they wish to know.

Bear this in mind and stay relevant when providing your answers and information; don't answer the questions you wanted to be asked, or twist irrelevant examples to suit the question. Again, this is a guaranteed method for not having your application progressed through to the next stage.

The basics

The first few pages are usually made up of basic information: personal details, education and training, and your previous employment. If you have all this information to hand this should not take a long time. However, not all application forms are designed with clarity in mind so, if you are very unsure about what information is required, use the contact information that should be provided in case of queries, or be bold and make a phone call directly to human resources (HR) or personnel to ask what to do. Better to check than make a mistake that rules you out of the process at an early stage.

Referees

It's also important that you have checked with your potential referees that they are still willing to support your application and that they may receive an email requesting a reference at short notice, so make sure you do this before you start submitting your applications. It's usual for companies to ask for one academic reference and one from a previous employer, so be organised with this in advance. Applications for academic research and teaching positions, if you are a postgraduate or postdoctoral student, will require three referees, so be prepared.

Answering competency questions

Where you will need to take your time is with the competency questions. It can be challenging to think of the most appropriate examples to show off your skills, especially when you are trying not to repeat yourself over several questions, and when you have limited words (150–200 words per answer is common) so you must be concise while still selling what you have to offer. If you have spent some time looking back over your previous work and extra-curricular experience then you should be able to find the material you need.

Typical examples of competency questions

- Have you ever had to explain something complex to someone with very little knowledge of the subject? How did you help them to understand?

- Tell us about a time when you worked as a team and there was conflict. How did you deal with this and what was the outcome?

- Describe a situation where you have solved a problem using creative thinking.

You will notice that, at this point, your scientific knowledge is not being asked about, although you may well be asked why you are applying for this particular job in this field. This is because the recruiter is looking for the broader range of employability skills discussed in Chapter 14; more specific technical skills can always be developed later on. While the scientific principles you have been studying will be useful in your work, you have to learn how the organisation that employs you applies them in practice and this can be very different from the theory.

Avoid the common mistakes

Before we look at how to put together an answer, one word of caution: do not send out too many applications. A common mistake is to fire out as many application forms as possible, in the hope that some of them will result in an interview. This is a waste of time, as you cannot conduct the quality research that 20–30 forms would require. It's a more productive approach to produce a small set of quality applications (fewer than 10) knowing that, when you submit them, you really did the best job on them you could and that they don't look too generic. Less is more when it comes to applications. Despite the horror stories in the media by people who 'sent out 200 application forms and still didn't get an interview', you can guarantee that those applications were not targeted to the employers' needs, nor did they present what the applicant had to offer in the way the employer wanted to see it.

How to structure answers to competency-based questions

Many candidates compose their answers to application form questions by starting with the first sentence, agonising over it and then struggling through to the end – a strategy in common with attempts at essay writing and just as exhausting. Start with bullet points and build your answer up in pieces, even for just a couple of hundred words; with so little space, you really need to make the most of what you have. Be as precise as possible: what is the main point you want the employer to remember? What was the learning you took away from a particular experience and how is that of value to your potential new company?

Use tried and trusted frameworks to help you

There are two frameworks you can use to structure your answers (they work well for interviews, too), and they are recommended by employers. The longer version is **STAR**.

Situation: brief setting of background scene so that the employer understands the context. Don't waste too many words here describing what was happening rather than getting to the point.

Task: what was it you were required or had decided to do?

Action: **what** you did, and **why** you decided to do it like that. This is crucial to your answer as it highlights your ability to synthesise information, act on it and defend your actions later on. It can also demonstrate your problem-solving skills. This section is the largest component of the answer, and you must provide **specific examples** of your actions here.

Result: this can be a specific outcome, such as increasing a company's profits by a certain percentage while you were on work experience, a great piece of feedback from a client or manager, or a specific learning point, such as what you personally took away from the experience. It is also okay to state that you learned how **not** to do something, and that you would take a different approach in the future, as this demonstrates reflection and learning.

Finally, and I can't stress this enough, make sure that your spelling and grammar throughout the answer are as perfect as you can make them. Don't be ruled out by avoidable mistakes when you have some great experience and skills to offer.

The shorter version of STAR is **CAR**, which stands for Context, Action and Result, which some people prefer. It may also be easier to recall under pressure, so can be helpful for answering questions 'live' in an interview.

Example application form answer

Let's look at a possible answer to the question, *'Tell us about a time when there was a problem in a team you were working in. How was this resolved and what was the outcome?'* Showing what you have learned from a challenging team situation shows that you can work with different personality types and put the work before any personal differences. It's also 99% likely that any role in science will require you to work in a team, at least part of the time. Using the STAR framework will help you to establish the context, show how you solved the problem and the results you obtained.

Situation: 'For my final year computer science project, teams were asked to develop a game for children that helped them develop their maths.'

Task: 'After a few weeks, it became obvious that one team member had stopped contributing to the work, not attending meetings or contributing any code. My team asked me to speak with them, as they felt I could handle the situation tactfully.'

Action: 'I arranged to meet privately with this team member, informally over coffee so that they did not have to deal with the whole team. I asked if they were having any problems, because I had noticed their lack of contributions; I thought this would be more sensitive than telling off this person for not working hard enough. They told me that a relative had been ill and they had lost focus on their work as a result, but hadn't liked to say anything to the team.'

Result: 'We agreed the team member would take on a smaller proportion of the work until they could contribute more fully, and this person thanked me for not being angry about their lack of work. They completed their share of the work as planned, and we submitted the project on time, receiving the second-highest mark in the year group.'

Analysis of the answer

This answer **demonstrates the applicant's approach to solving the problem**, that they were trusted by their teammates and that they were also able to approach a difficult situation with sensitivity and tact. There is also **a clear result** here: not only did the group do well in their project, but the troubled team member felt supported by their colleagues. The *answer is* **relevant**, demonstrates **learning** points and provides **specific evidence of the applicant's ability to defuse a conflict**. It also uses 'I', rather than 'we', to emphasise the applicant's particular contribution to the situation; too many candidates write as if on behalf of their entire project team, so focus on your own actions and their results. The answer is of course also written clearly and without errors.

How to produce an effective CV and covering letter package

While many applicants find the restrictions imposed on them by an application form frustrating, having the freedom to put together your own CV and covering letter presents its own challenges. This is because the employer is relying on you to match your skills and experience to their requirements as precisely as possible; too many candidates use the CV and covering letter as an opportunity to showcase interesting but irrelevant information and find it very hard to edit their package down into something concise.

> Remember at all times that both the letter **and** the CV need to be targeted at the specific job you are applying for, so try to see your application from the employer's point of view and ask yourself, 'So what?', each time you include something, as this will help you to evaluate the relevance of your chosen content.

There is no point in highlighting all your research skills and publications you may have, when the scientific role you are applying for may be more public facing. You need to play down the academic content and showcase your communication skills instead. Think carefully about where to place your emphasis.

The covering letter

As a career coach, 'What goes into a covering letter?' is one of the most common questions I am asked. The first rule of writing these letters is that they should be no more than one side of A4, including your address, the company's address, date and your sign off. While it's important to stay within these limits to show that you can be concise, many candidates actually don't include enough specific examples of their skills, making general statements such as 'I am an excellent team player.'

You need to provide **proof** of this, so that sentence should be rephrased along the lines of, 'I have excellent teamwork skills. For example, in our organic chemistry research project, one team member fell ill just before the deadline, and I both reorganised the group's task, with their agreement, as well as taking on additional work to my own. We submitted our project on time and received a mark of 72% despite the problems we encountered.' The latter provides a specific example of your contribution to the team, as well as a concrete result the employer can understand, so provide evidence of your skills with every statement.

Structuring a covering letter

A sample letter has not been included in this book as not only are there so many examples available online (see 'Further reading and resources'), but you also need to be able to produce tailored, individual letters, rather than slavishly copying a set format. Below is a typical structure you can adapt.

Getting started and introducing yourself

The letter should follow a standard business layout, with your home address (or the address where you want to receive any hard copy correspondence from the employer), and the address of the employer. Don't forget the date.

If at all possible, address the letter to a specific person; this makes a stronger impression than the generic 'Dear Sir/Madam'. You can always telephone the company switchboard to ask, and default to the generic greeting if they cannot supply a name. Avoid 'To whom it may concern', which is too impersonal.

Begin your letter by stating the position for which you are applying, where you saw it advertised, and summarising your current position: 'I am writing to apply for the post of nutritional therapist at Cityville Hospital, as advertised on the NHS website on 10 February. I am currently completing my BSc in Nutrition and Health Science at the University of Bigtown, and am on track for a 2.i.'

Why are you applying to them*?*

This is where you need to show off all the fruits of your research and resulting commercial awareness. For this application, the candidate would need to be clear on the following: why they want to work in nutritional therapy, why they want to work at Cityville Hospital in particular, what they know about the relevant hospital department and its work, and what they know about the broader trends in nutritional therapy. Do mention awards or projects the employer has been involved with, or any specialists you are looking forward to working with, as well as any features of the training that stand out to you, such as a mentoring scheme, or being able to work with clients as soon as you start. Most applicants neglect to do this section justice, so make sure you take the time to do your homework before you start writing and, as with the form, start with a bullet list of what you want to cover and then build it up gradually.

Why should they be interested in you*?*

This is the section where you should be focusing on matching your skills and experience precisely to what the employer is asking for. Make sure your letter is properly targeted. Focus on the main skills you feel you have to offer, and provide specific examples of them, using the STAR or CAR frameworks discussed above. This ensures that you will provide adequate evidence of your skills and prevents the letter becoming a series of general statements.

An important point: many applicants tie themselves in knots trying not to duplicate information from their CV in the covering letter. This is unnecessary as the CV and covering letter **should** overlap; the letter is there to draw attention to the highlights of the CV, like a trailer for a film. Think of the documents as two components of a package, with the letter introducing the CV, and you shouldn't go too far wrong.

To finish

Sign off politely and restate your interest in the post. This is also the place to mention if you have exams or booked holidays coming up that may conflict with interview timings, or if there is anything you need to explain in terms of disappointing grades or time out due to illness. For the latter, try to keep as positive a spin on things as possible. For example, 'My second-year grades were disappointing but, as you can see from my final year results, I learned a great deal about managing my time and achieved a 65% average.'

When it comes to illness or issues of a more personal nature, do remember that you are not obliged to disclose anything you choose not to. Simply stating that, 'A period of illness during the autumn of my final year obviously affected my grades, but I still completed my studies and anticipate no further problems in the future', is fine. It's okay to have experienced problems – it's unusual for anyone to complete their degree completely free of any difficulties – but you need to emphasise how you overcame them, what you learned, and that you are now fit for work. If you have a continuing health issue or a disability that will have a continuing impact, then seek advice from a careers adviser on how to address this in your application.

What can go wrong with a covering letter?

Not targeting the letter sufficiently is a common problem. Also, if you are writing several letters and using 'cut and paste', be absolutely sure that you have the correct company details on each letter! Ensure that you have enough specific examples in your section about your skills and experience, and that you have provided a good depth of commercial knowledge. Finally, check, cheque and check again for those all-important spelling, grammar and typing errors (did you spot the deliberate mistake?).

The CV

Because there are so many possible CV formats, of which a wide selection are available to you online, I will discuss the main principles of producing an effective CV so that you can think about what type would best showcase what you have to offer.

There is no such thing as a 'standard' CV, although you will see many that look very similar.

> The main point is to address the person specification for the job as accurately as you can and present the information in a format that the reader can take in as quickly and easily as possible.

A CV is not designed to be read word by word, but to be skimmed over for key information, so avoid being too 'wordy'.

Make the format suit you

The traditional type of CV format tends to present information in the following order: personal details, education, employment/work experience, positions of responsibility, awards/skills, interests, references. However, don't be afraid to move things around if you feel this would better highlight what you have to offer. For example, if you have some outstanding work experience or employment, you could put this section straight after the personal information at the top. Similarly, you can group related work experience under a heading of 'Relevant experience' to present it more coherently and stop some great information disappearing onto a second page. If you are a more mature candidate with gaps in employment for raising children or managing a household, a skills-based CV might suit you better, as it will highlight what you have to offer now and what is relevant to the job, and will help to gloss over gaps in your work history.

Profile or no profile?

Personal profiles at the top of a CV are increasingly common. However, if they are simply a general statement of your skills and achievements without any detail or supporting evidence – 'I am a hard-working biological sciences undergraduate with excellent teamwork and research capabilities seeking a challenging role in the pharmaceuticals industry' – then it's best left out. Isn't everyone hard working and looking for a great job? Without proof of your skills, or containing distinctive content, a profile is simply taking up valuable space on your CV where you can provide more specific examples of your abilities.

Get the length right

Unless you are applying for a specifically academic position, where you will need to list conference papers and publications, you must keep the CV to two pages maximum in length. Any longer, and it may well end up in the reject pile. Choose your best examples to highlight, and feel free to summarise the rest of your content. It's only the financial sector that seems to be requesting one page CVs recently, but one pagers can really demonstrate your ability to highlight your best points in the sciences, if done well; they can be put to good use to make the most of limited experience that may look thin when spread over two pages. However, produce **either** one full page **or** two full pages – one page and a half with a lot of yawning white space at the end looks unfinished and won't do you any favours.

Write concisely

Don't bother writing in full sentences. Use bullet lists to provide the information in a direct way, and start your phrases with verbs, such as 'Developed', 'Led', 'Took responsibility for' or 'Achieved'. Try to avoid passive constructions such as, 'The experiment was designed to achieve the maximum results in the shortest time.' Better to go for active constructions such as, 'Developed an experiment to achieve maximum results in the shortest time frame' – much more dynamic.

Use specific examples

You must provide specific evidence of your abilities, and resist falling into simply describing what a particular job required of you in the past. Remember to focus on the learning points unique to you, and the skills that you developed that you feel would be most relevant to the job.

Sell everything

Don't expect an employer to understand why you have included something on your CV that comes without any explanation. For example, 'Duke of Edinburgh Gold Award' tells them nothing. You need to explain how the skills you used to complete it could be useful in the job you want. For example: 'Duke of Edinburgh Gold Award: developed excellent skills in working under pressure when leading a climb in challenging weather conditions, getting my team home safely and on time,' could be very relevant to any science job that involves potentially working outside in adverse conditions.

Do include your interests

Employers are not hiring a walking skill set; they want to know about you more personally so that they can get a sense of whether you will fit into their organisation. Therefore, do include a summary of what you enjoy doing in your spare time, but remember to make it relevant to the job by drawing out the skills you are developing by doing them. For example: 'Regular yoga practice: keeps me healthy and helps me to relax and manage stress.'

Referee contact information

It is standard these days to simply state, 'References available on request' at the end of the CV. This leaves you space for more valuable information, as your references are unlikely to be taken up until you are considered to be a serious contender for the position. However, if you do have enough space, by all means include their contact information, remembering telephone numbers and email addresses, as this is the most common way for an employer to contact your referee. In terms of who to use, one academic referee and one from your previous employment is standard. It is also a courtesy to let your referees know how many applications you are submitting and to whom, and to keep them updated with your progress. It can also be helpful to provide them with your CV and an update of any activities you have undertaken that may help them to write you a good reference.

What can go wrong with a CV?

As with the form and covering letter, lack of targeting, not enough specific evidence, entries left to explain themselves, and the usual avoidable errors could all mean that your application is discarded, so be selective, be accurate and make all the content count.

Writing a statement in support of your application

Some employers will ask for a 'statement supporting your application' alongside or instead of an application form or covering letter. To complete one of these, take the same approach as for the covering letter, but do not format the document as a business letter. Use the same sections as for the covering letter to help you structure the statement, but you may well be permitted more space than one side of A4, so it's important that you think about the layout. Try to avoid presenting the employer with a couple of pages full of solid text, as this will be difficult for them to navigate.

Make use of headings to make the statement easier to read, highlighting your skills by section, such as 'Communication and interpersonal' or 'Technical', depending on the requirements of the job description. You can also use bullet lists to make the text easier to read. Again, try to see the document from the employer's viewpoint; how can you make it easier for them to see what you have to offer and how it matches their requirements? Sign off with a closing statement that reiterates your interest in the post, or similar, but make sure the statement ends neatly.

No vacancy being advertised? Make a speculative application

If you see an organisation that you would love to work for but they are not advertising a vacancy, then it is perfectly acceptable to send in what is known as a 'speculative application'. This will be a CV and covering letter, and you should follow the advice provided above on how to produce both documents. However, you will not be working to a job description, which makes this a more challenging task, as the employer will still be expecting you to tailor your application to their needs as much as possible.

Tailor your speculative application

Draw on your research and commercial awareness to put together a well-targeted application. While you may not have a job description to work to, you should be able to gain a good understanding of your chosen organisation's values and purpose from its website and other publications, so make sure that your CV and covering letter address these, demonstrating that you are the 'kind of person' that your chosen company typically employs. You should also be able to find out the skills required to do the work you are interested in by searching for related job descriptions online.

Finally, give human resources a call to find out who you need to address the application to, and take a chance – even if you are not offered a position in the short term, your application could be kept on file for a future vacancy, or could result in some useful, short-term work experience.

The advice provided in this chapter should help you to produce a well-researched and appropriately targeted application. A targeted application will always have a better chance of securing you an interview, so take your time over it. If you need reassurance that you are on the right lines, do ask for impartial feedback from a careers adviser, so that you can avoid any obvious mistakes and submit the best application you can.

16

Surviving the
selection process

This chapter explains the different ways in which you are likely to be assessed by a science recruiter, as part of the recruitment process. We will cover:

- knowing yourself, the role and the sector – a reminder

- dealing with competency-based questions

- dealing with strengths-based interviews

- presenting yourself and your body language in an interview

- telephone interviews

- graduate aptitude or psychometric tests

- assessment centres – dealing with group exercises, presentations and social activities

- before, during and after – a timeline for success.

Hopefully, all the hard work you put into your applications has paid off, and you have started receiving invitations to attend interviews and assessment. This can be when anxiety sets in, putting yourself under pressure to perform across a variety of tasks when you **really** want a particular job. However, with the right preparation, you have as good a chance as anyone of being the person who beats the rest of the candidates. Because there are so many resources available covering all the aspects of the selection process in great detail, this chapter provides an overview of what to expect and how to begin your preparation, which you can then follow up using the 'Further reading and resources'.

Knowing yourself, the role and the sector: a reminder

If you have already worked through Chapter 15, you will be familiar with the tripartite approach that was outlined for completing applications: know yourself, the company and the sector. This knowledge needs to be refreshed before you attend an interview or assessment centre, or you are in danger of being rejected. Therefore, start by spending some time thinking about your skills and experience, and be prepared to answer questions on the content you submitted in your application; ensure that you keep copies of everything you sent to the recruiter.

Start refreshing your memory a week or a few days before the interview so that everything is fresh in your mind. Remember why you applied for this particular post and get used to saying this out loud until it sounds convincing. Finally, make sure that you are up to speed with any developments concerning both your chosen organisation and sector. Don't be ignorant of the fact that your prospective laboratory has been just bought out by a larger company, for example, and not be able to speak with confidence about how this could affect the organisation. Keep checking the news, even on the morning of the interview, so that you don't get caught out and are able to answer commercial awareness questions such as, 'Tell me about a recent news item regarding developments in geoscience that interested you.' Yes, that kind of question really can come up!

'Showing a keen interest in a company and the people can get you a long way. At interview, I was quizzed heavily on the role and position of the company I was applying for. Being able to talk intelligibly about the industry and current trends indicates your interest and desire to work there.'

Software developer in the finance sector

Dealing with competency-based interviews

The most common form of interview question is based around assessing your competencies, or skills. Each question focuses around one or two particular skills in which the company needs you to be proficient. Competency questions rely on you to draw on past experiences and the lessons you learned in order to assess how well you might perform in that organisation in the future.

Your interview preparation must involve going back through your application to remind yourself of what you submitted, in case this content is used by the interviewer as a basis for their questions, and you must continue familiarising yourself with the company's values and ethos as set out on their website and in any literature you can find. If, for example, a company that makes medical equipment prides itself on its cutting-edge research, then you can guess that the working culture there will be conducted at a fast pace and that they probably value creativity; you should be prepared to answer questions about why this appeals to you and when you have been innovative in the past.

What is covered by competency questions?

What kind of competencies are you likely to be asked about? The majority of organisations require a broad range of transferable skills, as outlined in Chapter 14, and it's likely that questions related to teamwork, communication skills, problem solving and self-management could be asked. More science-specific skills may be tested as part of a more practical assessment such as a group exercise, or in an interview where you are presented with a problem and are asked to talk the recruiter through your thinking. An example of this could be making a case for the best site for exploration and development, if you are applying to be a water scientist, based on a selection of locations that you must evaluate and discuss.

Get plenty of practice

Getting plenty of practice with answering competency questions is paramount. You need to feel comfortable with choosing the most relevant example, structuring your answer and trying to tie it in to your chosen organisation's values and priorities. Too many people fall into the trap of using the interview to explain what they hope to **gain from** working with the company; try to pitch it more in terms of what skills and experience you will **bring to** the company, and you will be demonstrating the right attitude.

You can find plenty of practice questions online, and your university careers service should hold copies of books you can use. Make sure you practise questions that you wouldn't like to be asked, as well as those where you feel confident – you cannot predict what will come up. Remember that your friends may not be particularly well versed in what a good answer should be, so do check in with a careers professional, and get some informed feedback.

Structuring your answers

When it comes to structuring your answers, you should use either the STAR or CAR frameworks discussed in the previous chapter on making applications.

The STAR framework

Situation: brief description of the background context

Task: what were you being asked to do?

Action: what did you do, and why did you do it like that?

Result: outcomes, feedback, learning points

> The CAR framework
>
> **Context:** relevant background information and the task in hand
>
> **Action:** what did you do, and why did you do it like that?
>
> **Result:** outcomes, feedback, learning points

Having a structure in mind will help you to get the balance right, as well as helping to remind you where you are if you wander off the point.

Do not rehearse scripted answers

One final warning: don't memorise scripted answers to interview questions. Interviews are rarely the one-way interrogations that people imagine and should, when going well, feel more like a structured conversation. While they will have certain competencies that they must cover with you, many interviewers will be comfortable following up on details in your answers, and you will not be able to produce pre-scripted answers for this kind of process. Even if you prepared an answer on teamwork, how can you know which aspect of teamwork the recruiter will want to know about? Will they ask about your particular role within a team? How you persuaded another team member to do something they didn't want to do? How you dealt with conflict within the team?

Dealing with strengths-based interviews

Strengths-based interviews are slowly increasing in popularity with recruiters, and will provide you with a very different interview experience from something more competency-based. Many candidates are becoming very practised at answering competency questions, especially if they have been through the selection process several times, and it is becoming increasingly difficult to differentiate between well-qualified candidates. Some organisations have turned to strengths-based interviewing to make a clearer assessment of a candidate's personality and to avoid them producing tried and tested answers to competency questions.

In a strengths-based interview, the questions are personal and are designed to see if you will fit in with the company and therefore work efficiently and happily. The underlying rationale is that someone whose values are aligned with those of their employer is far more likely to engage positively with their work and produce the desired results for their company.

> Because the questions are so personal, you need to answer with honesty, as you are not being assessed on how well you can complete a task, but more on your attitude and approach to it.

What are strengths-based questions?

This type of interview will focus on areas such as what you naturally do well, what motivates you, what your preferences and values are, and understanding how you learn and perform at your best. Typical strengths-based questions could include the following.

- What energises you and why?

- What did you enjoy most about your university course?

- What makes you want to get out of bed in the morning?

- What tells you that you've had a good day?

- What challenges do you take on to stretch yourself?

- What kind of work would you do even if you didn't receive payment for it?

You cannot predict what the employer is looking for in your answer; this will be dependent on the nature of the organisation. Therefore, don't second-guess what the company wants, and answer with honesty.

Preparing for strengths-based questions

> To prepare for a strengths-based interview, fundamentally you need to know yourself.

It is crucial that when you look back at your previous experience for this kind of interview, you focus on what motivated you through a project, how you maintained a positive mindset, identify the circumstances that helped you perform to the best of your ability, and analyse why you made particular decisions. If asked why you chose your particular degree course, for example, you need to look in-depth at the factors important to you at the time, such as what you enjoyed studying at school and who had influenced you when you talked about your future.

Be as specific as you can

It's not enough with these types of interview to say that you just 'muddled through' or did what 'seemed right at the time'.

> Recruiters are looking for evidence of self-analysis and personal reflection: a willingness to really look at yourself and demonstrate how you have learned how to perform to the best of your ability.

But still be prepared for commercial awareness questions!

It is possible in a strengths-based interview that you will be asked about your prospective organisation and the area of science that interests you. These kinds of questions will probably focus more on your interest in the work and why you feel that the company suits you, rather than being an opportunity to showcase extensive research. If asked why you have applied to the organisation, emphasise how their values match yours and how well you feel you would fit into their culture.

Where do the STAR/CAR frameworks fit in with strengths-based questions?

In terms of structure, the STAR/CAR frameworks will not be applicable to strengths-based questions, as you will be speaking more reflectively. However, if you start using examples to illustrate how you motivated yourself through a solo project, then using these frameworks to structure your evidence can be helpful to keep you on track.

Presenting yourself and your body language in an interview

Nerves can make us say and do strange things in job interviews, so it's important to learn how to manage how we perform under pressure. An interview is a form of presentation. You are 'on show', being asked to think on your feet, and trying to persuade your audience of something; in this case, for them to give you the job you really want!

The effects of stress

This kind of stressful situation has resulted in some questionable behaviour in the interviews I have been involved with over the years. One candidate spent the entire time with one arm flung over his shoulder, scratching his back;

another started the interview sucking on a sweet which he spat out into his lap while talking and, even worse, retrieved and put back into his mouth! One of my colleagues has interviewed someone who completely unconsciously and systematically rolled their tie up and down for the whole interview.

Get a practice interview

A practice interview, if you can get one at your university or college careers service, will not only pinpoint any problems with your answers but can also provide valuable feedback on your body language and speech patterns. There has been a great deal of research carried out about the significance of non-verbal communication, the most frequently cited being that by engineer turned psychologist Albert Mehrabian, and it is widely agreed that both your body language and tone of voice can have more impact on your audience than the words you are speaking. It is crucial to get the whole package right so that your answers are supported, not undermined, by the way in which you present them.

Let's work through the different stages of a typical interview and look at where you need to be making the right impression.

First impressions

First impressions in interviews are crucial, as initially negative impressions can be very difficult to overcome. It's not to say that you cannot recover from a shaky start, but you will have to work hard to overcome a poor first assessment. An obvious example of this happened when I was conducting interviews myself, and a candidate mistook me for the secretary taking him to the 'real' interviewer and not only tried to get me to carry his bags, but was rather patronising. This made for an uncomfortable situation when he realised who I was and had to make up for such a poor start, and I was already 99% certain that this was not someone I could work with or who would fit into our team with that attitude.

Be professional with everyone you meet

Bear in mind that you will meet a range of staff members on the day of your interview, and it is important to treat receptionists and administrative staff with the same courtesy as you would a senior manager. Not only is this a professional way to behave in the workplace anyway, but it is also very likely that their opinion of you will be sought as part of the selection process.

Making your entrance

Get off to a positive start and enter the room with confidence and good posture. Avoid slouching, which is something we often unconsciously do when anxious in a bid to make ourselves appear 'smaller'. Make eye contact and smile at your interviewer(s). Remember that you need to demonstrate that you can perform even under the pressure of needing to impress.

Sit comfortably

When you sit down, take up all the space in your seat. Try to sit back, relax and breathe. I have seen many people hovering at the front of their chair, which makes them look nervous. While talking, you should not be afraid to gesture and move – this is natural and, the more enthusiastic you are, the more animated you are likely to become. If you feel that you are moving too much, or that you don't know what to do with your hands, just bring them back to your lap. For men, it's important to avoid playing with loose change or keys in your pockets – this is surprisingly common. Women can often fiddle with jewellery or with their hair, so it's important to identify what you tend to target under pressure and learn to leave it alone. Again, this is where feedback from a practice interview can come in handy.

What to wear

This is not always as straightforward as it seems, as the level of formality will depend on the organisation. For the majority of interviews for science roles, a suit is going to be the safe choice. Keep your look clean, with minimal fussy details. Fragrance should also be kept to a minimum, as scents can be very powerful. You need to avoid overwhelming your interviewer with your favourite perfume or aftershave. Make up should be kept to enough to look groomed but not overdone; an appointment at a make-up counter run by one of the big cosmetics brands can often provide you with the skills and ideas you need, if you are not confident in this area.

What if a suit is not appropriate?

If you are applying to a small company, or somewhere the dress code is very casual, it may look incongruous if you arrive in a formal suit. Something more in the line of smart-casual (jacket, but no tie, for example, or clean and pressed jeans with a jacket) might be more appropriate. You can always make a quick call to find out what is expected so that you don't get caught out on the day. In any event, it's better to be overdressed and be able to take off a jacket and dress down your outfit, than to arrive and find that you have made an error and are far too casual; it's the latter that can undermine your confidence much more than the former.

A few other points

I have been asked many questions about issues in an interview that may seem minor but which have worried people in the past simply out of nerves, so I will address a few of them here.

- Should you accept a cup of coffee or tea? If the drink comes in a cup and saucer and you are shaky with nerves, then the clattering of crockery can highlight your anxiety. It's also advisable to avoid taking in caffeine if you are nervous, so accept water instead, which should come in a non-noisy glass or cup, and will hydrate you far more effectively.

- How firm should the handshake be? Mid-way between limp and bone crushing! Try it out on a friend if you're not sure. Really engage with a handshake, offering your entire hand and not just the tips of your fingers, and match it with eye contact and a warm smile.

- What if you need to make an urgent visit to the loo? These things happen, especially when we are nervous, as this is part of the way in which the body reacts to stress. Just excuse yourself politely; they can't refuse to let you go, and they can't carry on the interview without you!

- What happens if you don't understand the question or don't hear it clearly? It's absolutely fine to ask for clarification, and this is far more professional than simply pushing ahead and providing an irrelevant answer. Just don't do it for every question or you will appear not to be paying attention. If you are being interviewed in a second language, then the interviewer should take this into consideration.

- Can you take your CV with you? Absolutely. In fact, it is advisable to take with you copies of your application and any documents received from the company prior to the interview, so that you can refer to them if necessary. However, reminding yourself of what you submitted should be part of your preparation, as you don't want to be constantly looking at your CV for inspiration.

- What kind of questions should you ask at the end? Wait until you have been offered the position before asking questions about salary and holidays! Instead, show your interest by asking about training and development, or issues to do with the company that you may have read about. You can even ask the interviewer what they like most about their job, or what a typical day is like for a new recruit. All these topics provide sources for questions demonstrating your interest in the company.

- And finally, what happens at the end? Your interviewer should indicate when the session is finished and what will happen next. However, if they don't mention when they will be in touch with you, it's fine to ask. Finish by thanking them for their time and be prepared for goodbye handshakes. It's a smart idea to write down the questions you were asked, as well as noting down the examples you used, in case you are invited back for a second interview.

Telephone interviews

Telephone interviews have become a common part of the selection process, and are used by large organisations that will receive significant numbers of applications, and where the job may include significant amounts of verbal communication, including consulting within the science field. They are very cost-effective for organisations to use, and the average length of time is about 30 minutes.

Some applicants report that these interviews are conducted quickly with a lot of questions being asked, as well as verbal reasoning tests and, in some cases, role play, so be prepared for any eventuality. Companies using telephone interviews who employ science graduates include GlaxoSmithKline and Shell, so it's likely that this will feature as part of your application process.

Why use telephone interviews?

This extra interview step allows a company to filter out candidates that they do not wish to progress to a face-to-face interview, and allows them to assess your motivation and commercial knowledge. Telephone interviews are often carried out by the graduate recruitment team or members of HR, and sometimes by an agency on behalf of the company to which you are applying. All these interviewers will be assessing you against very specific criteria, so it's important to prepare appropriately and be ready for an interview experience where your voice is going to be your most important tool.

Preparing for a telephone interview

When preparing for a telephone interview, the advice above on competency interviews will be appropriate. And, while you won't be face to face with your interviewer, you still need to be in the right mindset for the task, so don't do the interview in your pyjamas, with housemates milling around. It can help a great deal if you are wearing something appropriately professional, have a table set out with everything you need, and explain to everyone in your living space that you mustn't be disturbed for a certain amount of time. If this is problematic, it may be possible to arrange to use a private space or office at your university or college careers service, so do ask. Switch off any gadgets that are liable to disturb you, and spend a few minutes before the phone is due to ring doing some slow breathing to relax you.

During a telephone interview

Stay aware of your posture. Open your chest and let your shoulders sink down so that you can breathe fully and open up your diaphragm. This will make you more easily understood than if you are hunched over the phone and will help to keep you relaxed.

Convey as much of your personality as you can down the phone. Be warm and enthusiastic, and try to smile; you can 'hear' when people are smiling, so make sure this is communicated to the interviewer. This approach will help you to develop rapport with the person at the other end, which is always harder without being able to see them, but non-verbal communication will still be apparent, so think carefully about your tone of voice and the clarity of your speech.

> Imagine the person is in the room with you and that you can see each other, and you will achieve the desired effect.

It's also possible that you may be asked to carry out your interview via Skype. In this case, it is essential that you present yourself appropriately and ensure that you are happy with what the interviewer can see behind you!

Graduate aptitude or psychometric tests

It is common to have to take online numerical and verbal reasoning tests before progressing to an interview. Even if your chosen science role will not require a high level of numeracy, many companies use these tests as another way to filter out potential candidates who do not reach an established benchmark early on in selection. The tests are developed by specialist companies using occupational psychologists, are standardised and carefully scored, and are usually carried out on a computer.

Get plenty of practice for tests

There is a wealth of material available that can help you to practise the different kinds of tests. Look at the 'Further reading and resources' section for specific titles and websites. What follows is a general guide to what to expect and some strategies for completing the tests to the best of your ability. It is generally the case that the more practice you get, the better your performance will become; familiarise yourself with the format of the questions and get used to working through them quickly and accurately.

Keep testing in perspective

An important point to bear in mind is that all the different kinds of tests represent just one aspect of the entire recruitment process, and an organisation will look at a range of different factors before making a decision about you. Do note however that people with certain kinds of disabilities may be disadvantaged by some of these tests, so it is important to disclose any potential issues, such as dyslexia, Asperger's or dyscalculia, early on so that alternative arrangements can be agreed. This can also open up a discussion as to any workplace support you need should you be offered the job.

Aptitude, ability and intelligence tests

It is helpful to have a calculator handy to complete these tests. The results may be used in comparison with your application form and interview to help recruiters make a decision, or they could also be used to help compare you with other candidates within 'normed' groups. It is not expected that you will finish all the questions in a test; they usually become more difficult as you progress, and accuracy will become more important. Some employers may also use negative marking, so concentrate on getting correct answers rather than attempting more but getting them wrong. Verbal reasoning tests are usually the most straightforward and simply require careful reading to be able to answer 'agree/disagree/cannot say'.

Numerical tests

Some of these tests require you to extract data from graphs, tables and diagrams, while others will expect you to be able to perform calculations using ratios, percentages and fractions, the most likely application of number within a commercial organisation. More specific mathematical and technical ability is likely to be tested at a later stage during the selection process and be tied more directly to your specific job role, if necessary. Mathematical tests may also require spatial reasoning, and may ask you to mentally rotate two-dimensional objects across three dimensions.

Recruiters recommend that the best way to prepare for numerical tests is to get hold of a GCSE maths revision book and work through it, as this level should be sufficient to see you through the initial stages.

Personality tests

Most employers want to ensure they recruit someone who can not only do the job, but can carry out the work in a way that best fits that organisation. There is little point in trying to second-guess the answers to personality questions, as they are closer in nature to strengths-based interviewing than to competency questions. They are also usually designed specifically for a company's profile by specialist psychologists.

Go with your initial reaction to a question, as this is often your most honest answer. The questions will also be asked in several different ways to compensate for anyone trying to convey a specific kind of 'profile' that they think the company wants. You can have a look at several kinds of personality tests online to get a feel for the kinds of questions you may be asked, such as a simplified version of the Myers Briggs-Type Indicator (MBTI) test: www.humanmetrics.com/cgi-win/jtypes2.asp, the Keirsey Temperament Sorter: keirsey.com, and another simple version of MBTI on the BBC website: ssl.bbc.co.uk/labuk/experiments/personality.

Programming tests for computer science

If you are a computer science student or seeking to enter this field with a related degree, it is likely that you will be given a programming test as part of the selection process. This may include the use of pseudocode, flowcharting and assembly languages. You may also face multiple choice questions, a 10 minute syntax checking test, UML diagrams, questions about firewalls and proxy servers (for a research-based job), and mathematical questions requiring an 'out of the box' approach to solve.

A student from the University of Kent offers the following advice:

'When doing the syntax checking, it can be more productive to answer the questions **not** in the order as they appear, but looking for the type X questions and then answering the type Y questions. This way you don't have to keep switching the rules in your head. I've done the same test in both ways and found the second way was more productive.'

See www.kent.ac.uk/careers/psychotests.htm for advice on how to pass graduate aptitude tests.

You may also encounter a day of solving highly complex problems known as the **Parity IT Aptitude Test**, which is difficult to prepare for; you need to turn up with your problem-solving and technical skills ready to apply to different challenges. You will be given four or five hours to solve a set of lengthy problems based on mathematics and programming, allowing you to take comfort and refreshment breaks. Have a good retractable pencil and eraser to hand for these tests, and full instructions will be provided, so read them carefully and prepare to do the best job you can.

Assessment centres: dealing with group exercises, presentations and social activities

Assessment or selection centres are used by larger organisations that recruit nationally and on a global scale, and usually follow a successful initial application and interview. Because you get to demonstrate your skills across a range of areas, they can be more accurate at predicting your success in the workplace than just an interview, which can be very subjective. Some people have also learned from experience how to perform well at interviews, but then do not go on to perform as expected in the job role, so assessment centres are considered to be a fair way of assessing your suitability.

What to expect

Running an assessment centre is about as close as the recruiter can get to seeing you in your job role and this helps them to make a more informed decision. You will be scored by an assessor as you carry out tasks that can include presentations, group exercises, role plays and e-tray exercises. This kind of testing can take place over a day or two, and you should be given plenty of warning about what to expect. The activities will usually be run at a hotel hired for the purpose or at a training centre owned by the company. Any overnight stays or meals will be organised for you by the recruiter, and you should be able to claim back travel expenses.

Points to bear in mind

The stress involved in getting through an assessment centre usually comes from being closely observed, as well as the fact that you will be tested alongside another six to eight candidates with whom you must work as professionally as possible. Though the prospect of up to two days of observed tests is daunting, it is important to remember that only 5%–10% of all applicants get as far as an assessment centre, and because they are expensive for employers to run, you will only be invited if they feel you are a serious contender for the job.

Be aware that you may not be directly competing against the other candidates with whom you will be working; there could be several positions available, so be professional in your approach and think about how to contribute to the team you are working in, rather than being aggressively competitive and standing out to the assessors in the wrong way. One candidate applying for an analytical chemist role with Procter and Gamble was surprised to be in an assessment centre group with seven other students, of whom four were applying for engineering positions, two for roles in microbiology and only one other for the chemistry job.

Dealing with the different elements of an assessment centre

Group exercises

There are several types of activities that you may be asked to carry out with a group of candidates, and these could involve completing a task of some kind, having a conversation about a set topic, or trying to solve a problem related to the job you are applying for.

> Importantly, no matter how technical the science role you are applying for, employers such as Procter and Gamble, Unilever and GlaxoSmithKline will focus their assessment centre tasks around business and their core company values, so be prepared for group exercises based on budgeting for research and development, and exploring commercial concerns, and not on technical knowledge. Technical questions may form part of one-to-one interviews or presentations instead.

In all cases, you will be thoroughly briefed and provided with the information you need to complete the activity. It is important that you say enough for the assessor to mark you on; staying quiet will not do you any favours. Similarly, do not dominate but be diplomatic. You need to strike the right balance and be assertive, as well as encouraging other candidates who may be hesitant to contribute. Keeping an eye on the time to ensure that the task is completed – a very important aspect of the activity – can also be a useful role to take on.

Presentations

Most people find presenting quite a stressful experience, but there are ways in which to manage the pressure. If you are set the topic before the assessment centre, then take full advantage and research and practise as comprehensively as you can. Under no circumstances should you let the presentation you do under test conditions be the first time that you have done a complete run-through of your content. Even if you are only set the topic on the day, you need to allocate time during your preparation period to run through the talk completely at least once to test the timings and to make sure you move logically between sections.

Give your presentation a clear, logical structure

Make sure that your presentation has a complete structure: an introduction, clearly delineated sections that progress logically, and a clear conclusion. Try to demonstrate your thinking as well as any questions raised by the topic. If you have done your research into the company and your science sector trends, then you should have enough examples with which to illustrate your ideas, but don't panic if the topic is unfamiliar; the assessors will still be looking at your problem solving more than your background knowledge. It's also easy to overestimate what you can cover in a short timeframe. Build your content around the key messages that you want your audience to remember and don't add detail for the sake of it. Keep the structure easy to follow and make your points with clarity.

Be aware of your body language when presenting

When presenting, use the body language cues mentioned in the above section on interviews. Remember to make eye contact and maintain a professional, positive attitude. Stand with your legs roughly under your hips so that you have a stable base – crossing your legs can make you very unbalanced – and avoid fiddling with hair, jewellery and clothing. Try to avoid reading directly from a script, as this is not really presenting, but use prompts instead and deliver in a more spontaneous way. If you are not provided with PowerPoint, then you can write out your points on a sheet of flipchart paper, on a whiteboard, or an index card. Your assessors will appreciate that you will be nervous, but you should aim to present as professionally as possible. Again, take advantage of any workshops or training at your university or college if this is a weak area for you, and start getting some feedback on where you need to improve.

Dealing with presentation nerves

Presenting can make many people feel anxious and panicky. Your body releases a chemical cocktail of adrenaline and cortisol into your system to give you the extra energy it needs to deal with the situation, but this can feel unpleasant. Try to think of this more positively as fuel to get you through the presentation, in the same way that a stage actor needs adrenaline to help them perform. Keep some water nearby in case you also experience a dry mouth, which is a common side effect of stress.

If it helps you to feel more in control, finding a private place to do some slow breathing before the presentation can be very calming. Try breathing in for a slow count of four, holding for a count of two, and then breathing out in a controlled way for a slow count of four. If your chosen role requires client-facing or stressful work, then it is important to demonstrate that you have coping strategies and can rise to the challenge.

Tests

Any aptitude or personality tests that you may have to take at an assessment centre should conform to the same principles as those you may have completed earlier on in the application process. Remember that aptitude tests require both speed and accuracy, while personality tests need honest responses. If you know that these are coming up, then getting as much practice as possible before the day is essential.

Interviews

It is not uncommon for an interview to form part of an assessment centre programme, even if you have already had one as part of the application process. The guidance provided above on dealing with interviews still applies. It is possible that this interview will be conducted by more senior members of staff or by the person who would be your line manager. They may also follow up on your answers from your first interview, so be prepared to go into more depth; this is why it is a good idea to keep track of what you put in your applications and to make a note of what you were asked the first time around.

E-tray/inbox exercise

Often conducted on a computer, these exercises are designed to test how well you can prioritise and summarise information, as well as react to unforeseen changes to a task. You will usually be presented with a screen that looks like a typical email inbox, and will be asked to decide in what order to answer the messages. You may need to pay special attention to some of them, and to provide answers which summarise the information you have received, testing your reasoning and organisational skills. All of this will be carried out under a strict time limit, and the assessors may decide to complicate things by sending emails to you mid-way through the exercise, or even to telephone you as part of the assessment.

Your ability to produce a professional email and take a telephone call in a business-like manner is obviously important, so make sure you are familiar with workplace etiquette: Ciara Woods' book, *Everything You Need to Know at Work*, is very helpful here and you can find it in the 'Further reading and resources' section.

Socialising

There will be breaks and meals as part of the assessment centre and, while you are not being formally assessed here, it is still important to bear in mind that you are being observed. As with the group exercises, get involved with the conversation, ask questions about the company and show your interest. It's not the best time to discuss anything controversial, or to be sharing any anecdotes that may raise the eyebrows of your potential employers; remember that you are still 'on duty'. If alcohol is on offer, then it's tempting to indulge to help you relax but be aware of your limits; if even a small amount has a tendency to take the edge off your professional demeanour then it's best avoided. You may also need to be up early and ready to impress the next morning, so enjoy the dinner but make sure you have enough time to relax properly and get a good night's sleep

And when it's all over?

The assessment centre is usually the final part of the selection process before the job offers are made, so you should know very quickly if you have been successful. Some centres are structured so that candidates who do not perform to the required standards by the mid-point of the tests are sent home early, with only the more promising ones allowed to proceed, but you should be told in advance if this is a possibility.

If you are unsuccessful, then the employer should offer you feedback on what you should have done differently and how you can improve. If feedback is not offered, then you should not be shy in asking for it, as most employers are happy to provide some guidance after taking you so far into their selection process.

Before, during and after: your timeline for success

To finish, here is a summary of practical points you may wish to consider before, during and after your interview or assessment centre.

Before

- Make sure that you have carried out your research. A last minute check of the news on the day of the interview can help avoid any embarrassing mistakes if you are asked about very recent developments.

- Remember to have several examples in mind for the different competencies or strengths that are the focus of your chosen organisation.

- Have copies of any correspondence exchanged between you and the recruiter, including copies of your application form, CV and covering letter.

- Keep any contact information for the recruiter with you, and programme their number into your mobile in case of any problems. For example, if your train is delayed, let them know immediately as they may be able to rearrange the schedule and allow you to be interviewed later.

- Pack your bag the night before with everything you need. A notepad and pen, or tablet device, will be useful for capturing the interview questions at the end of the day. Healthy snacks and a bottle of water to keep your blood sugar and hydration levels balanced during a long day can also be helpful to manage your energy.

- Decide what you are going to wear and have it clean and ready to go. If it's all new, wear it at home a few times to get used to how everything feels, and don't wear brand new shoes on the day in case they create too much discomfort.

During

- This is mainly covered above, but in summary remember to maintain a professional and positive approach at all times, with everyone you meet.

- Make sure your handshake is firm, and make lots of friendly eye contact.

- Ask for clarity if there is anything you are uncertain about.

- Don't let a badly executed activity put you off, or let yourself be derailed by a bad interview answer. Treat each new question as a new opportunity to impress.

- At an assessment centre, remember to strike the balance between being aggressive and assertive. You need to give the assessors something to mark without dominating every discussion.

- Maintain your professional attitude throughout any more social activities.

After

- Find a quiet place for a cup of tea or coffee and make notes about what you were asked, as well as the examples you provided. Reflect on what you felt you did well, and where you might have improved.

- Send an email to the recruiter as soon as possible, reiterating your interest in the post and thanking them for their time. This can sometimes make the difference if there is difficulty choosing between two evenly matched candidates.

- Talk through the experience with a friend or career professional, if that will help you to draw out any learning points.

This advice should cover most eventualities and help you to be best prepared for all the different ways in which an employer may assess your suitability. The final chapter will now look at your first months in your new job and how best to position yourself for professional development and growth in your career.

17

Developing as a professional and your next career steps

This final chapter looks at how to manage your professional development now that you are in your chosen science role, as well as what kind of skills and strengths you will need to develop to make the right impression in the workplace. This chapter includes:

- how to make the right impression in your first months on the job

- dealing with challenges

- next steps.

Your initial months in your first science role are your opportunity to lay down solid foundations for your future prospects, as well as to develop professional habits that will make a positive impression on your manager and colleagues. While it will be perfectly acceptable to need to ask questions in your first weeks, you will be expected to work independently quite quickly, so it pays to know how you best motivate and organise yourself to get the job done: something you should now be very familiar with from answering all those application and selection questions.

How to make the right impression in your first months on the job

You may already have come across the term 'day one skills'. This phrase refers to the competencies which, as a new graduate, you should be able to put into practice as soon as you start your new role. While areas such as medical and veterinary sciences have very specific skill sets that 'day one' employees should be able to deploy, you should think about what you are bringing to your new workplace in terms of not only your science-specific abilities but also your professional skills and attitude.

Managing yourself, your time and your attitude

While some of the advice that follows may seem obvious, it is based on feedback from employers about the attitude they like to see in their workplace. The majority of organisations tend to 'recruit for enthusiasm and train for skills', and they want to see a very positive, 'can do' attitude from the start, according to the Council for British Industry (CBI).

'A lot of my work has been self-led, so a level of self-discipline is needed to keep the work on track. I also have several strands on the go, so a level of organisation and multi-tasking is required.'

Dr James Matthews, university research assistant

Points to bear in mind

Arrive early

Most laboratory and office jobs in the science sector work on a nine to five day but, if you take 15 minutes to sort yourself out when you arrive, getting yourself a coffee, greeting colleagues and getting equipment running, then you're not really starting 'work' at nine and may find it difficult to be ready punctually when you need to be at a meeting due to start dead on nine o'clock. Arrive a little early to give yourself time to get organised and show enthusiasm. If traffic or public transport delays mean that you usually make it in just on the stroke of nine, then accept that you need to leave home earlier. Don't waste precious time in the mornings figuring out what you are going to wear or thinking about what to take for lunch. Establish an evening routine of packing what you need and checking your diary for the following day, and your mornings will run much more smoothly.

Don't be first out of the door at the end of the day

It will be noticed if you are usually the last person to arrive and the first person to leave. Use your first weeks to assess the company culture. There may be days when it's considered acceptable to leave bang on time, or even a little early, such as on Fridays, but make sure you work out what the 'unwritten rules' are. It is important to maintain your work–life balance and not stay late every night, but you want to make a positive impression by leaving when you have reached an appropriate point in your work and not just because the clock says it's time to go.

Maintain a diary and set some goals

Time management will take some time out of your day in terms of planning, but this is time well invested to avoid missing important targets. Be clear on both the final and any interim deadlines for the projects you are working on, and monitor these as you progress. Set these up as weekly and daily goals that you can easily see, maybe on a wall planner or on a gadget such as a tablet, on which you can set up automatic reminders.

It's also worth getting into the habit of immediately writing down any requests or thoughts about your work that come to you in a notebook, and adding these to your diary. This means that you are unlikely to forget a request, and will make you feel more in control.

If you struggle with your motivation, then start by making a list at the beginning of the week of what you intend to achieve and compare this with an end of the week list of what you actually completed. You will easily be able to see what tasks you avoid; these should be the first tasks you tackle on Monday morning.

Tasks that you completely loathe, such as cleaning down equipment or field kit, can be completed with the promise of a reward at the end of it: for example, buying your favourite magazine on the way home or an evening out after work.

Stay on top of emails

We all receive large numbers of emails, many of them just clogging up our inbox. Resist the temptation to keep your email open all day. This is too much of a distraction, and stopping to read new messages as they come in can prevent you from focusing on other tasks. Your approach to email becomes one of 'fire fighting', rather than a strategic response to dealing with your messages. Set specific times when you check and act on your emails. When you do open them, decide what to do with the message immediately. Reply or follow up on an action, make a note in your diary as to when you will act on it, or file it in the 'delete' folder – those are the only three options if you do not wish your email inbox to grow to unmanageable proportions.

Maintain a positive attitude

When you first start your graduate position, you may be asked to carry out tasks that you don't expect. However, everyone needs to complete tasks that are usually avoided, such as dealing with difficult clients, or taking care of annoying paperwork. Show willing by doing your share of this kind of work, and offer to help out colleagues, which will always be appreciated. If you are asked to stay late because an important task needs to be completed, and there is no reason for you to get home in a hurry, then show a positive attitude and stay. This should not be a regular scenario – if it is, then you need to discuss your workload with your manager – but, if it happens occasionally and it will help the team, join in and help everyone to get the job done.

Working with your team

While there are plenty of theories out there about what makes a good team, what happens in practice can be challenging. You need to be prepared to deal with personality clashes, political agendas and skill imbalances, while still working to meet a deadline. For example, a colleague may prefer having lots of time on a project but, if you are employed within the oil industry, commercial pressures can require you to move very quickly. You may have to step in and help your colleague to work more effectively, so that they don't hold the project back.

Much of a team's success will depend on the willingness of individual members to set their egos aside and work towards the common goal. Ideally, the goals of the team, individual and organisation should all be aligned, which is why you should be happy with your choice of company culture before you accept the job.

It is inevitable that there will be people in your team that you do not like, or whose working practices are dissimilar to your own. Your challenge is to accept this variation in how people get their job done and, if they deliver on time and to the agreed standards, there is no reason why you should expect them to do things differently.

Indeed, if you have your sights set on having management responsibility later in your career, then accepting that your team may work very differently from your own practice is part of learning to trust those who work for you.

To be a good colleague and a valued member of your team:

- get involved and volunteer for tasks

- be polite and positive as much as you can

- acknowledge the contributions and hard work of others

- be a team player – put your preferences aside when necessary

- don't take criticism personally – try to apply it to your job and how you do it

- keep personal problems out of work, if you can, unless your manager needs to know about something serious that could impact on your work and team

- don't ever say in private what you wouldn't say in public or to someone's face.

Managing your manager and your continuing professional development

It is possible that you will differ in how you approach your work from your line manager.

> The trick to not disagreeing with your boss over every task you carry out and how you do it is to learn to 'manage your manager'. This means that you should try to see a task from your manager's point of view and present your solution or method in the language that they use.

It is also important, especially in the early days of your job, to listen carefully to any feedback offered by your manager, and not to take offence. There may be established systems that you are expected to adhere to, and bypassing them may cause problems, so always ask if you are not sure; it's probably best not to make your own decisions on important topics until you are used to how your company works.

You may also be asked to set some goals for the first few months with your manager as part of what is known as continuing professional development or CPD, so use this time to develop your skills and deliver good quality work, and then be prepared to take on board any feedback. It is good practice that feedback be delivered to you in a timely manner (as soon as an action has taken place), relate to a specific event and should help you to move forward. If feedback comes long after the event and is vague and unhelpful, it is appropriate to ask for clarification to help you learn. These goals may then develop into an annual review of your work, so be prepared to reflect on your progress, identify successes as well as problems, and think about any training you could ask for to help you do improve your performance. You may want to ensure that you are on track to become a Chartered Scientist, for example, and become accredited by the relevant professional body in your field, so it will be important to attend the right courses and conferences in your early career years.

Dealing with challenges

The majority of your working day should generally run smoothly. However, there will inevitably be obstacles to overcome and these frequently come in the form of other people and behaviour that you may find challenging. Sadly, bullies exist as much in the workplace as they do in school, and some of them may now have power, which can exacerbate the worst of their behaviour. You may also come across people who are lazy and rely on others to carry their share of the workload, or chronic moaners who try to drag everyone down.

Learning how to deal with these kinds of behaviours and maintain your positive attitude is crucial. You need to establish your own boundaries for acceptable behaviour and let people know how you wish to be treated, as well as cope with any problems that may arise from dealing with the behaviours of others. This is why resilience is highly prized as an attribute in the workplace and why you need to demonstrate assertiveness. These qualities will help you to deal with professional setbacks. Working in the sciences can bring commercial pressures if your organisation develops and sells products, financial ones such as those within the National Health Service due to budget cuts, or research targets in academia – you need to be prepared to deal with problems.

Developing resilience

Resilience is appearing with increasing regularity in the lists of skills and attributes that employers expect their recruits to possess. If you have ever experienced a personal failure, such as failing important exams, your resilience will determine how readily you come back from that adversity as well as what you learn and take forward. Employers do not want you to crumble when an experiment unexpectedly goes wrong or a client creates a drama; they want you to solve the problem and keep things moving in the right direction.

Psychologist Charlotte Style (*Brilliant Positive Psychology*, 2011, page 129) lists the qualities of a resilient person as follows:

- optimistic and hopeful

- able to solve problems

- has self-belief but is not arrogant

- can maintain self-control and use emotions appropriately

- is able to find meaning and benefit in adversity

- can use humour

- has a good toolbox of coping strategies

- is able to learn, forgive and move on.

This is really all summed up by the positive, can-do attitude mentioned in the introduction to this chapter that employers want you to demonstrate. If you're not sure that you possess resilience, think back to a time when you experienced a failure or disappointment. How did you feel about it? What actions did you take to deal with it? Did you learn anything about yourself that you have since put into practice in a positive way? You can usually take some kind of lesson even from the most negative experience, but it may take time to be able to adopt a more balanced perspective and see the positive aspects.

Try not to 'catastrophise' if you have a serious problem, and see everything as pointless. Instead, start by accepting that you have a problem, apologising and offering to fix anything that was specifically your fault. This shows honesty and integrity, another two fundamental professional attributes. Think about what **specifically** went wrong to get some perspective, rather than seeing the whole situation as irredeemable. Identify any positives that you can. Plan ahead to avoid making the same mistake in the future, and remember that we usually learn more from failure than success.

To best manage stress

- Get organised. Develop the systems you need to get your job done effectively and don't delay difficult tasks. Attack them head on and get them finished, or you will build up stress simply from putting things off.

- Develop as much autonomy as you can in your job role. Understand what motivates you and set your own goals for individual days or tasks.

- Accept what is beyond your control and accept change. Don't waste energy by fighting what you can't alter – develop your coping strategies instead.

- Look after your personal health and wellbeing. Eat a balanced diet that is low in sugar and processed foods, and rich in nutrients. Take regular exercise to offload any excess adrenaline, and enjoy being social with colleagues, friends and family.

Developing your assertiveness

Most people have experienced the feeling at work that they were unable to say 'no', or that they have been taken advantage of in some way. This can leave you feeling powerless and very stressed so, as well as developing your resilience, it's also important that you can learn to be assertive. Being assertive can often be confused with the need to be aggressive to get what you want, but these are not the same kind of behaviours at all.

Aggressive behaviour

When we display aggression, we show little regard for the feelings of those around us. We can be hurtful and cruel. Aggressive people push themselves forward at the expense of others, and can sometimes use intimidation, including threatening body language and tone of voice, to get what they want. They do not value anyone else's ideas or feelings.

Submissive behaviour

At the other end of the spectrum, there are submissive or passive behaviours. While being less intimidating, a submissive person on your team can wreak havoc by not speaking up at an appropriate time and then creating dissent behind the scenes. When people behave submissively, they hide what they feel and then seethe quietly, erupting into temper or tears later on, leaving others mystified as to why they are so upset. They also find it hard to say 'no' and then they develop resentment towards the person who gave them the work, apologise when something is not their fault, and generally feel undervalued within their team.

Assertive behaviour

Between these two extremes is assertiveness, and this is what we aspire to. Assertive people can disagree with others by criticising an idea and not the person, demonstrating respect for their colleagues. They will not humiliate someone publicly, but will have an honest conversation with them in private, if there is a problem. They are honest about what they feel and express it directly, but without using anger or tears to get their way. They can stand their ground and say 'no' when they have to, but they also know when to concede when a battle is not worth fighting.

An example of assertiveness would be if your manager asks you to work late in the lab but you have a very important family occasion to get home to. You can refuse politely and offer an alternative solution to the problem that may require you to get in a little earlier the next day, or to take some work home with you. If the experiment needs monitoring, could a colleague cover this for you if you agree to take on some of their work in return? This way everyone stays happy and the work is still completed on time.

Next steps

When you have been in your job for a while and feel that you have thoroughly got to grips with it, it may be time to think about how to develop. It is not necessary to leave your role in order to grow; instead, you might want to have a conversation with your line manager about any training from a relevant professional body to increase your skill set, taking on more responsibility, or volunteering for a project that could give you experience of working with a different team. Even if your request cannot be accommodated immediately, it can be factored into your CPD for a later date.

Being in the right position for promotion

If you wish to be considered for greater responsibility, including taking on the management of others, it is vital that you position yourself accordingly and get noticed in the right way.

You need to develop a solid reputation for being someone who delivers their work on time and to a high quality, who volunteers for projects rather than waits for them to be assigned, takes up their fair share of the workload and occasionally more, and who offers suggestions for getting work completed productively and with greater efficiency.

It also helps to be seen as a team player and someone who can communicate well with all their colleagues; it can be difficult for someone who is naturally independent and has idiosyncratic working habits to be promoted, as they may find it hard to work for the greater good of the organisation and to accept that their team may adopt different working practices from their own.

While many people feel uncomfortable with the idea, you also need to ensure that your manager knows what you are achieving, especially if you deliver work early or receive particularly good feedback from a client or colleague.

Send your manager a quick email to let them know that something has gone particularly well. If you keep all your hard work quiet, then it can't be taken into consideration when senior staff are considering who to approach to lead a new project.

Changing fields – transferring your skills and experience outside of science

Hopefully, you will enjoy the first months of your career in science and start to feel like a valued member of your team. However, it may be the case that there has been an unfortunate mismatch either between you and your organisation or, more broadly, between you and your choice of work. This doesn't have to be a disaster, but you will need to use your resilience to help you assess your options and keep moving forward.

Use your contacts to find new opportunities

If it's the case that the job role is fine but the company doesn't suit you, then it's time to start using contacts and scour job advertisements to work out where you can move to. Find out where openings may be coming up, or make discreet speculative applications to other companies. This may be a long game requiring patience, so it is important to maintain your professional approach to your current job until you can move on. In this way, you should be able to leave with a good reference and your head held high. You will need to explain your reasons for leaving as positively as possible to potential new employers; it is imperative that you do not denigrate your old company.

It is far better in the long term to make a firm decision to find work that suits you better and move on, than to remain unhappy for the sake of looking consistent on your CV. It may be the case that working in a pharmaceutical research lab just doesn't suit you. However, it may be possible to stay within the same industry and move into the sales side, working directly with clients instead.

Leaving science completely

If it turns out that the science sector is not what you expected and you wish to look more broadly at your options, then there is also good news for you. According to Prospects, the majority of graduate recruiters don't mind what your degree subject was in – they want evidence of the general employability skills detailed in Chapter 14 as well as a positive attitude to work. Having a degree in physics, chemistry or mathematics does not determine the job role you will be successful in and you may be surprised at the diverse range of jobs taken on by the students in your graduating year.

Look at Destinations of Leavers (DLHE) statistics for ideas

It can be helpful to ask your careers service if you can see their statistics for Destinations of Leavers from Higher Education (DLHE). These are collected around January–February, providing a 'snapshot' of where everyone is six months after graduation and could offer you some ideas as to where you might move on to. Have another look at Chapter 13 on career planning for exercises to help generate some options, and get talking to friends and contacts about their work and what they enjoy.

Retraining

Changing sectors may involve some retraining, so you will need to look into how to fund this. For example, if you decided to move from being a software engineer into international development, you would need to take a master's degree in this area as well as get some volunteering experience on your CV to make this a viable option. It's always worth having a chat with prospective employers to check what they need from you before you apply, or to find out what the job is really like. You don't want to move from one job you hate to another, so take the time to get some work shadowing or volunteering to ensure that you are making the right decision.

Stay positive about your decision

Finally, present your choice to move out of science and into a different employment sector as positively as you can.

> Think about new challenges you could take on, new areas to learn about, or skills you wish to develop, rather than dwelling negatively on why you wanted to get out of your former organisation.

Talk to a careers adviser to get impartial advice and to help you weigh up your options before committing to a new path. Again, this could all take time, but think about leaving science as a positive decision that will help you move forward to a fulfilling career, rather than hanging on to a job that you dislike. You may even want to look into self-employment, if your first science role has enabled you to develop skills you could offer on a freelance basis, and this is worth considering as an option if you have found it difficult to work within the hierarchy of a larger organisation and are happier working independently and under your own motivation.

Finally — remember that your happiness at work is **your** responsibility, so take positive action and start selling all the amazing employability skills that you have to offer to potential new employers! I wish you the very best of luck with your career choices.

Further reading and resources

Career planning

- Bolles, Richard N, *What Color is Your Parachute? A Practical Manual for Job Hunters & Career Changers* (Ten Speed Press, 2013)

- Dunning, Donna, *What's Your Type of Career? Find Your Perfect Career by Using Your Personality Type* (Nicholas Brealey Publishing, 2010)

- Houghton, Anita, *Finding Square Holes* (Crown House Publishing, 2005)

- LaPorte, Danielle, *The Firestarter Sessions: A Soulful and Practical Guide to Creating Success on Your Own Terms* (Hay House, 2012)

- Lees, John, *How to Get a Job You'll Love* (McGraw-Hill Professional, 2012)

- McConnell, Carmel, *Soultrader: Find Purpose and You'll Find Success* (Momentum, 2002)

- McConnell, Carmel, *Make Money, Be Happy* (Prentice Hall, 2004)

- Taylor, Denise, *How to Get a Job in a Recession* (Brook House Press, 2009)

Applications and selection

- Bryon, Mike, *How to Pass Graduate Psychometric Tests* (Kogan Page, 2011)

- Jones, Stephanie, *Psychological Testing* (Harriman House Publishing, 2010)

- Lees, John, *The Interview Expert* (Pearson Business, 2011)

- Lees, John, *Job Interviews: Top Answers to Tough Questions* (McGraw-Hill Professional, 2012)

- Mills, Corinne, *You're Hired! How to Write a Brilliant CV* (Trotman, 2009)

- Smith, Heidi, *How to Pass Numerical Reasoning Tests* (Kogan Page, 2011)

- Tolley, Harry and Thomas, Ken, *How to Pass Verbal Reasoning Tests* (Kogan Page, 2010)

- Tolley, Harry and Wood, Robert, *How to Succeed at an Assessment Centre* (Kogan Page, 2011)

Professional development

- Kirton, Bill, *Brilliant Workplace Skills for Students & Graduates* (Prentice Hall, 2011)

- Style, Charlotte, *Brilliant Positive Psychology* (Prentice Hall, 2010)

- Trought, Frances, *Brilliant Employability Skills* (Prentice Hall, 2011)

- Woods, Ciara, *Everything You Need to Know at Work: A Complete Manual of Workplace Skills* (Prentice Hall, 2002)

Skills development

- Adair, John, *Effective Leadership* (Pan Books, 2009)

- Belbin, R Meredith, *Team Roles at Work* (Butterworth Heinemann, 2010)

- Clayton, Mike, *Brilliant Time Management* (Prentice Hall, 2010)

- Egolf, Donald B, *Forming, Storming, Norming, Peforming: Successful Communication in Groups and Teams* (iUniverse, 2001). Covers Tuckman's theories on teams

- White, William J, *From Day One: CEO Advice to Launch an Extraordinary Career* (Financial Times/Prentice Hall, 2005)

Useful websites

Note: websites for individual occupations are listed at the end of each job role in Part 1.

- All About Careers: www.allaboutcareers.com. Aimed at 16–24 year olds interested in graduate careers. Contains useful job role information.

- Business Balls: www.businessballs.com. Career help and business training.

- Confederation of British Industry (CBI): www.cbi.org.uk. Lobbying organisation for UK business. Useful source of employability and skills information.

- Find a PhD: www.findaphd.com. Searchable database of PhD opportunities and other postgraduate research positions.

- GOV.UK: www.gov.uk/business. Government information on starting and financing a business.

- Harvard Business Review: www.hbr.org. Useful and informative articles and research on professional skills and workplace issues

- Health & Care Professions Council: www.hpc-uk.org. For entry into the healthcare professions, check here to see if your degree or course is registered.

- High Fliers: www.highfliers.co.uk. Publisher of regular surveys into the graduate labour market and recruitment.

- Institute of Physics: www.iop.org. Advancing physics for the benefit of society.

- Jobs.ac.uk: jobs.ac.uk. Searchable database of academic jobs.

- LinkedIn: http://uk.linkedin.com. Professional networking site. Also contains company information and useful news items.

- National Careers Service: https://nationalcareersservice.direct. gov.uk/Pages/Home.aspx. Information about job roles, training and funding.

- NHS Careers: www.nhscareers.nhs.uk. Advice on careers within the National Health Service.

- National College for Teaching & Leadership: www.education.gov.uk/ get-into-teaching. Information about careers in teaching.

- Nature: www.nature.com. International publication on scientific and medical developments.

- New Scientist: www.newscientist.com. International publication offering information about scientific developments and jobs.

- Outset: www.outset.org. Organisation supporting new businesses and start-ups.

- Prospects: www.prospects.ac.uk. The UK's largest website for information about graduate jobs.

- Royal Society of Chemistry: www.rsc.org. Network for those working in chemistry, as well as a publisher and source of events.

- Science Careers: http://sciencecareers.sciencemag.org. Searchable database for jobs, from *Science* magazine.

- ScienceGrrl: www.sciencegrrl.co.uk. Inspiring women in science.

- TARGETjobs: http://targetjobs.co.uk. Information on careers and job roles, as well as vacancies.

- Teach First: www.teachfirst.org.uk. Charity training graduates with leadership potential to become inspiring teachers.

- You Tube: www.youtube.com. Search for videos here from universities and science organisations to find out more about working in science in the UK, as well as on career development and progression.

Bibliography

Books

- Clayton, Mike, *Brilliant Time Management* (Prentice Hall, 2010)

- Houghton, Anita, *Finding Square Holes* (Crown House Publishing, 2005)

- Jay, Ros, *Get What You Want at Work* (Prentice Hall, 2003)

- Knight, Alice, *How to Become a Clinical Psychologist* (Routledge, 2002)

- LaPorte, Danielle, *The Firestarter Sessions: A Soulful and Practical Guide to Creating Success on Your Own Terms* (Hay House, 2012)

- Lees, John, *How to Get a Job You'll Love* (McGraw-Hill Professional, 2012)

- McConnell, Carmel, *Soultrader: Find Purpose and You'll Find Success* (Momentum, 2002)

- Shahar, Tal-Ben, *Happier: Can You Learn to Be Happy?* (McGraw-Hill Professional, 2008)

- Style, Charlotte, *Brilliant Positive Psychology* (Prentice Hall, 2010)

- White, William J, *From Day One: CEO Advice to Launch an Extraordinary Career* (Financial Times/Prentice Hall, 2005)

- Woods, Ciara, *Everything You Need to Know at Work: A Complete Manual of Workplace Skills* (Prentice Hall, 2002)

Websites

- All About Careers: www.allaboutcareers.com

- Business Balls: www.businessballs.com

- Confederation of British Industry (CBI): www.cbi.org.uk

- Guardian Careers: careers.theguardian.com

- Harvard Business Review: www.hbr.org

  - Goleman, Daniel, 'Resilience for the Rest of Us': http://blogs.hbr.org/cs/2011/04/resilience_for_the_rest_of_us.html

  - Seligman, Martin, 'Building Resilience': http://hbr.org/2011/04/building-resilience

- Health & Care Professions Council: www.hpc-uk.org

- High Fliers: www.highfliers.co.uk

- National Careers Service: https://nationalcareersservice.direct.gov.uk/Pages/Home.aspx

- NHS Careers: www.nhscareers.nhs.uk

- National College for Teaching & Leadership: www.education.gov.uk/get-into-teaching

- Nature: www.nature.com

- Outset: www.outset.org

- Prospects: www.prospects.ac.uk

- Science Careers: http://sciencecareers.sciencemag.org

- ScienceGrrl: www.sciencegrrl.co.uk

- TARGETjobs: http://targetjobs.co.uk

- University of Central Lancashire Careers Service: www.uclan.ac.uk/students/employability/futures/careers_advice.php

- University of Bristol Careers Service: www.bris.ac.uk/careers

- University of Kent Careers Advisory Service: www.kent.ac.uk/careers

- wiseGEEK: www.wisegeek.com

Index of Advertisers